AAT

NVQ TECHNICIAN

REVISION **COMPANION** Units 8 & 9

Managing Performance
& Controlling Resources

BPP LEARNING MEDIA

Eighth edition May 2009
First edition 2002

ISBN 9780 7517 6717 9 (previous ISBN 9780 7517 4635 8)

British Library Cataloguing-in-Publication Data
A catalogue record for this book is available from the British Library

Published by

BPP Learning Media Ltd
BPP House
Aldine Place
London
W12 8AA

www.bpp.com/learningmedia

Printed in Great Britain

Your learning materials, published by BPP Learning Media Ltd, are printed on paper sourced from sustainable, managed forests.

We are grateful to the AAT for permission to reproduce specimen assessments and examples from previous exam based assessments. All answers have been prepared by BPP Learning Media Ltd.

CONTENTS

INTRODUCTION

This is BPP Learning Media's AAT NVQ Technician Revision Companion for Unit 8, Contributing to the Management of Performance and the Enhancement of Value, and Unit 9, Contributing to the Planning and Control of Resources. It is part of an integrated package of AAT materials.

It has been written in conjunction with the BPP Course Companion and has been carefully designed to enable students to practise all aspects of the requirements of the Standards of Competence and performance criteria. It is fully up to date as at May 2009 and reflects the Standards of Competence and the exams set to date.

This Revision Companion contains these key features:

- graded activities corresponding to each chapter of the Course Companion
- five practice exam based assessments for each unit, including tasks from AAT assessments up to and including December 2008.

All activities and practice assessments have full answers prepared by BPP Learning Media Ltd.

The emphasis in all activities and questions is on the practical application of the skills acquired.

All activities and practice assessments have full answers prepared by BPP Learning Media Ltd.

Tutors adopting our Companions (minimum of ten Course Companions and ten Revision Companions per Unit, or ten Combined Companions as appropriate) are entitled to free access to the Lecturers' Area resources, including the Tutor Companion. To obtain your log-in, e-mail lecturersvc@bpp.com.

Home Study students are also entitled to access to additional resources. You will have received your log-in details on registration.

If you have any comments about this book, please e-mail helendarch@bpp.com or write to Helen Darch, AAT range manager, BPP Learning Media Ltd, BPP House, Aldine Place, London W12 8AA.

chapter 1: INTRODUCTION TO MANAGEMENT ACCOUNTING

1 Explain the differences between financial accounting and management accounting. Ensure that you cover the following points:

- the main purposes of each form of accounting
- the users of each type of information
- the format of financial accounts and management accounts

2 Complete the following sentences:

i) The three main purposes of management accounting are ...., ... and ....

ii) If production levels decrease then total variable costs will ....

iii) The stores department in a manufacturing organisation is an example of a .... cost centre

iv) Costs which cannot be directly attributed to a unit of production are known as .... costs

v) When service cost centre costs are divided between the production cost centres this is known as .... of costs

vi) The range of activity levels over which a fixed cost is anticipated to remain fixed is known as the .... range

3 For each of the following statements determine if they are true or false:

		True/false
i)	Management accounts must be audited by an external auditor	....
ii)	As production levels fall fixed costs per unit will rise	....
iii)	A semi-variable cost is one which is fixed for a certain range of activity and then increases and is fixed again for a further range of activity	....
iv)	As production levels rise the variable costs per unit will remain constant	....
v)	The salary of the production manager is an indirect cost	....
vi)	Absorption of overheads is the process of allocating overheads to relevant cost centres	....

4 At a production level of 16,000 units a production cost totals £54,400. At a production level of 22,000 units the same cost totals £68,200. Is this a variable cost?

5 The following details are available for four types of costs at two activity levels:

Cost type	*Cost at 1,000 units*	*Cost at 1,500 units*
I	£7,000	£10,500
II	£11,000	£12,500
III	£12,000	£12,000
IV	£3,800	£5,700

Classify each cost by behaviour:

Cost I

Cost II

Cost III

Cost IV

6 Given below are eight graphs illustrating a variety of cost behaviours. From the list of eight cost behaviours or descriptions given below (i to viii) match each graph to a cost behaviour or description.

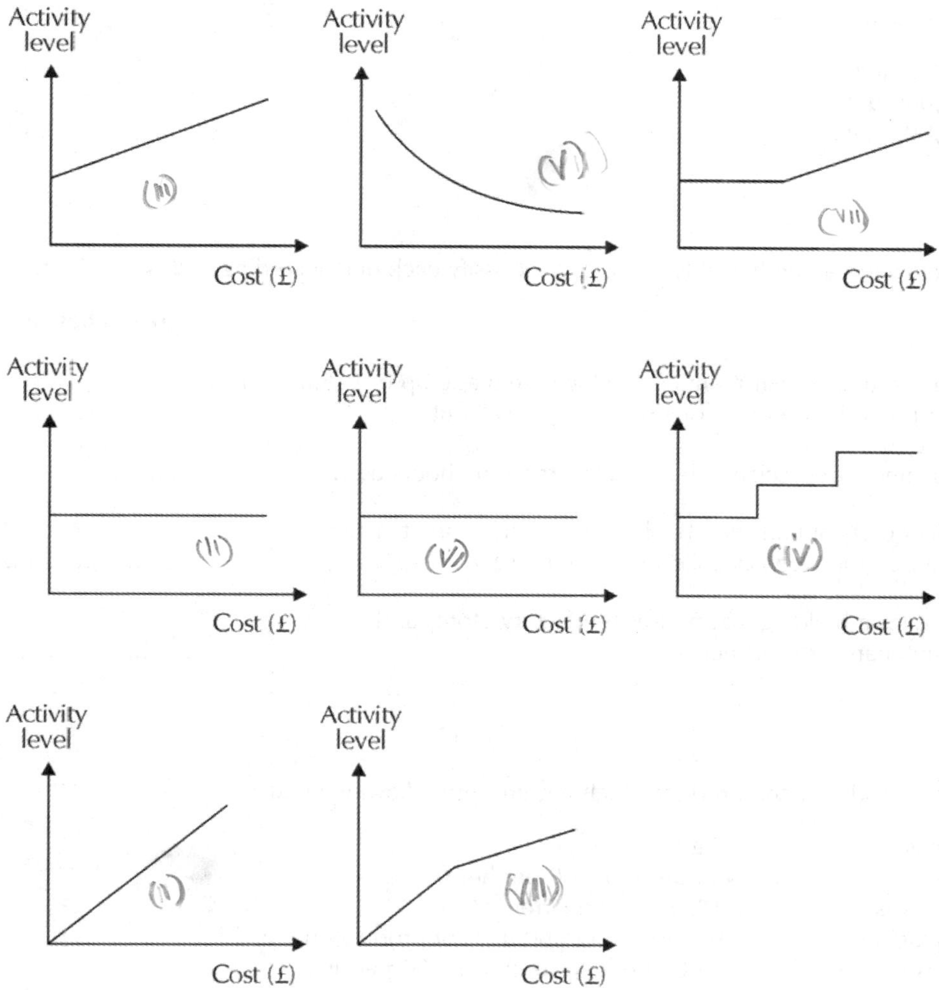

i) total variable cost

ii) total fixed cost

iii) semi-variable cost

iv) stepped cost

v) fixed cost per unit

vi) variable cost per unit

vii) materials cost with trade discount offered for purchases over a certain level

viii) production workers' wages who are paid per unit produced with a guaranteed weekly minimum wage

7 A manufacturing business anticipates that its variable costs and fixed costs will be £32,000 and £25,000 respectively at a production level of 10,000 units.

You are to produce a schedule showing the total production cost and the cost per unit at each of the following activity levels:

i) 8,000 units
ii) 12,000 units
iii) 15,000 units

8 Given below are a number of types of cost – classify each one according to its behaviour:

		Cost behaviour
i)	Maintenance department costs which are made up of £25,000 of salaries and an average of £500 cost per call out	....
ii)	Machinery depreciation based upon machine hours used	....
iii)	Salary costs of nursery school teachers where one teacher is required for every six children in the nursery	....
iv)	Rent for a building that houses the factory, stores and maintenance departments	....

9 A business produces one product which requires the following inputs:

Direct materials	6 kg @ £4.80 per kg
Direct labour	4 hours @ £7.00 per hour
Building costs	£18,000 per quarter
Leased machines	£600 for every 600 units of production
Stores costs	£3,000 per quarter plus £3.00 per unit

i) What is the total cost of production and the cost per unit at each of the following quarterly production levels:

a) 1,000 units
b) 1,500 units
c) 2,000 units

ii) Explain why the cost per unit is different at each level of production.

10 A business produces one product in its factory which has two production departments, cutting and finishing. There is one service department, stores, which spends 80% of its time servicing the cutting department and the remainder servicing the finishing department.

The expected costs of producing 50,000 units in the following quarter are as follows:

Direct materials	£16.00 per unit
Direct labour	3 hours cutting @ £7.50 per hour
	2 hours finishing @ £6.80 per hour
Cutting overheads	£380,000
Finishing overheads	£280,000
Stores overheads	£120,000

It is estimated that in each of the cost centres 60% of the overheads are variable and the remainder are fixed.

Determine the cost per unit of production under the following costing methods:

i) Absorption costing – fixed and variable overheads are to be absorbed on a direct labour hour basis

ii) Marginal costing

11 To help decision making during budget preparation, your supervisor has prepared the following estimates of sales revenue and cost behaviour for a one-year period, relating to one of your organisation's products.

Activity	60%	100%
Sales and production (thousands of units)	36	60
	£'000	£'000
Sales	432	720
Production costs – variable and fixed	366	510
Sales, distribution and administration costs – variable and fixed	126	150

The normal level of activity for the current year is 60,000 units, and fixed costs are incurred evenly throughout the year.

There were no stocks of the product at the start of the quarter, in which 16,500 units were made and 13,500 units were sold. Actual fixed costs were the same as budgeted.

Tasks

a) Calculate the following using absorption costing.

i) The amount of fixed production costs absorbed by the product
ii) The over/under absorption of fixed product costs
iii) The profit for the quarter

b) Calculate the net profit or loss for the quarter using marginal costing

You may assume that sales revenue and variable costs per unit are as budgeted.

12 a) A company absorbs overheads on a machine hour basis. Actual machine hours were 22,435, actual overheads were £496,500 and there was over absorption of overheads of £64,375.

Task

Calculate the overhead absorption rate to the nearest £.

b) When opening stocks were 8,500 litres and closing stocks were 6,750 litres, a firm had a profit of £27,400 using marginal costing.

Task

Assuming the fixed overhead absorption rate was £2 per litre, calculate the profit using absorption costing.

c) Actual overheads were £496,980 and actual machine hours were 16,566. Budgeted overheads were £475,2C0.

Task

Based on the data above and assuming that the budgeted overhead absorption rate was £32 per hour, calculate the budgeted number of machine hours (to the nearest hour).

13 You are employed as an accounts assistant in the management accounting department of Charleroi Aircon Ltd, the UK subsidiary of a major French group. Charleroi design and install industrial air-conditioning systems. The company is based in Birmingham.

Charleroi's usual pricing policy is to use direct costs (equipment and installation labour) plus a mark-up of 50% to establish the selling price for an air-conditioning installation.

Alice Devereaux, Charleroi's sales manager, is about to tender for a contract (quotation HMG/012) to install air-conditioning in some government offices in Exeter which are being refurbished.

Alice is also about to bid for a contract (quotation CFG/013) to install the air-conditioning in a furniture store which is being built in Gloucester. This job is very similar to an earlier one for the same customer.

Alice has asked Mark Langton, Charleroi's management accountant, to second you to the sales department to assist her in developing better pricing and cost models. Alice is particularly keen to experiment with activity based costing (ABC) as Mark is in the process of designing an ABC system for the company. She has asked you to investigate the profitability of quotations HMG/012 and CFG/013.

You have obtained the following information about the two jobs.

Estimates related to contracts HMG/012 and CFG/013		
Contract number:	*HMG/012*	*CFG/013*
Equipment: cost number of items purchased	£175,000 650	£120,000 410
Direct labour: hours hourly rate	10,000 £13	6,000 £11
Design hours	1,280	620
Distance from Birmingham office (miles round-trip)	320	90
Engineer site visits required	30	10

You have managed to obtain the following overhead information from Mark's ABC working papers.

ABC details for overhead activities connected with air conditioning installation contracts			
Activity	*Budgeted cost pool* £pa	*Cost driver*	*Cost driver units pa*
Design department	675,000	Design hours	25,000
Site engineers	370,000	Miles travelled	185,000
Purchasing department	105,000	Items purchased	15,000
Payroll department	75,000	Direct hours	300,000
Site management	750,000	Direct hours	300,000
Post-installation inspection	80,000	Items purchased	20,000

Tasks

a) Calculate the price for each of jobs HMG/012 and CFG/013.

b) Prepare a schedule setting out the activity-based overhead costs for each of jobs HMG/012 and CFG/013.

c) Write a memo to Alice setting out the profitability of each contract. Include a breakdown of costs into their main elements, plus details of the projected profits as a percentage of selling price and as a percentage of total cost.

14 You are employed as a financial analyst at Drampton plc, a computer retailer. Drampton plc has recently taken over Little Ltd, a small company making personal computers and servers. Little appears to make all of its profits from servers. Drampton's finance director tells you that Little's fixed overheads are currently charged to production using standard labour hours and gives you their standard cost of making PCs and servers. These are shown below.

Little Ltd: Standard cost per computer

Model	*Server*	*PC*
Annual budgeted volume	5	5,000
Unit standard cost		
	£	£
Material and labour	50,000	500
Fixed overhead	4,000	40
Standard cost per unit	54,000	540

The finance director asks for your help and suggests you reclassify the fixed overheads between the two models using activity-based costing. You are given the following information.

- **Budgeted total annual fixed overheads**

	£
Set-up costs	10,000
Rent and power (production area)	120,000
Rent (stores area)	50,000
Salaries of store issue staff	40,000
Total	220,000

Every time Little makes a server, it has to stop making PCs and rearrange the factory layout. The cost of this is shown as set-up costs. If the factory did not make any servers these costs would be eliminated.

- **Cost drivers**

	Server	*PC*	*Total*
Number of set-ups	5	0	5
Number of weeks of production	10	40	50
Floor area of stores (square metres)	400	400	800
Number of issues of stock	2,000	8,000	10,000

Task

Prepare a note for Drampton's finance director. In the note, you should use the cost drivers to do the following.

a) Reallocate Little's budgeted total fixed annual overheads between server and PC production.
b) Show the revised unit fixed overheads for each of the two types of unit.

15 Explain what is meant by a net present value and why it is used in project appraisal.

chapter 2: COLLECTION OF DATA

1 For each of the following sources of data state whether they are primary or secondary data:

		Primary/secondary
i)	Retail Price Index	Sec.
ii)	Stock Exchange share price listings	Sec.
iii)	Analysis of sales of a company by product	prim
iv)	Trade Association inter-firm comparisons	Sec.
v)	A company's aged debtor listing	prim.

2 Complete the following sentences:

i) The Retail Price Index is an indication of the level of ......inflation...... in the UK

ii) Quantitative data can be either ......financial...... or ......non-financial...... data

iii) The National Statistics are published in 11 separate ......themes......

iv) A good alternative to pure random sampling are ......quasi-random...... sampling methods

v) When sampling, the name given to all items that are to be considered is the ......population......

3 For each of the following statements determine whether they are true or false:

		True/false
i)	An analysis of purchase invoices to determine the average trade terms from suppliers is an example of secondary data	....
ii)	The number of days holiday taken per year by qualified staff in a firm of solicitors is non-financial quantitative data	....
iii)	A survey showing favourite holiday destinations is an example of qualitative data	....
iv)	Quota sampling is an example of random sampling	....

4 What quantitative information can be found from the purchase invoices of a business and how might this information be used?

5 Suggest where each of the following sources of information might be obtained:

		Source
i)	Local planning applications	....
ii)	The previous year's financial statements for a competitor company	....
iii)	Previous month's discounts allowed	....
iv)	Industry average profit margin	....
v)	Information about a competitor's success	....
vi)	Average sick days of employees per month	....

6 Explain what the National Statistics are and how they might be of use to a business.

7 Explain the following sampling methods and give an example of the circumstances in which each might be used and how the sample would be chosen:

i) random sampling
ii) systematic sampling
iii) stratified sampling

8 For each of the following situations discuss any appropriate and practical methods of choosing a sample:

i) an auditor wishes to check whether purchase invoices in a business are properly authorised prior to payment

ii) a train service provider wishes to assess the level of customer satisfaction with its service on a particular line

iii) a manufacturing business wishes to assess the level of defective products that are likely to be produced in each batch of production

9 The adult population of your organisation's Northern sales territory is 500,000. The territory is divided into a number of regions as follows.

Region	*Adult population* '000
Northia	90
Wester	10
Southam	140
Eastis	40
Midshire	120
Centrasia	100

In order to provide sales forecasting information, it has been decided to carry out a survey based on a 2% sample of the Northern sales territory's population.

Tasks

a) Describe how the sampling should be organised if the following methods are to be employed.

i) Simple random
ii) Cluster
iii) Stratified
iv) Systematic

b) Discuss which of these methods would be likely to give the most representative sample and why. Your answer should include discussion of the disadvantages of the other methods.

10 One of the ways of conducting surveys is by the use of questionnaires.

Task

Discuss the advantages and disadvantages of conducting surveys by questionnaire using each of the following methods.

a) Personal interview
b) Telephone
c) Postal

chapter 3:
TIME SERIES ANALYSIS AND INDEXATION

1 In the context of time series analysis explain what is meant by the following:

i) The trend
ii) Cyclical variations
iii) Seasonal variations
iv) Random variations

2 Given below are the production cost figures for the last nine months:

	£
March	104,500
April	110,300
May	112,800
June	109,400
July	117,600
August	116,000
September	119,200
October	122,300
November	120,500
December	119,300

Calculate a three-month moving average for these figures.

3 A new restaurant has recently been opened which only trades for five days a week. The takings have been increasing rapidly over the first four weeks since opening, as given below.

		£
Week 1	Day 1	600
	Day 2	700
	Day 3	1,000
	Day 4	1,200
	Day 5	1,500
Week 2	Day 1	680
	Day 2	750
	Day 3	1,250
	Day 4	1,400
	Day 5	1,860
Week 3	Day 1	820
	Day 2	1,030
	Day 3	1,940
	Day 4	2,100
	Day 5	2,500
Week 4	Day 1	1,000
	Day 2	1,320
	Day 3	1,560
	Day 4	2,290
	Day 5	2,670

You are to:

i) calculate the trend of the results using a five-day moving average

ii) calculate the daily seasonal variations on the assumption that the seasonal variations are additive

iii) comment upon how useful the trend and seasonal variation figures might be in this situation for forecasting future restaurant takings

4 Given below are the quarterly sales figures for a small business:

		£
2005	Quarter 3	50,600
	Quarter 4	52,800
2006	Quarter 1	55,600
	Quarter 2	48,600
	Quarter 3	51,200
	Quarter 4	53,900
2007	Quarter 1	58,000
	Quarter 2	49,800
	Quarter 3	53,000
	Quarter 4	54,600
2008	Quarter 1	60,100
	Quarter 2	50,700
	Quarter 3	54,200
	Quarter 4	55,200

You are to:

i) calculate the trend of the sales figures using a centred four quarter moving average

ii) calculate the seasonal variations on the assumption that the seasonal variations are additive

iii) using the spreadsheet given below enter appropriate formulae in order for the spreadsheet package to calculate the trend using a centred four quarter moving average

	A	B	C	D	E
1					
2					
3					
4					
5					
6					
7					
8					
9					
10					
11					
12					
13					
14					
15					
16					
17					
18					
19					
20					
21					
22					
23					
24					
25					
26					
27					

5 A business uses time series analysis and has found that the predicted trend of sales for the next four quarters and historical seasonal variations are as follows:

	Predicted trend	*Seasonal variation*
	£	£
Quarter 1	418,500	+21,500
Quarter 2	420,400	+30,400
Quarter 3	422,500	–16,700
Quarter 4	423,800	–35,200

What are the predicted actual sales figures for these four quarters?

6 Given below are the production cost figures for a business and the Retail Price Index for the last six months.

	£	RPI
January	129,600	171.1
February	129,700	172.0
March	130,400	172.2
April	131,600	173.0
May	130,500	174.1
June	131,600	174.3

i) Express each month's production cost figures in terms of January's prices.

ii) Explain what the figures in part i) indicate.

iii) Express each month's production cost figures in terms of June's prices.

iv) Explain what the figures in part iii) indicate.

v) Is this the same conclusion that was drawn when the production costs were expressed in terms of January's prices?

7 Given below are the quarterly sales figures for a business for the last two years.

		Sales £
2007	Quarter 1	126,500
	Quarter 2	130,500
	Quarter 3	131,400
	Quarter 4	132,500
2008	Quarter 1	133,100
	Quarter 2	135,600
	Quarter 3	136,500
	Quarter 4	137,100

i) Calculate an index for these sales with quarter 1 2007 as the base period.

ii) Explain what the index indicates about the sales.

iii) You are now also given the industry average price index for each of the quarters:

		Average price index
2007	Quarter 1	135.4
	Quarter 2	138.2
	Quarter 3	141.7
	Quarter 4	142.3
2008	Quarter 1	144.4
	Quarter 2	146.2
	Quarter 3	147.5
	Quarter 4	149.1

Express each quarters sales in terms of quarter 4 2006 average prices.

iv) Calculate an index using the price adjusted figures from iii) with quarter 1 2005 as the base year.

v) Explain what the index indicates about the sales. Is there any difference between the situation shown by this index and the situation shown by the index in ii).

8 a) AB Ltd set the standard cost of material C at £3.50 per litre when an index of material prices stood at 115. The index now stands at 145.

Task

Calculate the updated standard cost.

b) Culver Ltd decides to buy a machine from a company in ABC country for 100,000 ABC dollars, when the rate of exchange is 10 ABC dollars to the £. Payment for the machine occurs when the exchange rate is 11.2 ABC dollars to the £.

Task

Calculate the difference between the planned cost and actual cost of the machine.

9 The following data show the sa es of the product sold by your company in the period 2006 to 2008.

Year	*Quarter 1*	*Quarter 2*	*Quarter 3*	*Quarter 4*
	£'000	£'000	£'000	£'000
2006	86	42	57	112
2007	81	39	55	107
2008	77	35	52	99

Tasks

a) Plot the data and comment on them.

b) By means of a moving average find the trend.

c) The seasonal adjustments are as follows.

Quarter 1	*Quarter 2*	*Quarter 3*	*Quarter 4*
+9	–32	–16	+39

Give the sales for 2008 seasonally adjusted.

d) Forecast sales for each quarter of 2009 using a 'rule-of-thumb' approach and comment on the likely accuracy of your forecasts.

10 You have collected the following data on your company's quarterly sales in recent years.

	Quarter			
	1	*2*	*3*	*4*
	Units	Units	Units	Units
2006	200	110	320	240
2007	214	118	334	260
2008	220	124	340	278

As part of the sales budget preparation you have been asked to analyse this data.

Tasks

a) Calculate a moving average of quarterly sales.
b) Calculate the average seasonal variations.

chapter 4: STANDARD COSTING

1 A business budgeted to produce 2,680 units of one of its products during the month of May. The product uses 5 kg of raw material with a standard cost of £4.00 per kg. During the month the actual production was 2,800 units using 14,400 kg of raw materials costing £60,480.

You are to calculate:

i) the total materials cost variance
ii) the materials price variance
iii) the materials usage variance

2 A business has the following standard cost card for one unit of its product:

Direct materials	4 kg @ £3 per kg	£12
Direct labour	3 hours @ £9 per hour	£27
Fixed overheads	3 hours @ £4 per hour	£12

The budgeted production level is 12,000 units.

The actual results for the period are:

Production	11,400 units
Materials 44,800 kgs	£150,480

You are to calculate:

i) the total materials cost variance
ii) the materials price variance
iii) the materials usage variance

3 Production of product Z1 for the month of November in a manufacturing business was 12,100 units using 54,900 hours of direct labour costing £410,200. The standard cost card shows that the standard labour input for a unit of Z1 is 4.5 hours at a rate of £7.30 per hour.

You are to calculate:

i) the total labour cost variance
ii) the labour rate variance
iii) the labour efficiency variance

4 A business has the following standard cost card for one unit of its product:

Direct materials	4 kg @ £3 per kg	£12
Direct labour	3 hours @ £9 per hour	£27
Fixed overheads	3 hours @ £4 per hour	£12

The budgeted production leve is 12,000 units.

The actual results for the period are:

Production	11,400 units
Labour 34,700 hours	£316,400

You are to calculate:

i) the total labour cost variance
ii) the labour rate variance
iii) the labour efficiency variance

5 A business has budgeted to produce and sell 10,000 units of its single product. The standard cost per unit is as follows:

Direct materials	£18
Direct labour	£13
Fixed production overhead	£7

During the period the actual results were:

Production and sales	11,500 units
Fixed production overheads	£75,000

You are to calculate:

i) the fixed overhead expenditure variance
ii) the fixed overhead volume variance

6 A business has a single product into which fixed overheads are absorbed on the basis of labour hours. The standard cost card shows that fixed overheads are to be absorbed on the basis of 6 labour hours per unit at a rate of £7.60 per hour. The budgeted level of production is 50,000 units.

The actual results for the period were that fixed overheads were £2,200,000 and that the actual hours worked were 310,000 and the actual units produced were 52,000.

a) You are to calculate:

   i) the fixed overhead expenditure variance
   ii) the fixed overhead volume variance

b) Split the fixed overhead volume variance into the efficiency variance and the capacity variance

7 A business incurred fixed overheads of £203,000 in the month of May. The fixed overheads are absorbed into units of production at the rate of £3.60 per direct labour hour. The actual production during the month was 13,200 units although the budget had been for 14,000 units. The standard labour cost for the production is 4 hours per unit at an hourly rate of £8.00. During the month 50,000 labour hours were worked at a total cost of £403,600.

You are to calculate:

i) the budgeted fixed overhead for the month
ii) the fixed overhead expenditure variance
iii) the fixed overhead volume variance
iv) the fixed overhead efficiency variance
v) the fixed overhead capacity variance

8 The standard cost card for a business's product is shown below:

	£
Direct materials 4.8 kg at £2.80 per kg	13.44
Direct labour 2.5 hours at £8.50 per hour	21.25
Fixed overheads 2.5 hours at £1.60 per hour	4.00
	38.69

The budgeted production was for 1,100 units in the month of July. The actual costs during the month of July for the production of 1,240 units were as follows:

	£
Direct materials 5,800 kg	17,100
Direct labour 3,280 hours	27,060
Fixed overheads	4,650

You are to:

i) calculate the materials price and usage variances

ii) calculate the labour rate and efficiency variances

iii) calculate the fixed overhead expenditure, efficiency and capacity variances

iv) prepare a reconciliation statement reconciling the standard cost of the production to the actual cost

9 XYZ Ltd is planning to make 120,000 units per period of a new product. The following standards have been set.

		Per unit
Direct material A		1.2 kgs at £11 per kg
Direct material B		4.7 kgs at £6 per kg
Direct labour:	Operation 1	42 minutes
	Operation 2	37 minutes
	Operation 3	11 minutes

Overheads are absorbed at the rate of £30 per labour hour. All direct operatives are paid at the rate of £8 per hour.

Actual results for the period were as follows.

Production 126,000 units

Direct labour cost £1.7m for 215,000 clock hours

Material A cost £1.65m for 150,000 kgs

Material B cost £3.6m for 590,000 kgs

Tasks

a) Calculate the standard cost for one unit.
b) Calculate the labour rate and efficiency variances.
c) Calculate the material price and usage variances.

10 A manufacturing company has provided you with the following data which relates to component RYX, for the period which has just ended.

	Budget	*Actual*
Number of labour hours	8,400	7,980
Production units	1,200	1,100
Overhead cost (all fixed)	£22,260	£25,536

Overheads are absorbed at a rate per standard labour hour.

Tasks

a) Calculate the fixed production overhead cost variance and the following subsidiary variances.

i) Expenditure
ii) Efficiency
iii) Capacity

b) Provide a summary statement of these four variances.

11 You are employed as part of the management accounting team in a large industrial company which operates a four-weekly system of management reporting. Your division makes a single product, the Omega, and, because of the nature of the production process, there is no work in progress at any time.

The group management accountant has completed the calculation of the material and labour standard costing variances for the current period to 1 April but has not had the time to complete any other variances. Details of the variances already calculated are reproduced in the working papers below, along with other standard costing data.

Standard costing and budget data – four weeks ended 1 April

	Quantity	*Unit price*	*Cost per unit*
Material (kgs)	7	£25.00	£175
Labour (hours)	40	£7.50	£300
Fixed overheads (hours)	40	£12.50	£500
			£975
	Units	*Standard unit cost*	*Standard cost of production*
Budgeted production for the four weeks	4,100	£975	£3,997,500

Working papers

Actual production and expenditure for the four weeks ended 1 April

Units produced	3,850
Cost of 30,000 kgs of materials consumed	£795,000
Cost of 159,000 labour hours worked	£1,225,000
Expenditure on fixed overheads	£2,195,000

Material and labour variances

Material price variance	£45,000 (A)
Material usage variance	£76,250 (A)
Labour rate variance	£32,500 (A)
Labour efficiency variance	£37,500 (A)

Tasks

You have been requested to do the following.

a) Calculate the following variances.

   i) The fixed overhead expenditure variance
   ii) The fixed overhead volume variance
   iii) The fixed overhead capacity variance
   iv) The fixed overhead efficiency variance

b) Prepare a report for presentation to the production director reconciling the standard cost of production for the period with the actual cost of production.

c) The production director, who has only recently been appointed, is unfamiliar with fixed overhead variances. Because of this, the group management accountant has asked you to prepare a brief memo to the production director.

   Your memo should do the following.

   i) Outline the similarities and differences between fixed overhead variances and other cost variances such as the material and labour variances.

   ii) Explain what is meant by the fixed overhead expenditure, volume, capacity and efficiency variances, and show, by way of examples, how these can be of help to the production director in the planning and controlling of the division.

chapter 5: STANDARD COSTING – FURTHER ASPECTS

1 What factors should be taken into account when setting the standard cost of labour for a product?

2 What are the main problems with using ideal standards in a business?

3 State possible reasons for each of the following variances which are all independent of each other:

i) a favourable materials price variance
ii) a favourable materials usage variance
iii) an adverse labour rate variance
iv) an adverse labour efficiency variance

4 State the factors that may be a cause of each of the following variances (either favourable or adverse):

i) fixed overhead volume variance
ii) fixed overhead efficiency variance
iii) fixed overhead capacity variance

5 i) A business has had to use a less-skilled grade of labour in its production process for the last week. What effect is this likely to have on the variances for the week?

ii) A factory had a machine breakdown which resulted in three days of production delays last month. What effect is this likely to have on the variances for the month?

6 Given below is the operating statement for a manufacturing business for the last month:

Reconciliation of standard cost of actual production to actual cost – March 2009

	Variances		
	Adverse	*Favourable*	
	£	£	£
Standard cost of actual production			672,500
Variances:			
Materials price	24,300		
Materials usage		6,780	
Labour rate	10,600		
Labour efficiency		10,300	
Fixed overhead expenditure		7,490	
Fixed overhead capacity		4,800	
Fixed overhead efficiency		6,100	
	34,900	35,470	
Add: adverse variances			34,900
Less: favourable variances			(35,470)
Actual cost of production			671,930

A number of factors about the month's production have been discovered:

- at the end of the previous month a new warehouse had been purchased which has meant a saving in warehouse rental
- six new machines were installed at the start of the month which are more power efficient than the old machines, but also more expensive, causing a larger depreciation charge
- there was an unexpected increase in the materials price during the month and when other suppliers were contacted it was found that they were all charging approximately the same price for the materials
- a higher than normal skilled grade of labour was used during the month due to staff shortages. The production process is a skilled process and the benefit has been that these employees, although more expensive, have produced the goods faster and with less wastage. This particular group of employees are also keen to work overtime and, as the business wishes to build up stock levels, advantage of this has been taken.

Suggest what effect the combination of the factors given above might have had on the reported variances and make suggestions as to any action that should be taken in light of these factors.

7 The standard direct materials cost for a business's product is:

6 kg @ £8.00 per kg £48.00

During the month of October production was 7,400 units of the product and the actual materials cost was £397,400 for 45,100 kgs. The price of the materials has been unexpectedly increased to £8.50 per kg for the whole month.

i) Calculate the total materials price variance.

ii) Show how the total materials price variance can be analysed into the planning element that has been caused by the price increase and the control element caused by other factors.

iii) How would this affect how responsibility for the variance was assessed?

8 A business's product has a standard direct material cost of £26.00 (4 kgs @ £6.50 per kg). During the month of March the total production of the product was 2,500 units using 10,600 kgs of materials at a total cost of £73,140. During the month the price was unexpectedly increased due to a shortage of the material to £7.00 per kg.

i) Calculate the total materials price variance and analyse this into the planning variance due to price increase and the control variance due to other factors.

ii) How would the analysis of the sub-variances affect how the responsibility for the total variance would be assessed?

9 A business makes a product which uses a raw material which has a standard cost of £7.00 per kg. Each unit of the product requires 5 kgs of this material. The price of the materials for the last few years has been subjected to a time series analysis and the following percentage seasonal variations have been seen to occur.

Jan–Mar	–6%
Apr–June	+8%
July–Aug	+11%
Sept–Dec	–13%

During March 18,000 units of the product were made and the price paid for the 92,000 kgs of material was £631,200.

What is the total materials price variance and how can this be analysed to show the planning variance due to the season and the control variance due to other factors?

10 The standard cost of direct materials for a product is made up of 8 kgs of material at an average standard cost of £4.00 per kg. It has been noted over the years that the cost of the material fluctuates on a seasonal basis around the average standard cost as follows:

Jan–Mar	+12%
Apr–June	+18%
July–Sept	–16%
Oct–Dec	–14%

In the month of June the actual production was 5,000 units and 42,300 kgs of material were used at a cost of £194,580.

What is the total materials price variance, the planning variance caused by the seasonal price change and the control variance caused by other factors?

11 a) You are employed as the assistant management accountant in the group accountant's office of Hampstead plc. Hampstead recently acquired Finchley Ltd, a small company making a specialist product called the Alpha. Standard marginal costing is used by all the companies within the group and, from 1 August 2008, Finchley Ltd will also be required to use standard marginal costing in its management reports. Part of your job is to manage the implementation of standard marginal costing at Finchley Ltd.

John Wade, the managing director of Finchley, is not clear how the change will help him as a manager. He has always found Finchley's existing absorption costing system sufficient. By way of example, he shows you a summary of his management accounts for the three months to 31 May 2008. These are reproduced below.

Statement of budgeted and actual cost of Alpha production – 3 months ended 31 May 2008

	Actual		*Budget*		*Variance*
Alpha production (units)		10,000		12,000	
	Inputs	£	*Inputs*	£	£
Materials	32,000 m	377,600	36,000 m	432,000	54,400
Labour	70,000 hrs	422,800	72,000 hrs	450,000	27,200
Fixed overhead absorbed		330,000		396,000	66,000
Fixed overhead unabsorbed		75,000		0	(75,000)
		1,205,400		1,278,000	72,600

John Wade is not convinced that standard marginal costing will help him to manage Finchley. 'My current system tells me all I need to know,' he said. 'As you can see, we are £72,600 below budget which is really excellent given that we lost production as a result of a serious machine breakdown.'

To help John Wade understand the benefits of standard marginal costing, you agree to prepare a statement for the three months ended 31 May 2008 reconciling the standard cost of production to the actual cost of production.

Tasks

i) Use the budget data to determine the following.

1) The standard marginal cost per Alpha
2) The standard cost of actual Alpha production for the three months to 31 May 2004

ii) Calculate the following variances.

1) Material price variance
2) Material usage variance
3) Labour rate variance
4) Labour efficiency variance
5) Fixed overhead expenditure variance

iii) Write a short memo to John Wade. You memo should:

1) include a statement reconciling the actual cost of production to the standard cost of production;

2) give TWO reasons why your variances might differ from those in his original management accounting statement despite using the same basic data;

3) **briefly** discuss ONE further reason why your reconciliation statement provides improved management information.

b) On receiving your memo, John Wade informs you that the machine breakdown resulted in the workforce having to be paid for 12,000 hours even though no production took place, and that an index of material prices stood at 466.70 when the budget was prepared but at 420.03 when the material was purchased.

Task

Using this new information, prepare a revised statement reconciling the standard cost of production to the actual cost of production. Your statement should subdivide both the labour variances into those parts arising from the machine breakdown and those parts arising from normal production, and the material price variance into that part due to the change in the index and that part arising for other reasons.

12 a) Pronto Ltd was recently established in the UK to assemble cars. All parts are sent directly to the UK in the form of a kit by Pronto's owner from its headquarters in a country called Erehwon.

The contract between Pronto and its owner is a fixed price contract per kit and the contract specifies zero faults in all of the parts. This fixed price was used to establish the standard cost per kit. Despite this, the managing director of Pronto, Richard Jones, is concerned to receive the following statement from the management accounting department where you are employed as an accounting technician.

	September 2008	*October 2008*	*November 2008*
Kits delivered	2,000	2,100	2,050
Actual cost invoiced	£12,059,535	£11,385,495	£10,848,600
Unit cost per kit to nearest £	£6,030	£5,422	£5,292

Richard Jones cannot understand why, with a fixed price contract and guaranteed quality, the unit cost should vary over the three months. He provides you with the following information.

- The contract's cost was fixed in Erehwon dollars of $54,243 per kit.
- There has been no change in the agreed cost of the parts and no other costs incurred.

On further investigation you discover that the exchange rate between the UK pound and the Erehwon dollar was as follows.

At time of contract	*September 2008*	*October 2008*	*November 2008*
$9.80	$9.00	$10.00	$10.25

Task

Prepare a memo to Richard Jones. Your memo should include the following.

i) A calculation of:

1) the UK cost per kit at the time the contract was agreed;

2) the UK cost of the kits delivered using the exchange rates given for each of the three months;

3) the price variance due to exchange rate differences for each of the three months;

4) any usage variance in each of the three months, assuming no other reason for the price variance;

ii) A brief discussion about whether price variances due to exchange rate differences should be excluded from any standard costing report prepared for the production manager of Pronto Ltd.

b) Pronto uses a highly mechanised and computerised moving assembly line known as a track to build the cars. Although individual employees are assigned to particular parts of the track, they work in teams. If the production of cars slows below the speed of the track, teams help each other to maintain the speed of the track and the production of cars. Because of this approach, labour is viewed as a fixed cost and machine hours (the hours that the track is in use) are used to charge overheads to production.

For the week ended 28 November 2008, the management accounting department has prepared a statement of budgeted and actual fixed overhead for Richard Jones. This is reproduced below.

Pronto Ltd: Budgeted and actual fixed overheads – week ended 28 November 2008

	Budget	*Actual*
Car production	560	500
Machine (or track) hours of production	140	126
Fixed overheads	£	£
Rent and rates	16,000	16,000
Maintenance and depreciation	10,000	13,000
Power	75,000	71,000
Labour	739,000	742,000
Total	840,000	842,000

Richard Jones finds that the statement is not particularly helpful as it does not give him sufficient information to manage the company. He asks for your help.

Tasks

In preparation for a meeting with Richard Jones, do the following.

i) Calculate the following.

1) Budgeted overheads per machine (or track) hour
2) Budgeted number of cars produced per machine (or track) hour
3) Standard hours of actual production

ii) Calculate the following variances using the information identified in (i).

1) Fixed overhead expenditure variance
2) Fixed overhead volume variance
3) Fixed overhead efficiency variance
4) Fixed overhead capacity variance

iii) Prepare a statement for the week ended 28 November 2008 reconciling the fixed overheads incurred to the fixed overheads absorbed in production.

13 a) You are employed as a management accountant in the head office of Travel Holdings plc. Travel Holdings owns a number of transport businesses. One of them is Travel Ferries Ltd. Travel Ferries operates ferries which carry passengers and vehicles across a large river. Each year, standard costs are used to develop the budget for Travel Ferries Ltd. The latest budgeted and actual operating results are reproduced below.

Travel Ferries Ltd Budgeted and actual operating results for the year to 30 November 2008				
Operating data		*Budget*		*Actual*
Number of ferry crossings		6,480		5,760
Operating hours of ferries		7,776		7,488
Cost data		£		£
Fuel	1,244,160 litres	497,664	1,232,800 litres	567,088
Labour	93,312 hours	699,840	89,856 hours	696,384
Fixed overheads		466,560		472,440
Cost of operations		1,664,064		1,735,912

Other accounting information

- Fuel and labour are variable costs.
- Fixed overheads are absorbed on the basis of budgeted **operating hours**.

One of your duties is to prepare costing information and a standard costing reconciliation statement for the chief executive of Travel Holdings.

Tasks

i) Calculate the following information.

1) The standard price of fuel per litre
2) The standard litres of fuel for 5,760 ferry crossings
3) The standard labour rate per hour
4) The standard labour hours for 5,760 ferry crossings
5) The standard fixed overhead cost per budgeted operating hour
6) The standard operating hours for 5,760 crossings
7) The standard fixed overhead cost absorbed by the actual 5,760 ferry crossings

ii) Using the data provided in the operating results and your answers to part i), calculate the following variances.

1) The material price variance for the fuel
2) The material usage variance for the fuel
3) The labour rate variance
4) The labour efficiency variance
5) The fixed overhead expenditure variance
6) The fixed overhead volume variance
7) The fixed overhead capacity variance
8) The fixed overhead efficiency variance

iii) Prepare a statement reconciling the actual cost of operations to the standard cost of operations for the year to 30 November 2008.

b) On receiving your reconciliation statement, the chief executive is concerned about the large number of adverse variances. She is particularly concerned about the excessive cost of fuel used during the year. A colleague gives you the following information.

- The actual market price of fuel per litre during the year was 20% higher than the standard price.
- Fuel used directly varies with the number of operating hours.
- The difference between the standard and actual operating hours for the 5,760 ferry crossings arose entirely because of weather conditions.

Tasks

Write a memo to the chief executive. Your memo should do the following.

i) Subdivide the material price variance into two parts.

1) That part arising from the standard price being different from the actual market price of fuel

2) The part due to other reasons

ii) Identify ONE variance which is not controllable and give ONE reason why the variance is not controllable.

iii) Identify TWO variances which are controllable and which should be investigated. For each variance, give ONE reason why it is controllable.

14 a) You are the assistant management accountant at the Bare Foot Hotel complex on the tropical island of St Nicolas. The hotel complex is a luxury development. All meals and entertainment are included in the price of the holidays and guests only have to pay for drinks.

The Bare Foot complex aims to create a relaxing atmosphere. Because of this, meals are available throughout the day and guests can eat as many times as they wish.

The draft performance report for the hotel for the seven days ended 27 November 2008 is reproduced below.

Bare Foot Hotel Complex
Draft performance report for seven days ended 27 November 2008

	Notes		*Budget*		*Actual*
Guests			540		648
		$	$	$	$
Variable costs					
Meal costs	1		34,020		49,896
Catering staff costs	2,3		3,780		5,280
Total variable costs			37,800		55,176
Fixed overhead costs					
Salaries of other staff		5,840		6,000	
Local taxes		4,500		4,200	
Light, heat and power		2,500		2,600	
Depreciation of buildings and equipment		5,000		4,000	
Entertainment		20,500		21,000	
Total fixed overheads			38,340		37,800
Total cost of providing for guests			76,140		92,976

Notes

1 Budgeted cost of meals: number of guests × 3 meals per day × 7 days × $3 per meal

2 Budged cost of catering staff: each member of the catering staff is to prepare and serve 12 meals per hour. Cost = (number of guests × 3 meals per day × 7 days ÷ 12 meals per hour) × $4 per hour.

3 Actual hours worked by catering staff = 1,200 hours

Other notes

The amount of food per meal has been kept under strict portion control. Since preparing the draft performance report, however, it has been discovered that guests have eaten, on average, four meals per day.

You report to Alice Groves, the general manager of the hotel, who feels that the format of the draft performance report could be improved to provide her with more meaningful management information. She suggests that the budgeted and actual data given in the existing draft performance report is rearranged in the form of a standard costing report.

Tasks

i) Use the budget data, the actual data and the notes to the performance report to calculate the following for the seven days ended 27 November 2008.

1) The actual number of meals served

2) The standard number of meals which should have been served for the actual number of guests

3) The actual hourly rate paid to catering staff

4) The standard hours allowed for catering staff to serve three meals per day for the actual number of guests

5) The standard fixed overhead per guest

6) The total standard cost for the actual number of guests

ii) Use the data given in the task and your answers to part a) i) to calculate the following variances for the seven days ended 27 November 2008.

1) The material price variance for meals served

2) The material usage variance for meals served

3) The labour rate variance for catering staff

4) The labour efficiency variance for catering staff, based on a standard of three meals served per guest per day

5) The fixed overhead expenditure variance

6) The fixed overhead volume variance on the assumption that the fixed overhead absorption rate is based on the budgeted number of guests per seven days

iii) Prepare a statement reconciling the standard cost for the actual number of guests to the actual cost for the actual number of guests for the seven days ended 27 November 2008.

b) On receiving your reconciliation statement, Alice Groves asks the following questions.

- How much of the labour efficiency variance is due to guests taking, on average, four meals per day rather than the three provided for in the budget and how much is due to other reasons?

- Would it be feasible to subdivide the fixed overhead volume variance into a capacity and efficiency variance?

Task

Write a memo to Alice Groves. Your memo should do the following.

i) Divide the labour efficiency variance into that part due to guests taking more meals than planned and that part due to other efficiency reasons.

ii) Explain the meaning of the fixed overhead capacity and efficiency variances.

iii) Briefly discuss whether or not it is feasible to calculate the fixed overhead capacity and efficiency variances for the Bare Foot Hotel complex.

15 You are employed as a financial analyst at Drampton plc, a computer retailer. One of your duties is to prepare a standard costing reconciliation statement for the finance director.

The company sells two types of computer, personal computers (PCs) for individual use and servers for large organisations. PCs are sold by advertising in newspapers. Customers telephone Drampton to place an order and the telephone call is answered by trained operators. Drampton pays the cost of the telephone call. The total standard cost of one phone call is shown below.

Standard cost of one call

Expense	**Quantity**	**Cost**	**Cost per call**
			£
Telephone cost	1 unit	£0.07 per unit	0.07
Operators' wages	6 minutes	£7.00 per hour	0.70
Fixed overheads [1]	6 minutes	£6.50 per hour	0.65
Standard cost of one telephone call			1.42

[1] Fixed overheads are based on budgeted operator hours.

Drampton's finance director gives you the following information for the three months ended 31 May 2008.

- Budgeted number of calls 900,000 calls
- Actual number of calls 1,000,000 calls
- Actual expenses

	Quantity	*Cost*
		£
Telephone cost	1,200,000 units	79,200
Operators' wages	114,000 hours	877,800
Fixed overheads		540,400
Actual cost of actual operations		1,497,400

Tasks

a) Calculate the following information.

i) Actual cost of a telephone unit
ii) Actual hourly wage rate of operators
iii) Standard number of operator hours for 1,000,000 calls
iv) Budgeted cost of fixed overheads for the three months ended 31 May 2008
v) Budgeted number of operator hours for the three months ended 31 May 2008
vi) Standard cost of actual operations

b) Using the data given and your answers to part a), calculate the following variances.

i) Price variance for telephone calls
ii) Usage variance for telephone calls
iii) Labour rate variance for the telephone operators
iv) Labour efficiency variance for the telephone operators

v) Fixed overhead expenditure variance
vi) Fixed overheard volume variance
vii) Fixed overhead capacity variance
viii) Fixed overhead efficiency variance

c) Prepare a statement for the three months ended 31 May 2008 reconciling the standard cost of actual operations to the actual cost of actual operations.

16 Croxton Ltd makes a specialised chemical, X14, in barrels at its factory. The factory has two departments: the processing department and the finishing department. Because of the technology involved, Croxton apportions both budgeted and actual total factory fixed overheads between the two departments on the basis of budgeted machine hours.

The standard absorption cost per barrel of X14 in the processing department, and the budgeted production for the five weeks ended 31 May 2008, are shown below.

Processing department: standard cost per barrel of X14

Input	*Quantity*	*Standard price/rate*	*Cost*
			£
Material	10 litres	£60 per litre	600
Labour	8 labour hrs	£8 per labour hr	64
Fixed overheads	16 machine hrs	£20 per machine hr	320
Standard absorption cost per barrel			984
Budgeted production 5 weeks ending 31 May 2008			45 barrels

You are employed by Croxton Ltd as an accounting technician. One of your duties is to prepare standard costing reconciliation statements. Croxton's finance director gives you the following information for the five weeks ended 31 May 2008.

Total factory budgeted and actual data

- Factory budgeted machine hours 1,152 machine hours
- Factory budgeted fixed overheads £23,040
- Factory actual fixed overheads £26,000
- Budgeted **and** actual factory fixed overheads are apportioned between the processing and finishing departments **on the basis of budgeted machine hours**.

Processing department actual data

- Actual costs

	Total costs
Materials at £58.50 per litre	£23,985
Labour (328 hours)	£2,788

■ Actual production output	40 barrels
■ Actual machine hours worked	656 hours

- There was no work in progress at any stage.

Tasks

a) Calculate the following information for the processing department.

i) Actual litres of material used
ii) Standard litres of material required for 40 barrels of X14
iii) Average actual labour rate per hour
iv) Standard labour hours required for 40 barrels of X14
v) Budgeted number of machine hours
vi) Budgeted fixed overheads
vii) Actual fixed overheads
viii) Standard machine hours produced
ix) Standard absorption cost of actual production
x) Actual absorption cost of actual production

b) Using data given and your answers to part a), calculate the following variances for the processing department.

i) Material price variance
ii) Material usage variance
iii) Labour rate variance
iv) Labour efficiency variance
v) Fixed overhead expenditure variance
vi) Fixed overhead volume variance
vii) Fixed overhead efficiency variance
viii) Fixed overhead capacity variance

c) Prepare a statement for the five weeks ended 31 May 2008 reconciling the standard absorption cost of actual production with the actual absorption cost of actual production.

d) Judith Green is the production manager of the processing department. You show her the statement reconciling the actual and standard costs of actual production. Judith then gives you the following additional information.

– When the standard costs were agreed, a price index for the material used in making the X14 was 140, but during the five weeks ended 31 May it was 133.

– Actual production output was 40 barrels but Croxton had to make 41 barrels of X14 as one barrel had to be scrapped on completion. This was because the barrel was damaged. The scrapped barrel had no value.

- If labour hours worked exceed 320 hours per five weeks, overtime is incurred. The overtime premium is £8.00 per hour of overtime.
- There is just one customer for the X14. The customer purchased 40 barrels during the five weeks ended 31 May 2008.

Judith believes there is no need to examine the variances any further, for a number of reasons.

- The material price variance clearly shows that the purchasing department is efficient.
- The labour rate, labour efficiency and material usage variances were entirely due to the one scrapped barrel.
- Fixed overheads are not controllable by the processing department.

Write a memo to Judith Green. In your memo you should do the following.

i) Use the material price index to identify a revised standard price for the materials used in X14.

ii) Subdivide the material price variance calculated in task b) i) into that part due to the change in the price index and that part due to other reasons.

iii) Briefly explain whether the material price variance calculated in task b) i) arose from efficiencies in the purchasing department.

iv) Explain whether the one scrapped barrel might fully account for the following.

   1) Material usage variance
   2) Labour efficiency variance
   3) Labour rate variance

v) Give ONE reason why the fixed overheads might not be controllable by the processing department.

chapter 6: PERFORMANCE INDICATORS

1 Given below are the production figures for a factory for the last four months.

	November	*December*	*January*	*February*
Output in units	64,300	68,900	62,100	60,200
Budgeted output	65,000	65,000	60,000	62,000
Hours worked	98,200	107,300	90,200	92,000

The standard time for each unit of production is 1.5 hours.

Calculate the following performance indicators for each of the four months:

i) actual hours per unit
ii) efficiency ratio
iii) capacity ratio
iv) activity ratio

2 What is productivity? Does increased productivity always lead to increased profit? Give examples of increases in productivity that will lead to increased profit and examples that will not necessarily lead to increased profit.

3 Suggest possible measures of productivity for each of the following types of organisation:

i) a taxi firm
ii) a hospital
iii) a motorbike courier service
iv) a firm of accountants
v) a retail store
vi) a maker of handmade pottery

4 You are given the following information about a small manufacturing business for the year ending 31 March:

Sales revenue	£1,447,600
Cost of materials used	£736,500
Cost of bought in services	£316,900
Number of employees	15

What is the total value added and the value added per employee?

5 Given below are production and sales figures for a manufacturing organisation for the last three months:

	January	*February*	*March*
Production costs	£552,300	£568,500	£629,500
Production wages	£104,800	£98,300	£110,800
Output in units	8,540	8,670	9,320
Hours worked	8,635	7,820	9,280
Budgeted output	8,500	8,200	9,500
Sales revenue	£916,000	£923,000	£965,000
Number of employees	55	55	58

Production costs are made up of the materials for production and the bought in services required in the month. It is estimated that each unit takes 1.1 hours to produce.

a) Calculate the following performance indicators for each of the last three months and for the three months in total:

i) productivity per labour hour
ii) efficiency ratio
iii) capacity ratio
iv) activity ratio
v) cost per unit
vi) value added per employee

b) Comment briefly on what the performance indicators show about the business.

6 Given below is the summarised production information for a manufacturing organisation for the last month:

Budgeted production in units	15,000
Actual production in units	14,200
Labour hours worked	46,000
Standard hours for each unit	3

a) Calculate the following performance indicators and briefly explain what each one means:

i) efficiency ratio
ii) capacity ratio
iii) production volume ratio

b) Show how the three performance indicators calculated in part a) are related.

c) If the workforce had operated at 95% efficiency how many labour hours would have been saved last month?

7 A manufacturing organisation had a budgeted output planned for the quarter ending 31 March of 428,000 units but 467,800 units were in fact produced. The standard production time for each unit is 1.5 hours. The actual hours worked were 748,500 and the total production costs were £3,204,430.

Calculate the following performance indicators for the quarter:

i) cost per unit
ii) efficiency ratio
iii) capacity ratio
iv) activity ratio

8 Given below is the profit and loss account for a business for the year ending 31 March 2009 and a balance sheet at that date.

Profit and loss account

	£	£
Turnover		2,650,400
Cost of sales		
Opening stock	180,000	
Purchases	1,654,400	
	1,834,400	
Less: closing stock	191,200	
		1,643,200
Gross profit		1,007,200
Less: expenses		
Selling and distribution costs	328,400	
Administration expenses	342,200	
		670,600
Operating profit		336,600
Interest payable		36,000
		300,600
Tax		87,400
Profit after tax		213,200
Profit and loss reserve brought forward		374,300
Profit and loss reserve carried forward		587,500

Balance sheet

	£	£
Fixed assets		1,920,400
Current assets:		
Stock	191,200	
Debtors	399,400	
Bank	16,800	
	607,400	
Creditors	(190,300)	
Net current assets		417,100
		2,337,500
Less: long term loan		600,000
		1,737,500
Capital		1,000,000
Reserves		150,000
Profit and loss reserve		587,500
		1,737,500

a) Using the profit and loss account and balance sheet calculate the following performance indicators:

i) gross profit margin
ii) net profit margin
iii) return on capital employed
iv) asset turnover
v) fixed asset turnover
vi) current ratio
vii) quick ratio
viii) debtors' collection period
ix) stock turnover in days
x) creditors' payment period
xi) interest cover
xii) gearing ratio

b) If the creditors payment period was increased to 60 days what effect would this have on the cash balance?

9 Given below is a summary of a business's performance for the last six months:

	July	*Aug*	*Sept*	*Oct*	*Nov*	*Dec*
	£'000	£'000	£'000	£'000	£'000	£'000
Sales	560	540	500	550	580	600
Cost of sales	370	356	330	374	400	415
Expenses	123	119	110	116	122	131
Interest payable	–	–	–	3	3	3
Shareholders funds	440	445	458	468	480	490
Loan	–	–	–	50	50	50

a) For each month of the year you are to calculate the following performance indicators:

i) gross profit margin
ii) net profit margin
iii) percentage of expenses to sales
iv) return on capital employed
v) asset turnover

b) Comment on what the figures calculated in part a) show about the performance of the business over the last six months.

10 Given below is a summary of the performance of a business for the last three years:

	2006	*2007*	*2008*
	£'000	£'000	£'000
Sales	1,420	1,560	1,740
Cost of sales	850	950	1,080
Expenses	370	407	469
Interest	–	7	6
Capital and reserves	1,500	1,600	1,700
Long term loan	–	100	100
Fixed assets	1,100	1,300	1,500
Debtors	155	198	230
Stock	105	140	190
Creditors	140	162	193
Bank balance	280	224	73

For each of the three years you are to calculate the following performance measures and comment on what the measures indicate about the performance of the business over the period:

i) gross profit margin
ii) net profit margin
iii) return on capital employed
iv) asset turnover
v) fixed asset turnover
vi) current ratio
vii) quick ratio
viii) debtors' collection period
ix) stock turnover in days
x) creditors' payment period

11 A manufacturing business has three small divisions, North, South and Central. The figures for the last three months of 2006 for each division are given below:

	North	*South*	*Central*
	£	£	£
Financial details			
Sales	870,000	560,000	640,000
Opening stocks	34,000	41,000	34,000
Closing stocks	32,000	29,000	38,000
Purchases	590,000	380,000	420,000
Expenses	121,000	106,000	138,000
Capital	980,000	690,000	615,000
Creditors	103,400	42,600	66,700
Debtors	100,100	107,300	87,600
Non-financial details			
Factory floor area	500 sq m	400 sq m	420 sq m
Factory employees	18	12	15
Hours worked	8,500	5,800	7,000
Units produced	17,000	10,200	12,300

a) You are to calculate the following performance indicators for each division:

i) gross profit margin
ii) net profit margin
iii) return on capital employed
iv) asset turnover
v) stock turnover in months (using average stock)
vi) debtors' collection period in months
vii) creditors' payment period in months
viii) units produced per square metre of floor area
ix) units produced per employee
x) units produced per hour

b) Use the performance indicators calculated in a) to compare the performances of the three divisions for the three-month period.

12 i) A business operates on a gross profit margin of 48% and sales for the period were £380,000. What is the gross profit?

ii) A business operates on a gross profit margin of 34% and the gross profit made in the period was £425,000. What were the sales for the period?

iii) A business had sales of £85,000 in a month and with a gross profit margin of 40% and a net profit margin of 11.5%. What were the expenses for the month?

iv) A business has a return on capital employed of 11.6% and made a net profit for the period of £100,000. What is the capital employed?

v) A business has a net profit percentage of 8% and a return on capital employed of 10%. What is the asset turnover of the business?

vi) A business has opening stocks and closing stocks of £158,000 and £182,000 and made purchases during the year totalling £560,000. How many times did stock turnover during the year?

vii) A business has a debtor collection period of 48 days and the closing debtors figure is £96,000. What are the sales for the year?

13 A business has a gross profit margin of 42.3% for the year ending 31 December 2008 and had a gross profit margin of 44.6% for the year ending 31 December 2007. Suggest reasons for the change in gross profit margin.

14 Given below are the summarised profit and loss accounts and balance sheets of a business for the last two years.

Summarised profit and loss accounts

	Y/e 31 Dec 2008 £'000	*Y/e 31 Dec 2007* £'000
Turnover	602	564
Cost of sales	329	325
Gross profit	273	239
Expenses	163	143
Operating profit	110	96
Interest payable	10	10
Profit before tax	100	86
Tax	40	26
Retained profit	60	60
Profit and loss reserve b/f	240	180
Profit and loss reserve c/f	300	240

Summarised balance sheet

	31 Dec 2008		31 Dec 2007	
	£	£	£	£
Fixed assets		709		632
Current assets:				
Stock	28		32	
Debtors	66		68	
Cash	2		3	
	96		103	
Creditors	55		45	
Net current assets		41		58
		750		690
Long term loan		150		150
		600		540
Capital		300		300
Profit and loss reserve		300		240
		600		540

a) For each of the two years calculate the following performance indicators, based on total capital employed when relevant.

i) gross profit margin
ii) net profit margin
iii) return on capital employed
iv) asset turnover
v) fixed asset turnover
vi) current ratio
vii) quick ratio
viii) debtors' collection period
ix) stock turnover in days
x) creditors' payment period
xi) interest cover
xii) gearing ratio

b) Comment upon the performance of the business for the last two years basing your comments on the performance indicators calculated in part a).

15 What are the main limitations of ratio analysis?

16 Melosoven Ltd is a subsidiary company of Rengbaud plc and manufactures motor components. It is run as a separate entity from the parent company, however. Rengbaud plc monitors the performance of subsidiaries using a quarterly financial ratio analysis. Melosoven Ltd's factory is in Swansea.

You are employed as a financial analyst in Rengbaud plc's corporate finance department at the group's Leicestershire headquarters. Louise Simpson, the managing director of Melosoven Ltd, is at group head office for a meeting. She has called into your office with the last quarter's summary results which have just been faxed to her. Louise needs to have these figures analysed as quickly as possible and has obtained the agreement of Rob Hutchings, your immediate superior, for you to assist her.

Melosoven Ltd
Financial results for quarter 4

Operating statement			**Operating net assets at quarter end**		
	£'000	£'000		£'000	£'000
Sales		4,759	Fixed assets (NBV)		7,253
Materials	1,583				
Labour	1,196		Current assets		
Production overheads	1,201		Materials stocks	305	
		3,980	Work in progress	224	
Gross profit		779	Finished goods stocks	1,326	
Admin overheads		427	Debtors	2,040	
Operating profit		352	Bank and cash	83	
				3,978	
			Current liabilities		
Stock changes			Trade creditors	2,362	
Materials		+ 43	Other creditors	758	
Work in progress		0		3,120	
Finished goods		+ 231	Working capital		858
			Net assets		8,111

Tasks

a) Given that there are 91 days in quarter 4, prepare a table containing the following performance indicators for Melosoven Ltd for quarter 4.

i) The quarterly return on capital employed

ii) The operating profit margin as a percentage

iii) The quarterly asset turnover

iv) The average age of period-end debtors in days

v) The average age of period-end trade creditors in days

vi) The average age of period-end materials stocks in days

vii) The average age of period-end finished goods stocks in days

b) Louise needs a comparison between the quarter 4 results and those for the earlier quarters to take with her to a meeting at which Rengbaud plc's board will be reviewing the performance of Melosoven Ltd.

You are able to extract the following figures from Rengbaud plc's corporate information system.

Performance indicators for Melosoven Ltd for quarters 1 to 3

	Q1	*Q2*	*Q3*
Return on capital employed	4.3%	1.2%	2.8%
Operating profit margin	9.0%	2.6%	5.3%
Quarterly asset turnover	0.54	0.55	0.52
Age of debtors in days	39	38	44
Age of trade creditors in days	192	167	158
Age of materials stocks in days	29	24	18
Age of finished goods stocks in days	51	41	28

i) Given that Melosoven Ltd's business is not seasonal, update the above table to include Melosoven Ltd's quarter 4 figures.

ii) Write a briefing note to Louise comparing Melosoven Ltd's quarter 4 figures with those for quarters 1 to 3.

17 Middle plc owns two subsidiaries, East Ltd and West Ltd, producing soft drinks. Both companies rent their premises and both use plant of similar size and technology. Middle plc requires the plant in the subsidiaries to be written off over ten years using straight-line depreciation and assuming zero residual values.

East Ltd was established five years ago but West Ltd has only been established for two years. Goods returned by customers generally arise from quality failures and are destroyed. Financial and other data relating to the two companies are reproduced below.

Profit and loss accounts year to 30 November 2008

	West Ltd	*East Ltd*
	£'000	£'000
Turnover	18,000	17,600
Less Returns	90	176
Net turnover	17,910	17,424
Material	2,000	2,640
Labour	4,000	4,840
Production overheads*	3,000	3,080
Gross profit	8,910	6,864
Marketing	2,342	1,454
Research & development	1,650	1,010
Training	950	450
Administration	900	1,155
Operating profit	3,068	2,795

Balance sheets extracts at 30 November 2008

	West Ltd	*East Ltd*
	£'000	£'000
Plant	16,000	10,000
Depreciation to date	3,200	5,000
Net book value	12,800	5,000
Current assets	4,860	3,000
Current liabilities	(2,320)	(1,500)
Net assets	15,340	6,500

*Includes plant depreciation of £1,600,000 for West Ltd and £1,000,000 for East Ltd

Other data (000's litres)	*West Ltd*	*East Ltd*
Gross sales	20,000	22,000
Returns	100	220
Net sales	19,900	21,780
Orders received in year	20,173	22,854

You are employed by Middle plc as a member of a team monitoring the performance of subsidiaries within the group. Middle plc aims to provide its shareholders with the best possible return for their investment and to meet customers' expectations. It does this by comparing the performance of subsidiaries and using the more efficient ones for benchmarking.

Tasks

Your team leader, Angela Wade, has asked you to prepare a report evaluating the performance of West Ltd and East Ltd. Your report should do the following.

a) Calculate and explain the meaning of the following financial ratios for each company.

   i) The return on capital employed
   ii) The asset turnover
   iii) The sales (or operating profit) margin

b) Calculate the percentage cf faulty sales as a measure of the level of customer service for each company.

c) Identify ONE other possible measure of the level of customer service which could be derived from the accounting data.

d) Identify TWO limitations to your analysis in task a), using the data in the accounts.

18 a) You are employed by Micro Circuits Ltd as a financial analyst reporting to Angela Frear, the Director of Corporate Strategy. One of your responsibilities is to monitor the performance of subsidiaries within the group. Financial and other data relating to subsidiary A is reproduced below.

Subsidiary A

Profit and loss account year to 30 November 2008

	£'000	£'000
Sales		4,000
less returns		100
Turnover[1]		3,900
Material	230	
Labour	400	
Production overheads[2]	300	
Cost of production	930	
Opening finished stock	50	
Closing finished stock	(140)	
Cost of sales		840
Gross profit		3,060
Marketing	500	
Customer support	400	
Research and development	750	
Training	140	
Administration	295	2,085
Operating profit		975

Extract from balance sheet at 30 November 2008

	£'000	£'000	£'000
Fixed assets	*Land and buildings*	*Plant and machinery*	*Total*
Cost	2,000	2,500	4,500
Additions	–	1,800	1,800
	2,000	4,300	6,300
Accumulated dep'n	160	1,700	1,860
	1,840	2,600	4,440
Raw material stock	15		
Finished goods stock	140		
	155		
Debtors	325		
Cash and bank	40		
Creditors	(85)		
			435
Net assets			4,875

Other information

Notes

1. Analysis of turnover

	£'000		£'000
Regular customers	3,120	New products	1,560
New customers	780	Existing products	2,340
	3,900		3,900

2. Production overheads include £37,200 of reworked faulty production.

3. Orders received in the year totalled £4,550,000.

Task

Angela Frear asks you to calculate the following performance indicators in preparation for a board meeting.

i) The return on capital employed
ii) The asset turnover
iii) The sales (or operating profit) margin
iv) The average age of debtors in months
v) The average age of finished stock in months

b) One of the issues to be discussed at the board meeting is the usefulness of performance indicators. Angela Frear has recently attended a conference on creating and enhancing value.

Three criticisms were made of financial performance indicators.

- They could give misleading signals.
- They could be manipulated.
- They focus on the short term and do not take account of other key, non-financial performance indicators.

At the conference, Angela was introduced to the idea of the balanced scorecard. The balanced scorecard looks at performance measurement from four perspectives.

The financial perspective
This is concerned with satisfying shareholders. Examples include the return on capital employed and sales margin.

The customer perspective
This asks how customers view the business and is concerned with measures of customer satisfaction. Examples include speed of delivery and customer loyalty.

The internal perspective
This looks at the quality of the company's output in terms of technical excellence and customer needs. Examples would be striving towards total quality management and flexible production as well as unit cost.

The innovation and learning perspective
This is concerned with the continual improvement of existing products and the ability to develop new products as customers' needs change. An example would be the percentage of turnover attributable to new products.

Task

Angela Frear asks you to prepare briefing notes for the board meeting. Using the data from part a) where necessary, your notes should do the following.

i) Suggest ONE reason why the return on capital employed calculated in a) might be misleading.

ii) Identify ONE way of manipulating the sales (or operating profit) margin.

iii) Calculate the average delay in fulfilling orders.

iv) Identify ONE other possible measure of customer satisfaction other than the delay in fulfilling orders.

v) Calculate TWO indicators which may help to measure performance from an internal perspective.

vi) Calculate ONE performance indicator which would help to measure the innovation and learning perspective.

19 a) Travel Bus Ltd is owned by Travel Holdings plc. It operates in the town of Camford. Camford is an old town with few parking facilitates for motorists. Several years ago, the Town Council built a car park on the edge of the town and awarded Travel Bus the contract to carry motorists and their passengers between the car park and the centre of the town.

Originally, the Council charged motorists £4.00 per day for the use of the car park but, to encourage motorists not to take their cars into the town centre, parking has been free since 1 December 2007.

The journey between the car park and the town centre is the only service operated by Travel Bus Ltd in Camford. A summary of the results for the first two years of operations, together with the net assets associated with the route and other operating data, is reproduced below.

Operating statement year ended 30 November

	2007	2008
	£	£
Turnover	432,000	633,600
Fuel	129,600	185,328
Wages	112,000	142,000
Other variable costs	86,720	84,512
Gross profit	103,680	221,760
Bus road tax and insurance	22,000	24,000
Depreciation of buses	12,000	12,000
Maintenance of buses	32,400	28,512
Fixed garaging costs	29,840	32,140
Administration	42,000	49,076
Net profit/(loss)	(34,560)	76,032

Extract from balance sheet at 30 November

	2007	2008
	£	£
Buses	240,000	240,000
Accumulated depreciation	168,000	180,000
Net book value	72,000	60,000
Net current assets	14,400	35,040
	86,400	95,040

Other operating data	2007	2008
Fare per passenger journey	£0.80	£1.00
Miles per year	324,000	356,400
Miles per journey	18.0	18.0
Days per year	360	360
Wages per driver	£14,000	£14,200

Throughout the two years, the drivers were paid a basic wage per week, no bonuses were paid and no overtime was incurred.

In two weeks there will be a meeting between officials of the Town Council and the chief executive of Travel Holdings to discuss the performance of Travel Bus for the year to 30 November 2008. The previous year's performance indicators were as follows.

Gross profit margin	24%
Net profit margin	–8%
Return on capital employed	–40%
Asset turnover	5 times
Number of passengers in the year	540,000
Total cost per mile	£1.44
Number of journeys per day	50
Maintenance cost per mile	£0.10
Passengers per day	1,500
Passengers per journey	30
Number of drivers	8

Tasks

In preparation for the meeting, you have been asked to calculate the following performance indicators for the year to 30 November 2008.

i) Gross profit margin
ii) Net profit margin
iii) Return on capital employed
iv) Asset turnover
v) Number of passengers in the year
vi) Total cost per mile
vii) Number of journeys per day
viii) Maintenance cost per mile
ix) Passengers per day
x) Passengers per journey
xi) Number of drivers

b) On receiving your performance indicators, the chief executive of Travel Holdings raises the following issues with you.

- The drivers are claiming that the improved profitability of Travel Bus reflects their increased productivity.
- The managers believe that the change in performance is due to improved motivation arising from the introduction of performance related pay for managers during the year to 30 November 2008.
- The officials from the Town Council are concerned that Travel Bus is paying insufficient attention to satisfying passengers needs and safety.

The chief executive asks for your advice.

Task

Write a memo to the chief executive of Travel Holdings plc. Where relevant, you should make use of the data and answers to task a) to do the following.

i) Briefly discuss whether or not increased productivity always leads to increased profitability.

ii) Develop ONE possible measure of driver productivity and suggest whether or not the drivers' claim is valid.

iii) Suggest ONE reason, other than improved motivation, why the profitability of Travel Bus might have improved.

iv) 1) Suggest ONE existing performance indicator which might measure the satisfaction of passenger needs.

   2) Suggest ONE other possible performance indicator of passenger needs which cannot be measured from the existing performance data collected by Travel Bus.

v) 1) Suggest ONE existing performance indicator which might measure the safety aspect of Travel Bus's operations.

   2) Suggest ONE other possible performance indicator which cannot be measured from the existing performance data collected by Travel Bus.

20 You are employed as a financial analyst by Alderton Ltd, a chain of bookstores. Alderton's main competitor is Brandon Ltd. Extracts from the latest operating statements and balance sheets for both companies, together with other operating data, are shown below.

Statement of assets at 31 May 2008

	Alderton Ltd			Brandon Ltd		
	Leashold buildings	*Fixtures and fittings*	*Total*	*Leashold buildings*	*Fixtures and fittings*	*Total*
	£m	£m	£m	£m	£m	£m
Fixed assets						
Cost	500	200	700	200	80	280
Accumulated depreciation	100	80	180	184	56	240
Net book value	400	120	520	16	24	40
Net current assets						
Stocks		150			140	
Debtors		30			40	
Cash		5			50	
Creditors		(65)			(30)	
			120			200
			640			240

Operating statements for the year ended 31 May 2008

	Alderton Ltd		Brandon Ltd	
	£m	£m	£m	£m
Turnover		720		480
Opening stocks	60		200	
Purchases	450		150	
Less closing stock	(150)		(140)	
Cost of sales		360		210
Gross profit		360		270
Retail wages	60		40	
Depreciation buildings	10		4	
Depreciation fixtures and fittings	40		8	
Other expenses	70		80	
		180		132
Operating profit		180		138

Other operating data

	Alderton Ltd	*Brandon Ltd*
Square metres of floor space	240,000	200,000
Number of transactions	48,000,000	60,000,000
Number of employees	4,800	4,000

You report to Beverly Richards, the financial director of Alderton. Beverley has already calculated performance indicators for Alderton and these are shown below. She asks you to prepare similar indicators for Brandon Ltd. She tells you that Brandon did not have any bought-in services during the year ended 31 May 2008.

Alderton Ltd: performance indicators year ended 31 May 2008	
Sales margin	25%
Gross profit margin	50%
Asset turnover	1.125 times
Return on capital employed	28.125%
Average age of stocks	5 months
Average age of debtors	0.5 months
Added value per employee	£75,000
Average sales value per transaction	£15
Sales per employee	£150,000
Transactions per employee	10,000
Sales per square metre	£3,000

Tasks

a) Prepare the following performance indicators for Brandon Ltd.

i) Sales (or net profit) margin
ii) Gross profit margin
iii) Asset turnover
iv) Return on capital employed
v) Average age of stocks in months
vi) Average age of debtors in months
vii) Added value per employee
viii) Average sales value per transaction
ix) Sales per employee
x) Transactions per employee
xi) Sales per square metre

b) Beverley Richards gives you two pieces of information about the directors of Alderton.

- They are concerned about the differences in the performance indicators of the two companies.
- They currently use the return on capital employed as the main measure of efficiency and the asset turnover as the main measure of productivity.

She also tells you the following.

- During the year the average cost of books purchased by retailers had been falling.
- Alderton values stocks on a first-in-first out basis, but Brandon uses last-in first-out.
- Both companies use straight line depreciation assuming zero residual balances.

The directors have askec Beverley to prepare a report showing the reasons for the differences in the performance indicators and suggesting other possible ways of measuring productivity and efficiency. Beverley asks for your help.

Prepare draft notes for Beverley Richards. In the notes, you should do the following.

i) Explain what is meant by the following terms.

 1) Productivity
 2) Efficiency

ii) Give TWO possible reasons why there is a difference in the net book value of the fixed assets of the two companies.

iii) Show TWO ways the difference in the net book value of the fixed assets would affect the return on capital employed for Alderton.

iv) Explain the likely effect of the two different stock valuation policies on the operating profits and value of net assets of the two companies.

v) Give TWO limitations to using added value per employee as a measure of employee productivity.

vi) Suggest a valid alternative to asset turnover as a measure of employee productivity.

chapter 7: QUALITY

1 How would you define quality of products or services?

2 Define the four types of quality cost (prevention, appraisal, internal failure and external failure) and give three examples of each.

3 For each of the following state which type of cost of quality it is (prevention, appraisal, internal failure or external failure):

		Type of cost
i)	lost contribution on defective products sold as seconds	....
ii)	cost of replacing faulty products	....
iii)	claims from customers relating to defective products	....
iv)	products scrapped due to faulty raw materials	....
v)	training for quality control staff	....
vi)	maintenance of quality control equipment	....
vii)	performance testing of finished goods	....
viii)	costs of customer after sales service department	....
ix)	costs of inspection of raw materials	....
x)	costs of production delays due to re-working defective products discovered in quality inspection	....

4 A clothing manufacturer has had a number of events occurring recently:

i) the internal designers have designed a new type of zipper that should last much longer than normal zippers and should reduce returns of products

ii) one line of jumpers procuced over the last few months were produced on a faulty machine and have been returned by all the retailers who purchased them as the seams have come apart. Some of the retailers are considering suing the company for losses caused and it is almost certain that they will never purchase from the manufacturer again

iii) it has been discovered that the fabric used to make a large quantity of men's suits was flawed and these can now only be sold at a drastically reduced price as seconds

As a result of this discovery the manufacturer has introduced new inspection controls for raw materials.

Analyse each of these events and determine what effects they are likely to have on the various categories of quality costs – prevention, appraisal, internal failure and external failure.

5 Define explicit and implicit costs of quality. Give three examples of explicit costs of quality and three examples of implicit costs of quality.

6 A manufacturing business estimates that 3 out of every 1,000 of its products that is sold is defective in some way. When the goods are returned by customers they are replaced free of charge. It is estimated that 70% of customers who buy a faulty product will return it but that all customers who buy a faulty product will not buy from the business again. Each unit costs £10 to manufacture and is sold at a price of £15.

Due to quality inspections it is also estimated that 4,000 defective units a year are discovered before they are sold and these can then be sold as 'seconds' at a price of £11. The quality inspections cost £35,000 each year.

The unit sales of the product are 10 million each year.

Analyse and calculate the explicit costs of quality and determine whether there are any implicit costs of quality.

7 A manufacturing business estimates that it has to sell 7,500 defective units of its product at a 'seconds' price of £20 per unit. The normal selling price is £33 per unit and the inspection procedure that identifies these defective units costs £60,000.

What are the costs of quality and what type or types of quality cost are they?

8 A business estimates that one in 6,000 of its products are found to be faulty after sale. Of these it is estimated that 75% are returned by customers and can be repaired at a cost of £10 per product. It is felt that the customers who do not return the products will not buy the company's products again and the cost of advertising for replacement customers is £5,000 per annum. The customers that do return their products for repair are likely to purchase again from the business.

Total sales of the product are 8 million units each year.

List all of the costs of quality and the amount of that cost where possible. State into which category of cost of quality each cost falls.

9 A manufacturing organisation carries out quality inspections on its product and in the last year 5,200 defective units were discovered and had to be sold as seconds at a price of £108 compared with the normal selling price of £200. The costs of the quality inspections totalled £340,000 for the year.

Sales of the product are 1 million units each year and it is estimated that a further 1 in every 2,000 sales will be defective. Of these it is expected that 60% will be returned by customers and will be replaced free of charge. The cost of producing a unit of the product is £120. The customers who do not return their products are unlikely to buy the company's products again.

List all of the costs of quality incurred by the business and the amount of that cost if possible. State which type of cost of quality each cost is and whether it is an explicit cost or an implicit cost.

10 What is life-cycle costing?

11 Barnet Ltd is a small company owned by Hampstead plc. Barnet operates a job costing system making a specialist, expensive piece of hospital equipment.

Existing system

Currently, employees are assigned to individual jobs and materials are requisitioned from stores as needed. The standard and actual costs of labour and materials are recorded for each job. These job costs are totalled to produce the marginal cost of production. Fixed production costs – including the cost of storekeeping and inspection of deliveries and finished equipment – are then added to determine the standard and actual cost of production. Any costs of remedial work are included in the materials and labour for each job.

Proposed system

Carol Johnson, the chief executive of Barnet, has recently been to a seminar on modern manufacturing techniques. As a result, she is considering introducing Just-in-Time stock deliveries and Total Quality Management. Barnet would offer suppliers a long-term contract at a fixed price but suppliers would have to guarantee the quality of their materials.

In addition, she proposes that the workforce is organised as a single team with flexible work practices. This would mean employees helping each other as necessary, with no employee being allocated a particular job. If a job was delayed, the workforce would work overtime without payment in order for the job to be completed on time. In exchange, employees would be guaranteed a fixed weekly wage and time off when production was slack to make up for any overtime incurred.

Cost of quality

Carol has asked to meet you to discuss the implications of her proposals on the existing accounting system. She is particularly concerned to monitor the **cost of quality**. This is defined as the total of all costs incurred in preventing defects plus those costs involved in remedying defects once they have occurred. It is a single figure measuring all the explicit costs of quality – that is, those costs collected within the accounting system.

Task

In preparation for the meeting, produce **brief** notes. Your notes should:

a) identify FOUR general headings (or classifications) which make up the **cost of quality**;

b) give ONE example of a type of cost likely to be found within each category;

c) assuming Carol Johnson's proposals are accepted, state, with reasons, whether or not:

   i) a standard marginal costing system would still be of help to the managers;
   ii) it would still be meaningful to collect costs by each individual job;

d) identify ONE cost saving in Carol Johnson's proposals which would not be recorded in the existing costing system.

12 a) You are employed as the assistant management accountant with Local Engineering Ltd, a company which designs and makes a single product, the X4, used in the telecommunications industry. The company has a goods received store which employs staff who carry out random checks to ensure materials are of the correct specification. In addition to the random checks, a standard allowance is made for failures due to faulty materials at the completion stage and the normal practice is to charge the cost of any remedial work required to the cost of production for the month. Once delivered to the customer, any faults discovered in the X4 during its warranty period become an expense of the customer support department.

At the end of each month, management reports are prepared for the Board of Directors. These identify the cost of running the stores and the number of issues, the cost of production and the number of units manufactured, and the cost of customer support.

Jane Greenwood, Local Engineering's management accountant, has just returned from a board meeting to discuss a letter the company recently received from Universal Telecom, Local Engineering's largest customer. In the letter, Universal Telecom explained that it was determined to maintain its position as a world-class provider of telecommunication services and that there was serious concern about the quality of the units delivered by your company. At the meeting, Local Engineering Ltd's board responded by agreeing to establish a company-wide policy of implementing a Total Quality Management (TQM) programme, commencing with a revised model of the X4. Design work on the new model is scheduled to commence in six month's time.

One aspect of this will involve the management accounting department collecting the cost of quality. This is defined as the total of all costs incurred in preventing defects plus those costs involved in remedying defects once they have occurred within the accounting system – attributable to producing output that is not within its specification.

Task

As a first step towards the implementation of TQM, a meeting of the senior staff in the management accounting department has been called to discuss the role the department can play in making TQM a success. Jane Greenwood has asked you to prepare a brief background paper for the meeting.

Your paper should do the following.

i) Explain in outline what is meant by Total Quality Management.

ii) Briefly discuss why the current accounting system fails to highlight the cost of quality.

iii) Identify FOUR general categories (or classifications) of Local Engineering's activities where expenditure making up the explicit cost of quality will be found.

iv) Give ONE example of a cost found within each category.

v) Give ONE example of a cost of quality not normally identified by the accounting system.

b) Local Engineering Ltd has capacity to produce no more than 1,000 X4s per month and currently is able to sell all production immediately at a unit selling price of £1,250. A major component of the X4 is a complex circuit board. Spot checks are made on these boards by a team of specialist employees when they are received into stores. In May, 100 units were found to be faulty. Good components are then issued to production along with other material.

Upon completion, each X4 is tested. If there is a fault, this involves further remedial work prior to dispatch to customers. For the month of May, 45 units of the X4 had to be reworked because of subsequent faults discovered in the circuit board. This remedial work cost an additional £13,500 in labour charges.

Should a fault occur after delivery to the customer, Local Engineering is able to call upon a team of self-employed engineers to rectify the fault as part of its customer support function. The cost of the remedial work by the self-employed engineers carried out in May – and the number of times they were used – is shown as contractors under customer support.

Extract from the accounting records of Local Engineering Ltd for the month of May

	Units	£		Units	£
Purchases:			Production:		
Printed circuits	1,000	120,000	Printed circuits	900	108,000
Less returns	(100)	(12,000)	Other material		121,500
Net costs	900	108,000	Labour		193,500
Other material		121,500	Direct prod'n o/hd		450,000
Total purchases issued to production		229,500	Cost of production		873,000
Other direct stores costs:					
Goods received, labour costs and rent		54,000	Customer support:		
Inspection costs		10,000	Direct costs		36,000
Costs of returns	100	4,500	Contractors	54	24,300
Costs of stores		68,500			60,300

Task

As part of the continuing development of Total Quality Management, you are asked by Jane Greenwood to calculate the following:

i) The explicit **cost of quality** for Local Engineering Ltd for the month of May
ii) A further **cost of quality** not reported in the above accounting records.

chapter 8: BUDGETARY CONTROL SYSTEMS

1 a) What is a budget?

b) How can a budgetary system help management to perform their duties and carry out their responsibilities?

2 a) What is the difference between strategic plans and operational plans?

b) Explain how the management of a business will set the strategic plans and operational plans for the business.

3 Why is it important to produce a capital budget?

4 Briefly explain what figures would appear in each of the resource budgets that a manufacturing organisation would be likely to prepare and how these figures would be determined.

5 a) What is a key budget factor and why is it important?

b) Give three examples of possible key budget factors for a manufacturing organisation other than sales demand.

6 In each of the following situations suggest what may be the key budget factor:

i) A private nursing home with 140 beds. The home is situated in an area which has a large proportion of retired amongst the population and there is little difficulty in recruiting suitable staff.

ii) A vendor of ice cream in a busy shopping centre. The transportable stall can store a maximum of 50 litres of ice cream.

iii) A partnership of three skilled craftsmen making carved chess sets from wood and marble for home sales and exports to specific order. Sales demand is high and orders have to be frequently rejected.

iv) A manufacturer of CD players and hi-fi systems which are similar to those of other manufacturers and who distributes the systems amongst a number of small high street electrical retailers.

7 Briefly explain each of the following terms:

i) budget manual
ii) budget committee
iii) budget holder
iv) master budget

8 Explain the procedures that will be followed from the start of the budgeting process through to the completion of the master budget in a participative budgeting system.

9 What is a rolling budget and what benefits does it have?

10 Explain each of the following terms:

i) incremental budgeting
ii) zero-based budgeting
iii) activity-based budgeting

11 A company is considering its budget for next year and estimates that it will sell 300 units of product J during August and 600 units during September.

Each unit of product J requires eight hours of labour, the labour rate being £8 per hour.

It is company policy to hold stocks of finished goods at the end of each month equal to 50% of the following month's sales demand.

At the end of the production process the products are tested: it is usual for 10% of those tested to be faulty. It is not possible to rectify these faulty units.

Explain clearly, using the data above, how you would construct a spreadsheet to produce the labour requirements budget for August. Include a specimen cell layout diagram containing formulae which would be the basis for the spreadsheet.

chapter 9: FORECASTING INCOME

1 Forecasting is an important technique for budgeting purposes however it has limitations. Explain the general limitations of forecasting.

2 A business has analysed its historical sales data and has estimated that the trend of its sales figures in units over the last three years has been a 3.5% increase in each quarter. The sales in quarter 1 were 122,000 units.

The time series analysis has also indicated the following seasonal variations

Quarter 1	+6,000 units
Quarter 2	–8,000 units
Quarter 3	+12,000 units
Quarter 4	–10,000 units

Using this information what are the forecast sales in units for the remaining three quarters?

3 The trend figures for sales in units for a business for the four quarters of 2008 are given below:

Quarter 1	320,000
Quarter 2	325,000
Quarter 3	330,000
Quarter 4	335,000

The seasonal variations are expressed as follows:

Quarter 1	–18%
Quarter 2	+21%
Quarter 3	+7%
Quarter 4	–10%

What are the forecast sales for each of the quarters of 2009?

4 The sales data for the last three years have been subject to a time series analysis and the trend is that there is an increase of 2% per quarter in unit sales. The unit sales for quarter 4 of 2008 were 90,000 units.

The time series analysis also shows the following seasonal variations:

Quarter 1	–31%
Quarter 2	–3%
Quarter 3	+23%
Quarter 4	+11%

Forecast the unit sales for each of the four quarters of 2009.

5 The trend figures for sales in units for a business for the four quarters of 2008 and the seasonal variations are estimated as:

	Trend unit sales	*Seasonal variations*
Quarter 1	160,000 units	+7%
Quarter 2	164,500 units	+9%
Quarter 3	169,000 units	–3%
Quarter 4	173,500 units	–13%

What are the forecast sales in units for each of the quarters of 2009?

6 The sales of a business are considered by the sales director to have a distinct trend and regular seasonal variations. The recent quarterly sales have been as follows:

Units sold each quarter

Year	*Quarter 1*	*Quarter 2*	*Quarter 3*	*Quarter 4*
2006			1,900	2,300
2007	2,800	3,000	2,400	2,500
2008	3,200	3,400	2,500	2,700
2009	3,500	3,700*		

* estimated figure

You are to:

i) calculate the centred four quarter moving average trend figures

ii) calculate the seasonal variations using the additive method

iii) forecast the sales volume for quarter 3 of 2009

iv) suggest two reasons why there might be a difference between the forecast figure for sales in quarter 3 of 2009 and the actual figure

7 What are the limitations of using time series analysis to forecast figures?

8 a) Explain the five stages of the product life cycle and how costs and income will alter in each of the five stages.

b) How does knowledge of the product life cycle affect forecasting of future sales?

9 At which stage in the product life cycle is time series analysis likely to produce a fairly accurate figure for future sales?

10 The following spreadsheet is to be used to forecast the sales for the following year in both units and in value.

	A	B	C	D	E
1	Unit sales prices – £	150			
2	Annual sales volume – units	180,000			
3	Seasonal variation	–14%	–28%	+20%	+22%
4		Quarter 1	Quarter 2	Quarter 3	Quarter 4
5	Seasonal variation – units				
6	Quarterly volume – units				
7	Quarterly sales – £				

You are to:

i) insert formulae in rows 5, 6 and 7 of the spreadsheet in order to determine the quarterly figures for unit sales and sales value

ii) calculate the quarterly sales in units and in value

11 Star Fuels is a multinational oil company selling oil for industrial and domestic purposes through a network of distributors. Distributors purchase fuel oil from Star Fuels and then sell it on to their own customers.

A regular complaint of the distributors is that they either have to pay for the fuel on delivery to their storage tanks or be charged interest on a daily basis on the amount owed. This problem could be reduced if the distributors were able to forecast their demands more accurately.

You are employed as the Assistant Management Accountant to Northern Fuel Distributors Ltd, a major distributor of Star Fuels's fuel oils. You recently attended a meeting with Mary Lamberton, a member of Star Fuels's central staff. At the meeting, she demonstrated a statistical software package used for estimating demand for fuel oil. The user enters sales volumes per period and the package then calculates the least-squares regression equation for the data. This is in the form y = a + bx where x is the time period, y is the forecast and a and b are terms derived from the original data. Following further inputs by the user, the package can also estimate seasonal variations. Two forms of seasonal variation are calculated: the first calculates the seasonal variance as an absolute amount, the second as a percentage.

One week after the meeting, your copy of the software arrives at the head office of Northern Fuel Distributors Ltd and you immediately set about testing its capability. Purely for the purpose of testing, you assume seasonal variations occur quarterly. You enter this assumption along with the sales turnover figures for fuel oil for the last 20 quarters. Within moments, the software outputs the following information.

Regression line y = £2,000,000 + £40,000x

Seasonal variations

Quarter	*A*	*B*	*C*	*D*
Amount	+£350,000	+£250,000	–£400,000	–£200,000
Percentage	+15%	+10%	–15%	–10%

Quarter A refers to the first quarter of annual data, B to the second quarter, C to the third and D to the fourth. The pattern then repeats itself. In terms of the specific data you input, seasonal variation A refers to quarter 17, B to quarter 18, C to quarter 19 and D to quarter 20.

Actual sales turnover for quarters 17 to 20 was as follows.

Quarter	*17*	*18*	*19*	*20*
Sales turnover	£3,079,500	£3,002,400	£2,346,500	£2,490,200

Tasks

a) Making use of the formula derived by the software package, calculate the forecast sales turnover for quarters 17 to 20 using:

   i) the absolute seasonal variations;
   ii) the percentage seasonal variations.

b) i) From your answers to task a), determine which method of calculating seasonal variations gives the best estimate of actual sales turnover.

   ii) Having identified the preferred method, use that method to forecast the sales turnover for quarters 21 to 24.

c) Write a memorandum to your managing director. The memorandum should do the following.

   i) Explain what is meant by seasonal variations and seasonally adjusted data. Illustrate your explanation with examples relevant to Northern Fuel Distributors.

   ii) Suggest why your chosen method of seasonal adjustment might be more accurate.

   iii) Show how an understanding of seasonal variations and seasonally adjusted data can help Northern Fuel Distributors be more efficient.

   iv) Identify TWO weaknesses within your approach to forecasting undertaken in tasks a) and b).

chapter 10: FORECASTING EXPENDITURE

1 A business makes a single product, each unit of which requires 5 kgs of raw material. Unfortunately, due to a shortage of suppliers of the raw material, only 129,000 kgs will be available in the coming year. The materials are available on a monthly basis spread evenly over the year.

How many units of the product can be produced in total and each month?

2 The raw materials requirements for production for the next six months for a business are as follows:

	July	*Aug*	*Sept*	*Oct*	*Nov*	*Dec*
Raw materials requirements – kg	4,800	4,300	4,100	4,900	4,200	5,000

It is only possible to purchase 4,500 kg of the product each month.

a) What is the maximum shortage of raw materials over the six-month period in total if only the amount required each month is purchased, or the maximum amount if demand is greater than 4,500 kgs ?

b) How many kgs of the material should be purchased each month in order to maximise production and keep stock levels to the minimum possible?

What is the total shortage of raw materials over the six-month period under this policy?

3 How could a business try to alleviate the problem of shortage of materials if:

a) the shortage is a short-term problem and full supplies will be available after a few months; or

b) the shortage is a long-term problem?

4 The raw materials requirements for production for Selby Electronics for the next six months are as follows:

	May	*June*	*July*	*Aug*	*Sep*	*Oct*
Raw materials requirements – kg	9,500	10,200	10,200	9,300	10,200	10,300

Selby is only able to purchase 10,000 kgs of the material in each month.

a) How can the purchases be scheduled in order to ensure the maximum production over the six-month period together with the minimum possible stock level?

b) What is the total shortage of materials over the six-month period under the purchasing scheme in part a)?

5 A business produces a product which requires three hours of a highly skilled grade of labour per unit but the business currently only has 12 employees with the skills required. They normally work a 38-hour week although, by paying an overtime rate of double time, it has been possible to negotiate for each employee to work eight hours of overtime a week.

a) What is the maximum level of production each week?

b) Suggest ways in which the labour shortage problem could be solved.

6 In week 3 of the next quarter the sales demand for a business's product is expected to be for 1,860 units. Each unit requires four hours of direct labour time and the business employs 160 employees each working a 35-hour week. How much overtime would be required in order to meet demand with the current workforce?

7 A manufacturing organisation operates out of one factory with two identical production lines. The factory operates two seven-hour shifts each day for five days a week with the production lines working at full capacity. The production line is capable of producing 30 units of product per hour.

a) What is the maximum production for a week?

b) How could the business deal with this capacity problem if sales demand exceeds the maximum production level?

8 The sales and production in units for a business for the next six months are as follows:

	Jan	*Feb*	*Mar*	*Apr*	*May*	*June*
Production – units	3,600	2,900	3,200	3,100	3,400	4,000
Sales – units	3,500	3,000	3,000	3,200	3,500	3,800

The variable production costs are £10.50 per unit and the variable selling costs are £3.80 per unit.

What are the forecast figures for variable production and selling costs?

9 The direct materials cost for quarter 1 and quarter 2 of next year have been estimated in terms of current prices at £657,000 and £692,500 respectively. The current price index for these materials is 126.4 and the price index is estimated as 128.4 for quarter 1 of next year and 131.9 for quarter 2.

What are the forecast direct materials costs for quarters 1 and 2 of next year?

10 The production and sales levels for the next six months for a business are estimated as follows:

	Jan	*Feb*	*Mar*	*Apr*	*May*	*June*
Production – units	4,200	4,400	4,500	5,100	5,300	4,800
Sales – units	4,100	4,300	4,650	4,700	5,000	5,100

Variable production costs are currently £25.00 per unit and variable selling costs are £8.00 per unit. The price indices for the production costs and selling costs are currently 135.2 and 140.5 respectively.

The anticipated price indices for production and selling costs for the next six months are given below:

	Jan	*Feb*	*Mar*	*Apr*	*May*	*June*
Production costs index	137.3	139.0	139.6	140.3	141.2	143.0
Selling costs index	141.5	143.0	143.7	144.4	145.1	146.0

What are the forecast variable production costs and variable selling costs for each of the next six months?

11 A business rents its premises annually from 1 January to 31 December. The rent for the year ending 31 December 2008 was £65,000 but the business has been told by the letting company that there is to be a 5.5% increase for the year ended 31 December 2009.

The company incurred insurance premiums of £15,700 in the year ended 31 December 2008; it is widely thought that insurance premiums are likely to rise by 10% next year.

The power costs for the year ended 31 December 2008 were £84,000 and these normally increase in line with the average RPI each year.

The business is now trying to forecast its costs for the year ending 31 December 2009. The average RPI for 2008 was 166.3 and it is believed that the average RPI for 2009 will be 171.2.

Determine the forecast fixed costs for the year ending 31 December 2009.

12 The costs of a factory maintenance department appear to be partially dependent upon the number of machine hours operated each month. The machine hours and the maintenance department costs for the last six months are given below:

	Machine hours	*Maintenance cost*
		£
June	14,200	285,000
July	14,800	293,000
August	15,200	300,000
September	14,500	290,000
October	15,000	298,000
November	14,700	292,000

i) Estimate the variable cost per machine hour.
ii) Estimate the fixed costs of the maintenance department.

13 The activity levels and related production costs for the last six months of 2008 for a business have been as follows:

	Activity level	*Production cost*
	units	£
July	63,000	608,000
August	70,000	642,000
September	76,000	699,000
October	73,000	677,000
November	71,000	652,000
December	68,000	623,000

a) Estimate the fixed element of the production costs and the variable rate using the high-low method.

b) Estimate the production costs if the level of production is expected to be:

i) 74,000 units
ii) 90,000 units

c) Comment upon which of the two estimates of production costs calculated in ii) is likely to be most accurate and why.

14 a) What is the general equation of a straight line?

b) What do the figures a and b stand for in the equation of a straight line?

c) If the equation of a straight line defines a semi-variable cost what co the figures representing a and b in the equation mean?

15 The linear regression equation for production costs for a business is:

$$y = 138{,}000 + 6.4x$$

If production is expected to be 105,000 units in the next quarter what are the anticipated production costs?

16 The linear regression equation for the power costs of a factory is given as follows:

$$y = 80{,}000 + 0.5x$$

where x is the number of machine hours used in a period.

The anticipated machine hours for the next six months are:

	Machine hours
April	380,000
May	400,000
June	395,000
July	405,000
August	410,000
September	420,000

What are the forecasts for the power costs for the next six months?

17 The linear regression equation for the trend of sales in thousands of units per month based upon time series analysis of the figures for the last two years is:

$$y = 3.1 + 0.9x$$

What is the estimated sales trend for each of the first three months of next year?

18 A time series analysis of sales volumes each quarter for the last three years, 2006 to 2008, has identified the trend equation as follows:

$$y = 400 + 105x$$

where y is the sales volume and x is the time period.

The seasonal variations for each quarter have been calculated as:

Quarter 1	–175
Quarter 2	+225
Quarter 3	+150
Quarter 4	–200

Estimate the actual sales volume for each quarter of 2009.

chapter 11: PREPARING BUDGETS

1 A business has budgeted sales for the following period of 13,800 units of its product. The stocks at the start of the period are 2,100 units and these are to be reduced to 1,500 units at the end of the period. What is the production quantity for the period?

2 A business is preparing its production budget for the next quarter. It is estimated that 200,000 units of the product can be sold in the quarter and the opening stock is currently 35,000 units. The stock level is to be reduced by 30% by the end of the quarter.

What is the production budget for the quarter?

3 A production process has normal losses of 3% of completed output. If production of 16,200 good units is required how many units must be produced in total?

4 For budgeting purposes a business operates 13 four-week periods with five working days in each week.

The sales forecasts in units for the next four periods is as follows:

Period 4	*Period 5*	*Period 6*	*Period 7*
10,800 units	11,500 units	11,000 units	11,200 units

It is the business's policy to maintain closing stocks of finished goods at a level which is sufficient to cover 5 days of the next period's sales. The stocks of finished goods at the end of period 3 are 2,700 units.

The quality control procedures of the organisation have shown that 4% of completed production are found to be defective and are unsaleable.

a) Produce the production budget for periods 4 to 6.

b) Complete the following computer spreadsheet in order to determine the production budget for periods 4 to 6.

	A	B	C	D	E
1					
2					
3					
4					
5					
6					

5 A business requires 25,400 units of production in a period and each unit requires 5 kg of raw materials in the finished product. The production process has a normal loss of 10% during the production process. What is the total amount of the raw material required for the period?

6 A business is preparing its material usage budget for the next quarter for one its raw materials used in the production of one of its products. The production budget for the product is 40,000 units in the quarter.

Each unit of product requires 5 kgs of raw material. Opening stock of raw material is budgeted to be 30,000 kg and stock levels are to be reduced by 20% by the end of the quarter.

a) What is the usage budget for the raw material for the quarter?
b) What is the materials purchasing budget for the raw material for the year?

7 For budgeting purposes a business operates 13 four-week periods with five working days in each week.

The production budget in units for the next four periods is as follows:

Period 1	*Period 2*	*Period 3*	*Period 4*
32,000 units	35,000 units	40,000 units	48,000 units

Each completed unit of the product requires 8 kgs of raw material; however, the production process has a normal loss of 20% of materials input. Stock levels of raw materials are held in order to be sufficient to cover 5 days of gross production for the following period. The stocks of raw material at the start of period 1 are budgeted to be 64,000 kgs.

The price of each kilogram of raw material is £2.50 currently but is expected to rise by 4% in period 3.

a) You are required to produce for period 1, 2 and 3:

- the materials usage budget in units
- the materials purchasing budget in units
- the materials purchasing budget in pounds

b) Complete the following computer spreadsheet in order to produce the materials purchasing budget in both units and pounds.

	A	B	C	D	E
1		Period 1	Period 2	Period 3	Period 4
2	Production units	32,000	35,000	40,000	48,000
3					
4					
5					
6					
7					
8					

8 A product requires 18 labour hours for each unit. However 10% of working hours are non-productive. How long must an employee be paid for in order to produce 20 units?

9 A business wishes to produce 120,000 units of its product with a standard labour time of 4 hours per unit. The workforce are currently working at 120% efficiency. How long will it take to produce the units required?

10 For budgeting purposes a business has four quarters made up of 12 weeks each quarter and 5 working days in each week. The budgeted sales in units for quarters 1 and 2 are as follows:

	Quarter 1	*Quarter 2*
Budgeted sales	102,000 units	115,000 units

The stocks of finished goods at the start of quarter 1 are 17,000 units and it is the business policy to maintain closing finished goods stock levels at 10 days of the following quarter's budgeted sales.

The standard cost card indicates that each unit should take 5.5 labour hours however it is anticipated that during quarter 1, due to technical problems, the workforce will only be working at 95% efficiency.

You are to produce the production budget and the labour usage budget for quarter 1.

11 A business produces a single product, the Oliver. For budgeting purposes the year is divided into 13 four week periods with 5 working days each week. The forecast sales quantities for the first 5 periods of 2007 are as follows:

Period 1	*Period 2*	*Period 3*	*Period 4*	*Period 5*
3,000 units	3,400 units	3,900 units	3,500 units	4,000 units

i) The current selling price of the Oliver is £40 although it is anticipated that there will be a 6% price increase in Period 4.

ii) The closing stocks of finished goods are to be enough to cover 4 days of sales demand for the next period.

iii) 3% of production is defective and has to be scrapped with no scrap value.

iv) The stocks of finished goods at the start of period 1 will be 600 units.

v) Each unit of production requires 4 kgs of raw material X and the production process has a normal loss of 10% of the materials input into the process.

vi) It is policy to hold enough raw materials stocks to cover 7 days of the following period's production. The stock level at the start of period 1 is 4,200 kgs of raw material. The material usage for production in Period 5 is budgeted as 16,200 kgs.

vii) The standard time for production of one unit is 2 labour hour however due to necessary break times only 80% of the time worked is productive. The labour force are paid at a rate of £8 per hour but only 8,000 hours can be worked within the normal working hours any hours above 8,000 are overtime hours that are paid at time and a half.

For periods 1 to 4 you are to produce:

a) the sales budget in value
b) the production budget in units
c) the materials usage budget
d) the materials purchases budget in kgs
e) the labour budget in hours
f) the labour budget in value

12 A business produces two products, the Aye and the Bee. Both products use the same material and labour but in different proportions.

The previous policy has been to keep stocks of raw materials and finished goods at constant levels. However it has now been decided that closing stocks of finished goods should be expressed in terms of days' sales of the next quarter and that closing stocks of raw materials should be in terms of days' production for the next quarter.

The data provided by the sales and production departments are as follows:

	Aye	*Bee*
Budgeted sales (units) quarter 1	1,500	2,400
Budgeted sales (units) quarter 2	1,500	2,400
Budgeted material per unit (kg)	4	7
Budgeted labour hours per unit	10	7
Opening units of finished stock	160	300
Closing units of finished stock (days' sales next quarter)	5 days	5 days
Failure rate of finished production	2%	2.5%
Finance and other costs of holding a unit in stock per quarter	£6.00	£7.00

The failed units are only discovered after completion of the products and they have no resale value.

Other information available is as follows:

Weeks in each quarter	12 weeks
Days per week	5 days
Hours per week	35 hours
Number of employees	70 employees
Budgeted labour rate per hour	£8.00
Overtime premium for hours worked in excess of 35 hours per week	50%
Budgeted cost of material per kg	£10.00
Opening stock of raw materials	2,800 kgs
Closing stock of raw materials (days' production next quarter)	6 days
Financing and other costs of keeping 1 kg of raw material in stock per quarter	£2.00

a) Calculate the following information for quarter 1:

i) the number of production days
ii) the closing finished stock of Aye and Bee in units
iii) the labour hours available before overtime has to be paid

b) Prepare the following budgets for quarter 1:

i) the production budget in units for Aye and Bee, including any faulty production
ii) the materials purchases budget in kgs and value
iii) the production labour budget in hours and value, including any overtime payments

c) Calculate the savings arising from the change in required stock levels for quarter 1.

13 a) You have recently been promoted to the post of assistant management accountant with Northern Products Ltd, a company formed four years ago. The company has always used budgets to help plan its production of two products, the Exe and the Wye. Both products use the same material and labour but in different proportions.

You have been asked to prepare the budget for quarter 1, the twelve weeks ending 24 March 2009. In previous budgets, the closing stocks of both raw materials and finished products were the same as opening stocks. You questioned whether or not this was the most efficient policy for the company.

As a result, you have carried out an investigation into the stock levels required to meet the maximum likely sales demand for finished goods and production demand for raw materials. You conclude that closing stocks of finished goods should be expressed in terms of days sales for the next quarter and closing stocks of raw materials in terms of days production for the next quarter.

Your findings are included in the data below, which also shows data provided by the sales and production directors of Northern Products Ltd.

Product data	*Exe*	*Wye*
▪ Budgeted sales in units, quarter 1	930 units	1,320 units
▪ Budgeted sales in units, quarter 2	930 units	1,320 units
▪ Budgeted material per unit (litres)	6 litres	9 litres
▪ Budgeted labour hours per unit	12 hours	7 hours
▪ Opening units of finished stock	172 units	257 units
▪ Closing units of finished stock (days sales next quarter)	8 days	9 days
▪ Failure rate of finished production*	2%	3%
▪ Finance and other costs of keeping a unit in stock per quarter	£4.00	£5.00

*Failed products are only discovered on completion of production and have no residual value.

Other accounting data

▪ Weeks in accounting period	12 weeks
▪ Days per week for production and sales	5 days
▪ Hours per week	35 hours
▪ Number of employees	46 employees
▪ Budgeted labour rate per hour	£6.00
▪ Overtime premium for hours worked in excess of 35 hours per week	30%
▪ Budgeted cost of material per litre	£15.00
▪ Opening raw material stocks (litres)	1,878 litres
▪ Closing raw material stocks (days production next quarter)	5 days
▪ Financing and other costs of keeping a litre of raw material in stock per quarter	£1.00

Tasks

i) Calculate the following information for quarter 1, the 12 weeks ending 24 March 2009.

1) The number of production days
2) The closing finished stock for Exe and Wye in units
3) The labour hours available before overtime has to be paid

ii) Prepare the following budgets for quarter 1, the twelve weeks ending 24 March 2009.

1) The production budget in units for Exe and Wye, including any faulty production

2) The material purchases budget in litres and value

3) The production labour budget in hours and value, including any overtime payments

ii) Calculate the savings arising from the change in the required stock levels for the twelve weeks ending 24 March 2009.

b) On completing the budget for quarter 1, the production director of Northern Products Ltd tells you that the company is likely to introduce a third product, the Zed, in the near future. Because of this, he suggests that future budgets should be prepared using a spreadsheet. He explains that the use of spreadsheets to prepare budgets not only saves time but also provides flexibility by allowing the results of changes in the budget to be readily shown. The sales director is not convinced.

The production director suggests you demonstrate the advantages of budgets prepared on spreadsheets by using a template of a spreadsheet and sales data for the planned third product.

He gives you the following sales data he has received from the sales director.

- Estimated annual volume for Zed is 20,000 units.
- Planned unit selling price is £90.00.
- Seasonal variations are as follows.

1	+20%
2	+30%
3	–10%
4	–40%

Tasks

i) Calculate the budgeted volume of Zed for each quarter.

ii) Using the information provided by the sales director and a copy of the suggested spreadsheet template reproduced below. express the data provided by the sales director as formulae which would enable revised sales budgets to be calculated with the minimum of effort if sales price and annual volume were to change. (You may amend the template if desired to suit any spreadsheet with which you are familiar.)

A	B	C	D	E	F
1	Unit selling price	£90			
2	Annual volume	20,000			
3	Seasonal variations	20%	30%	– 10%	– 40%
4		Quarter 1	Quarter 2	Quarter 3	Quarter 4
5	Seasonal variations (units)				
6	Quarterly volume				
7	Quarterly turnover				

c) During quarters 1 to 3 of 2009 it became increasingly evident that there were problems with the supply of material. Shortages were so severe during quarter 3 that budgeted production quantities could not be met and closing stocks of both raw material and finished goods were eliminated. The situation did not improve during quarter 4, and the supplier warned that available supplies would be limited to 18,870 litres in quarter 1of 2010.

During quarter 4 it comes to light that a colleague charged with setting profit-maximising production plans during this period has simply been allocating half the material to production of Exes and the other half to production of Wyes. You have been asked to take over this task and ensure that the limited supply of material is allocated to production of the two products so as to ensure a profit-maximising production budget.

Task

Produce a revised production budget for period 1 of 2010 that maximises profit given that the total variable cost of the Exe is £240 and that of the Wye is £258, budgeted sales for quarter 1 of 2007 are 1,120 units of Exe and 1,480 units of Wye, the selling price of the Exe is £360, that of the Wye £420, and that there will be no opening or closing stocks of raw material or finished goods.

14 (a) Sandwell Ltd makes a single product, the Gamma. You are Sandwell's management accountant and you are responsible for preparing its operating budgets. The accounting year is divided into 13, four-week periods. There are five days in each week.

The sales director of Sandwell has recently completed the following forecast sales volume for the next five periods.

Sales forecast five periods to 18 November 2009

Period number	1	2	3	4	5
Four weeks ending	29 Jul	26 Aug	23 Sep	21 Oct	18 Nov
Number of Gammas	19,400	21,340	23,280	22,310	22,310

The production director provides you with the following information.

- On completion of production, 3% of the Gammas are found to be faulty and have to be scrapped. The faulty Gammas have no scrap value.
- Opening stocks: period 1, four weeks ending 29 July
  - Finished stock 3,880 Gammas
  - Raw materials 16,500 litres
- Closing stocks at the end of each period
  - Finished stock must equal 4 days' sales volume of Gammas in the next period.
  - Raw materials must equal 5 days' gross production in the next period.
- Each Gamma requires three litres of material costing £8 per litre.
- Each Gamma requires 0.5 hours of labour.
- Sandwell employs 70 production workers who each work a 40 hour week. Each employee is paid a guaranteed wage of £240 per week.
- The cost of any overtime is £9 per hour.

Tasks

Prepare the following budgets for the production director.

i) Gross production budget in Gammas (including faulty production) for each of the first four periods

ii) Material purchases budget in litres for each of the first three periods

iii) Cost of the material purchases for each of the first three periods

iv) Labour budget in hours for each of the first three periods including any overtime required in each period

v) Cost of the labour budget for each of the first three periods, including the cost of any overtime

b) After receiving your budgets, Sandwell's production director raises the following points.

- Overtime payments should only be made if absolutely necessary.
- The faulty Gammas are thought to be caused by poor work practices by some of the production workers although this is not known for certain.
- The 70 production workers work independently of one another in making Gammas.

Task

Write a memo to the production director. In your memo, you should do the following.

i) Explain and quantify the value of any possible overtime savings.

ii) Suggest ONE extra cost which might be necessary to achieve the overtime savings.

iii) Identify TWO advantages of sampling as a way of discovering reasons for the faulty Gammas.

iv) Briefly explain the difference between true (or simple) random sampling, systematic sampling and stratified sampling.

v) State which form of sampling Sandwell should use.

15 a) You are employed as an accounting technician by Guildshot Ltd, a company that makes statues. Statues are made in batches. A special powdered rock is added to water and poured into moulds. These moulds are then placed in ovens. Afterwards, the statues are removed from their moulds and inspected before being sold. At this inspection stage, some of the statues are found to be faulty and have to be destroyed. The faulty statues have no residual value.

Guildshot makes two types of statues, the Antelope and the Bear. Both use the same type of material and labour but in different amounts.

One of your duties is to prepare the production, material purchases and labour budgets for each four-week period. You are given the following information for period 8, the four weeks ending 26 July 2008.

	Antelope	*Bear*
Forecast sales		
■ Sales volume, period 8, four weeks ending 26 July 2008	141,120 units	95,000 units
Product information		
■ Opening finished stocks	30,576 units	25,175 units
■ Kilograms of powdered rock per statue	0.75 kg	0.50 kg
■ Production labour hours per statue	0.10 hours	0.05 hours
■ Faulty production	2%	5%

Material information	
■ Material: opening stock of powdered rock	30,000 kg
■ Material: closing stock of powdered rock	40,000 kg
■ Price per kilogram of powdered rock	£8.00
Labour information	
■ Number of production employees	140 employees
■ Days per week	5 days
■ Weeks per period	4 weeks
■ Hours per production employee per week	38 hours
■ Guaranteed weekly wage *	£228.00

* *The guaranteed weekly wage is paid even if hours produced are less than hours worked.*

Closing finished stocks

The closing finished stocks are based on the forecast sales volume for period 9, the four weeks ending 23 August 2008.

- Demand for the Antelope in period 9 is forecast to be 50% more than in period 8. The closing finished stock of Antelope statues for period 8 must be equal to four days' sales in period 9.
- Demand for the Bear statue in period 9 is forecast to be 30% more than in period 8. The closing finished stock of Bear statues for period 8 must be equal to five days' sales in period 9.

Other information

- The faulty production is only discovered after the statues have been made.
- For technical reasons, the company can only operate the ovens for five days per week.

Task

Prepare the following information for period 8, the four weeks ending 26 July 2008.

i) Production budget in units for Antelopes and Bears
ii) Material purchases budget in kilograms
iii) Cost of the materials purchases budget
iv) Labour budget in hours
v) Cost of the labour budget

b) Hilary Green is the production director for Guildshot. She tells you that there are likely to be material and labour shortages in period 9. For commercial reasons, the company must fully meet the demand for Bear statues. As a result it will not be able to meet all the demand for Antelope statues.

Hilary suggests it might be possible to meet the demand by producing extra Antelope statues in period 8. She gives you the following information.

- Because of the technology involved, Guildshot cannot increase the number of production employees and the existing employees cannot work any overtime. The maximum hours are limited to the 38 hours per week for each production employee.
- It would be possible to buy up to a maximum 3,000 extra kilograms of powdered rock in period 8.

Tasks

i) Calculate the maximum number of extra fault-free Antelope statues that could be made in period 8.

ii) Prepare a revised purchases budget in kilograms to include the production of the extra fault-free statues.

16 You are employed as an accounting technician in the management accounting department of Dobra Ltd. The company makes several chemicals and one of your jobs is to prepare quarterly budgets for the year ahead for each of the chemicals. There are 12 weeks in each quarter and five working days in each week.

The sales director gives you the following forecast of the number of tins of chemicals A120 to be sold in each quarter.

Sales forecast for tins of chemical A120 to 25 June 2009

Quarter number	1	2	3	4
12 weeks ending	19/9/2008	12/12/2008	19/3/2009	25/6/2009
Sales volume: number of tins	2,910	3,395	3,880	4,365

The production director gives you the following information.

- Production and sales volumes in the two quarters following quarter 4 will be the same as in quarter 4.
- Finished stocks:
  - Opening stocks for quarter 1 will be 582 tins.
  - Closing stocks in each quarter must equal 12 days sales volume of the next quarter.
- 3% of finished production is faulty and has to be destroyed. The faulty production has no scrap value.
- Each tin of A120 requires seven kilograms of raw materials.
- Raw material stocks:
  - Opening stocks for quarter 1 will be 2,170 kilograms.
  - Closing stocks in each quarter must equal 6 days gross production in the next quarter.
- The budgeted cost of material is £12.00 per kilogram.
- Each tin of A120 requires three labour hours.
- The company employs 29 production workers to make A120. Each worker is paid a guaranteed wage of £280 per week for a 35-hour week. If a worker works more than 35 hours a week, overtime is payable at £11.00 per hour.

Tasks

a) Prepare the following budgets for EACH of the first four quarters.

   i) Production budget in tins (including faulty production) for A120
   ii) Material purchases budget in kilograms
   iii) Cost of material purchases budget
   iv) Labour budget in hours, including any overtime required
   v) Cost of labour budget, including the cost of any overtime

b) The chief executive of Dobra is Jemma Hughes. After receiving your budgets, she gives you the following information.

   - Overtime should be avoided if possible. The company would be willing to increase the level of finished stocks if this reduced overtime.
   - There would be extra holding costs if finished stocks increased but these should be kept as low as possible.

   She also tells you that the company has been investigating the use of linear regression to help forecast sales. The sales director has plotted the last 24 quarterly actual sales and has calculated the linear regression formula y = a + bx as:

   y = 1,000 + 100x

   where y is the forecast sales trend measured in tins of A120, 1,000 is a constant and x is the quarter number. For quarter 1 of the year to 25 June 2009, x would therefore be 25.

   The sales director has also calculated the following seasonal variations based on the 24 observations.

Seasonal variations

	Quarter 1	Quarter 2	Quarter 3	Quarter 4
Seasonal variation (tins)	(500)	(300)	300	500

Write a memo to Jemma Hughes. In your memo you should do the following.

i) Prepare a revised budget of labour hours for each quarter to reduce overtime as much as possible.

ii) Prepare a revised production budget in tins for each quarter to take account of your planned reduction in overtime.

iii) Use the formula to forecast the trend for each of the quarters 1 to 4.

iv) Use the seasonal variations to forecast the sales volume for each of the quarters 1 to 4 for the year to 25 June 2009.

v) Identify THREE reasons why linear regression might not give accurate estimates of the demand for tins of A120.

chapter 12: RECONCILING BUDGETS AND ACTUAL FIGURES

1 Explain what is meant by a fixed budget and a flexed budget and how each is used in the management process.

2 The budget for production supervisors' costs for a period for a business at an activity level of 250,000 units is £15,000. One production supervisor is required for every 100,000 units of production. If actual production is 330,000 units what figure would appear in the flexed budget for production supervisors' costs?

3

	100,000 units	*120,000 units*
	£	£
Materials cost	240,000	288,000
Labour cost	124,000	144,000
Production overhead	38,000	38,000

How would each cost appear in a budget flexed to an actual activity level of 112,000 units?

4 The budgeted production overhead for a business is £524,000 at an activity level of 60,000 units and £664,000 at an activity level of 80,000 units. If the actual activity level is 72,000 units what is the flexed budget figure for production overhead?

5

	Quarter 4 budget
	£
Sales (20,000 units)	130,000
Material	(55,000)
Labour	(35,000)
Production overhead	(18,000)
Gross profit	22,000
General expenses	12,000
Operating profit	10,000

The details of the cost behaviour of each of the costs is given below:

Materials the materials cost is totally variable

Labour each operative can only produce 2,000 units each quarter – the cost of each operative is £3,500 each quarter

Production overhead the production overhead is a totally fixed cost

General expenses the general expenses are made up of a budgeted fixed cost of £6,400 and a variable element

Actual sales and production were in fact only 15,000 units during quarter 4. Prepare a flexed budget for an activity level of 15,000 units.

6 The budget for a manufacturing company for the month of March and the actual results for the month are given below:

	Budget	*Actual*
	28,000 units	*31,500 units*
	£	£
Sales	406,000	441,000
Materials	165,200	180,400
Labour	100,800	115,600
Production overhead	37,500	39,000
Gross profit	102,500	106,000
General expenses	55,600	68,900
Operating profit	46,900	37,100

The materials and labour costs are variable costs, the production overhead is a fixed cost and the general expenses are a semi-variable cost with a fixed element of £13,600

i) Calculate variances between the fixed budget and the actual results

ii) Prepare a flexed budget for the actual activity level and show the variances for each of the figures

iii) Comment on the differences shown by the two sets of variances

7 Given below is the original fixed budget for a manufacturing operation for quarter 2. However, as sales and production were subsequently anticipated to be higher than this budget made allowance for, a revised budget was also prepared. The actual results for quarter 2 are also given.

	Original budget 200,000 units		*Revised budget 240,000 units*		*Actual 230,000 units*	
	£	£	£	£	£	£
Sales		1,360,000		1,632,000		1,532,000
Materials	690,000		828,000		783,200	
Labour	387,000		449,000		423,600	
Production expenses	162,000		186,000		173,500	
Production cost		1,239,000		1,463,000		1,385,300
Gross profit		121,000		169,000		146,700
General expenses		72,000		72,000		74,700
Operating profit		49,000		97,000		72,000

Prepare a flexed budget to reflect the actual level of activity for the month and calculate the variances from that budget.

8 Given below is the budget for quarter 2 prepared using absorption costing principles. There were no opening stocks.

	Quarter 2 budget	
	£	£
Sales (50,000 units)		400,000
Materials	165,400	
Labour	69,800	
Production overhead	56,000	
Cost of production 56,000 units	291,200	
Less: closing stock	31,200	
Cost of sales		260,000
Gross profit		140,000
General expenses		52,000
Operating profit		88,000

The materials and labour costs are variable with the level of production but the production overhead and general expenses are both fixed costs.

i) Prepare the budget for quarter 2 using marginal costing principles.

ii) Reconcile the budgeted profit figure using absorption costing to the budgeted profit figure using marginal costing.

9 A business has an overhead absorption rate of £16.40 per unit produced. The budgeted fixed overhead was £3,034,000

What is the budgeted activity level for the period?

10 A business has the following budgeted and actual figures for a period:

Budgeted fixed overheads	£331,200
Actual fixed overhead	£315,000
Fixed overhead absorption rate	£1.20 per unit

What is the budgeted activity level?

11 The following information is known about a business's budgeted and actual figures:

Budgeted fixed overhead	£84,000
Budgeted activity level	24,000 units
Actual fixed overhead	£93,600
Under-absorption	£3,650

What was the actual activity level during the period?

12 The following information is known about a business's budgeted and actual figures:

Budgeted fixed overhead	£483,000
Budgeted activity level	70,000 units
Actual fixed overhead	£490,000
Over-absorption	£15,080

What was the actual level of activity?

13 Explain what is meant by the following terms:

i) a responsibility centre
ii) responsibility accounting
iii) an expense centre
iv) a profit centre

14 Why is it important that managerial performance is only judged on the basis of controllable variances?

15 Explain what is meant by feedback and feedforward.

16 Given below is the original fixed budget for a business's operations for the six months ending 31 March 2009 and the actual results for that period.

		Budget		*Actual*
Units		*30,000*		*34,000*
	£	£	£	£
Sales		660,000		697,000
Direct costs				
Materials	252,000		299,200	
Labour	180,000		192,600	
Factory power	83,600		88,600	
	515,600		580,400	
Fixed overheads	75,000		79,000	
Cost of sales		590,600		659,400
Operating profit		69,400		37,600

You are also provided with the following information:

i) The budget had assumed that there would be no closing stocks. However the actual production was 40,000 units with actual sales of 34,000 units

ii) The closing stocks of 6,000 units have been valued by including fixed overheads based upon the budgeted fixed overhead absorption rate

iii) The production employees are paid per week irrespective of the production level. The employees that were budgeted for are capable of producing a maximum of 45,000 units in a six-month period

iv) The budgeted and actual figures for factory power include a fixed cost element of £20,600

a) Calculate the following figures:

i) The budgeted selling price per unit
ii) The budgeted material cost per unit
iii) The budgeted marginal cost of factory power per unit
iv) The actual marginal cost of factory power per unit

b) Prepare a flexed budget operating statement for the actual activity level using marginal costing principles. Show variances for the sales and costs figures.

c) Give two reasons why the flexed budget operating statement shows different results from that of the original budget.

d) Give two reasons why the flexed budget operating statement might be a better measure of management performance than the original operating results.

17 a) Rivermede Ltd makes a single product called the Fasta. Last year, Steven Jones, the managing director of Rivermede Ltd, attended a course on budgetary control. As a result, he agreed to revise the way budgets were prepared in the company. Rather than imposing targets for managers, he encouraged participation by senior managers in the preparation of budgets.

An initial budget was prepared but Mike Fisher, the sales director, felt that the budgeted sales volume was set too high. He explained that setting too high a budgeted sales volume would mean that his sales staff would be de-motivated because they would not be able to achieve the sales volume. Steven Jones agreed to use the revised sales volume suggested by Mike Fisher.

Both the initial and revised budgets are reproduced below complete with the actual results for the year ended 31 May 2008.

Rivermede Ltd – budgeted and actual costs for the year ended 31 May 2008

	Original budget	*Revised budget*	*Actual results*	*Variances from revised budget*
Fasta production and sales (units)	24,000	20,000	22,000	2,000 (F)
	£	£	£	£
Variable costs				
Material	216,000	180,000	206,800	26,800 (A)
Labour	288,000	240,000	255,200	15,200 (A)
Semi-variable costs				
Heat, light and power	31,000	27,000	33,400	6,400 (A)
Fixed costs				
Rent, rates and depreciation	40,000	40,000	38,000	2,000 (F)
	575,000	487,000	533,400	46,400 (A)

Assumptions in the two budgets	
1	No change in input prices
2	No change in the quantity of variable inputs per Fasta

As the management accountant at Rivermede Ltd, one of your tasks is to check that invoices have been properly coded. On checking the actual invoices for heat, light and power for the year to 31 May 2008, you find that one invoice for £7,520 had been incorrectly coded. The invoice should have been coded to materials.

Tasks

i) Using the information in the original and revised budgets, identify the following.

1) The variable cost of material and labour per Fasta
2) The fixed and unit variable cost within heat, light and power

ii) Prepare a flexible budget, including variances, for Rivermede Ltd after correcting for the miscoding of the invoice.

b) On receiving your flexible budget statement, Steven Jones states that the total adverse variance is much less than the £46,400 shown in the original statement. He also draws your attention to the actual sales volume being greater than in the revised budget. He believes these results show that a participative approach to budgeting is better for the company and wants to discuss this belief at the next board meeting. Before doing so, Steven Jones asks for your comments.

Task

Write a memo to Steven Jones. Your memo should do the following.

i) **Briefly** explain why the flexible budgeting variances differ from those in the original statement given in the data to task a).

ii) Give TWO reasons why a favourable cost variance may have arisen other than through the introduction of participative budgeting.

iii) Give TWO reasons why the actual sales volume compared with the revised budget's sales volume may not be a measure of improved motivation following the introduction of participative budgeting.

18 a) HFD plc opened a new division on 1 December 2007. The division, HFD Processes Ltd, produces a special paint finish. Because of the technology, there can never be any work in progress. The original budget was developed on the assumption that there would be a loss in the initial year of operation and that there would be no closing stock of finished goods.

One year later, HFD Processes Ltd prepared its results for its first year of operations. The chief executive of HFD plc was pleased to see that, despite budgeting for an initial loss, the division had actually returned a profit of £74,400. As a result, the directors of HFD Processes were entitled to a substantial bonus. Details of the budget and actual results are reproduced below.

HFD Processes
Operating results for year ended 30 November 2008

	Budget		*Actual*	
Volume (units)		20,000		22,000
	£	£	£	£
Turnover		960,000		1,012,000
Direct costs				
Materials	240,000		261,800	
Production labour	260,000		240,240	
Light, heat and power	68,000		65,560	
	568,000		567,600	
Fixed overheads	400,000		370,000	
Cost of sales		968,000		937,600
Operating profit/(loss)		(8,000)		74,400

You are employed as a management accountant in the head office of HFD plc and have been asked to comment on the performance of HFD Processes Ltd. Attached to the budgeted and actual results were the relevant working papers. A summary of the contents of the working papers is reproduced below.

- The budget assumed no closing finished stocks. Actual production was 25,000 units and actual sales 22,000 units.
- Because of the technology involved, production employees are paid per week, irrespective of production levels. The employees assumed in the budget are capable of producing up to 26,000 units.
- The cost of material varies directly with production.
- The cost of light, heat and power includes a fixed standing charge. In the budget this fixed charge was calculated to be £20,000 per year. However, competition resulted in the supplier reducing the actual charge to £12,000 for the year.
- During the year, HFD Processes Ltd produced 25,000 units. The 3,000 units of closing finished stock were valued on the basis of direct cost plus 'normal' fixed overheads.

The number of units was used to apportion direct costs between the cost of sales and closing finished stock.

The budgeted fixed overhead of £20 per unit was used to calculate the fixed overheads in closing finished stocks.

The detailed composition of the cost of sales and closing stocks using these policies was as follows.

	Closing finished stocks	*Cost of sales*	*Cost of production*
Units	3,000	22,000	25,000
	£	£	£
Material	35,700	261,800	297,500
Production labour	32,760	240,240	273,000
Light, heat and power	8,940	65,560	74,500
Fixed overheads	60,000	370,000	430,000
	137,400	937,600	1,075,000

Tasks

i) Calculate the following.

1) The budgeted unit selling price
2) The budgeted material cost per unit
3) The budgeted marginal cost of light, heat and power per unit
4) The actual marginal cost of light, heat and power per unit

ii) Prepare a flexible budget statement for the operating results of HFD Processes Ltd using a **marginal costing** approach, identifying fixed costs for the year and showing any variances.

b) You present your flexible budget statement to the chief executive of HFD plc who is concerned that your findings appear different to those in the original operating results.

Task

You are asked to write a **brief** memo to the chief executive. In your memo, you should do the following.

i) Give TWO reasons why the flexible budget operating statement shows different results from the original operating results.

ii) Give ONE reason why the flexible budget operating statement might be a better measure of management performance than the original operating results.

19 a) Hall Ltd makes a product called the Omega. The budgeted and actual results for the year ended 30 November 2008 are shown below.

Hall Ltd: Budgeted and actual operating statement
Year ended 30 November 2008

	Budget	*Actual*
Sales volume (units)	36,000	35,000
	£	£
Turnover	1,440,000	1,365,000
Direct costs		
Material	432,000	500,000
Labour	216,000	232,000
Light, heat and power	92,000	96,000
Fixed overheads		
Depreciation	100,000	70,000
Other fixed overheads	400,000	420,000
Costs of production	1,240,000	1,318,000
less closing stock	–	164,750
Cost of sales	1,240,000	1,153,250
Operating profit	200,000	211,750

Ann Jones, the senior management accountant gives you the following information.

- Material and labour are variable costs.
- The budgeted total cost of light, heat and power includes a fixed element of £20,000.
- The **actual** cost of light, heat and power includes a fixed element of £12,000.
- There were no budgeted or actual opening stocks.
- During the year, actual production was 40,000 Omegas, of which 5,000 were unsold at the year end.
- The closing stock of 5,000 Omegas were valued at their actual direct cost plus an appropriate proportion of fixed overheads.
- The company did not purchase or sell any fixed assets during the year.
- There was no work in progress at any time.

Tasks

i) Calculate the following.

1) Budgeted selling price per Omega
2) Budgeted material cost per Omega
3) Budgeted labour cost per Omega
4) Budgeted variable cost of light, heat and power per Omega
5) The percentage of cost of production carried forward in closing stock

6) Total actual variable cost of sales by expenditure type
7) Total actual fixed costs

ii) Prepare a flexible budget statement using variable (or marginal) costing, showing the budgeted and actual results and any variances.

b) The chief executive of Hall Ltd is Harry Easton. On receiving the original budgeted and actual operating statement, he had been very pleased with the performance of Hall Ltd. After reading your revised statement, however, he is concerned about the changes in both the budgeted profits and actual profits and is considering investigating whether or not the managers of Hall Ltd were responsible for the differences. Ann Jones suggests you write a memo to the chief executive.

Task

Write a short memo to Harry Easton, the chief executive. In your memo you should do the following.

i) Briefly explain the main reason for the following.

1) The difference between the original budget and the budget you prepared in task a)

2) The difference between the original operating profit and the operating profit you prepared in task a)

ii) Give TWO possible reasons why the actual operating profit shown in task a) was greater than the budgeted operating profit despite a lower sales volume.

20 KBV Sound Ltd makes a CD player that is fitted to the cars made by KBV Motors.

You have recently been appointed as KBV Sounds assistant management accountant. You are responsible for preparing statements showing actual results against flexible budgets.

You have been given the working papers of the previous assistant management accountant. These contain the following.

- Two draft budgets for the year ended 31 May 2008. The first assumes a production and sales volume of 80,000 CD players. The second assumes a production and sales volume of 100,000 CD players. Any differences between the two budgets arose entirely from the different volumes assumed.
- The actual operating results for the year.
- A note stating there were no opening or closing stocks of any sort.
- A note stating that there were no purchases or sales of fixed assets during the year.

The draft budgets and actual results from the working papers are shown below.

KBV Sound Ltd: budgets and actual results for the year ended 31 May 2008						
	Draft budgets				Actual results	
CD player production and sales volume	80,000		100,000		140,000	
	£'000	£'000	£'000	£'000	£'000	£'000
Conversion costs						
Labour	640		760		972	
Light, heat and power	370		450		586	
Rent, rates and insurance	200		200		200	
Depreciation	150		150		132	
		1,360		1,560		1,890
Bought-in materials		1,600		2,000		3,220
Total expense		2,960		3,560		5,110
Turnover		3,200		4,000		6,440
Operating profit		240		440		1,330

Tasks

a) Calculate the following data.

i) Budgeted selling price per CD player
ii) Budgeted bought-in material cost per CD player
iii) Budgeted variable cost of labour per CD player
iv) Budgeted total labour fixed cost
v) Budgeted variable cost of light, heat and power per CD player
vi) Budgeted total light, heat and power fixed cost

b) Prepare a flexible budget statement showing the budgeted and actual results and any variances.

c) Mike Jones is the personnel manager of KBV Sound. He believes the high profits of £1,330,000 are due to increased effort by the managers following the introduction of performance related pay on 1 June 2007. He explains the scheme to you.

- The bought-in materials for the CD players are purchased from outside suppliers but the conversion costs – those manufacturing costs that transform the raw materials into the finished product – are all provided by KBV Sound.
- The only customer for the CD player is the parent company, KBV Motors. Because of this, there is no market price and so the price has had to be negotiated.
- It was agreed that the price of the CD players sold to KBV Motors should be twice the cost of the bought-in materials.

- Additional performance related payments are based on the following.
  - Exceeding the annual budgeted volume of sales
  - Increasing the actual profit per CD player above the budgeted profit per CD player
- The budgeted sales volume for the year was 100,000 CD players and the budgeted profit per CD player was £4.40.
- The actual sales volume for the year was 140,000 and the actual profit per CD player was £9.50.

Write a memo to Mike Jones. In your memo you should do the following.

i) Use the data in the question to explain THREE reasons why profits might have improved even without the introduction of performance related pay.

ii) Identify THREE general conditions necessary for performance related pay to lead to improved performance.

UNIT 8

PRACTICE EXAM 1

HEETME LTD

These tasks were set by the AAT in December 2008

Time allowed: 3 hours plus 15 minutes' reading time

INSTRUCTIONS

This exam paper is in TWO sections.

You must show competence in BOTH sections. So, try to complete EVERY task in BOTH sections.

Section 1 contains 3 tasks and Section 2 contains 3 tasks.

You should include all your workings and essential calculations in your answers.

Both sections are based on the information below about HeetMe Ltd.

SECTION 1 (Suggested time allowance: 90 minutes)

DATA

HeetMe Ltd manufactures solar panels. The solar panels heat water for commercial purposes. The company has several divisions including the Solar Panels (SP) Division.

You work as an Accounting Technician reporting to the Finance Director.

The SP Division operates a standard cost system in which:

- purchases of materials are recorded at standard cost
- direct material and direct labour costs are variable
- production overheads are fixed and absorbed on a labour hours basis

The budgeted activity and actual results for the month of November 2008 are as follows:

	Budget		Actual	
Production units (solar panels)		2,000		2,100
Direct materials (paint)	1,000 litres	£25,000	1,150 litres	£29,900
Direct material (glass)	10,000 kilograms	£120,000	10,500 Kilograms	£147,000
Direct labour	4,000 hours	£28,000	4,000 hours	£28,000
Fixed overheads		£120,000		£130,000
Total cost		£293,000		£334,900

Task 1.1

a) Calculate the following for November:

i) standard cost per litre of paint
ii) standard usage of glass per solar panel
iii) actual labour rate per hour
iv) standard labour hours for actual production
v) total budgeted cost per solar panel
vi) total standard cost of actual production

b) Calculate the following variances, if any, for November:

i) direct material (glass) price variance
ii) direct material (glass) usage variance
iii) direct labour rate variance
iv) direct labour efficiency variance
v) fixed overhead expenditure variance
vi) fixed overhead efficiency variance

c) Briefly explain how adverse and favourable variances affect the reported profit or loss for the period.

ADDITIONAL DATA

The Production Director has reviewed the variances and has given you the following information.

- A better quality glass was purchased than that priced in the budget.
- The improved quality of glass meant that the solar panels could be made more quickly.
- The company operates a just in time production process and does not manufacture for stock.
- The 4,000 labour hours used could have produced a total of 2,600 solar panels but the orders were only for 2,100 units.

d) **Using the information provided by the Production Director, draft a report analysing the following variances you calculated in 1.1 b) above.**

i) direct material (glass) price variance
ii) direct material (glass) usage variance
iii) direct labour rate variance
iv) direct labour efficiency variance

Your answer should refer to both the variances you calculated and the information provided by the Production Director.

DATA

The Finance Director has asked you to write some notes to help in the training of a junior accounting technician. The notes are to explain the calculation of the total direct material (paint) variance and how this variance can be split into a price variance and a usage variance.

Task 1.2

Prepare notes using the information given in task 1.1 above including a calculation and explanation of the following variances:

a) the total direct material (paint) variance
b) the direct material (paint) price variance
c) the direct material (paint) usage variance

DATA

The Production Director has asked for your help. She has been given an equation and information to estimate the cost of glass for January and February 2009.

The equation is Y = a + bX, where:

- X is the time period in months
- the value for X in November 2008 is 29
- the value for X in December 2008 is 30
- Y is the cost of glass
- the constant "a" is 9 and constant "b" is 0.1

The cost of glass is set on the first day of each month and is not changed during the month.

Task 1.3

Calculate the expected price of glass per kilogram for January and February 2009.

Nov	Dec	Jan	Feb
y = 9 + 0.1(29)	9 + 0.1(30)	9 + 0.1(31)	9 + 0.1(32)
y = 11.9	y = 12	12.1	12.2

SECTION 2 (Suggested time allowance: 90 minutes)

ADDITIONAL DATA

HeetMe Ltd has been reviewing the quality of the solar panels and has engineered two new products, the SP2000 and the SP3000.

The SP2000 is a low quality product with an economic life of 5 years. The SP3000 is a high quality product with an economic life of 20 years.

The Sales Director has provided information about the expected demand and price for the SP2000 and SP3000 for the coming year.

- SP2000 will be priced at £200 per panel and demand is expected to be around 9,000 units per year.
- SP3000 will be priced at £300 per panel and demand is expected to be around 5,000 units per year.

Forecast profit and loss account

	SP2000	*SP3000*
Volume	9,000 units	5,000 units
	£	£
Turnover	1,800,000	1,500,000
Cost of production		
Direct materials (glass)	540,000	300,000
Direct labour	126,000	175,000
Fixed production overheads	120,000	120,000
Total cost of sales	786,000	595,000
Gross profit	**1,014,000**	**905,000**
Selling and distribution costs	400,000	400,000
Administration costs	200,000	200,000
Operating profit	**414,000**	**305,000**

Extracts from the forecast balance sheet

	£	£
Stock of material (glass)	60,000	60,000
Stock of finished goods	NIL	NIL
Turnover	2,014,000	1,905,000

Task 2.1

a) Calculate the following performance indicators for BOTH companies:

i) Gross profit margin
ii) Operating profit margin
iii) Direct materials cost per unit
iv) Direct labour cost per unit
v) Fixed production overheads cost per unit
vi) Return on net assets
vii) Raw materials stock turnover in days

b) Draft a report for the Finance Director covering the following:

i) an explanation of why the gross profit margin is different for each product. Your answer should refer to the following and explain their effect on the gross profit margin:

– sales price per unit
– materials, labour and fixed cost per unit

ii) an assessment of the return on net assets for each product.

ADDITIONAL DATA

The information in task 2.1 above ignored the cost of failure rates in the manufacture of the SP2000. The production process is based upon 2 hours of labour and results in a failure rate of 10% at the end of production.

The SP3000 production process is more robust and based on 5 hours of labour and results in a failure rate of nil.

Task 2.2

Calculate for SP2000 the following:

a) the revised production in units required to make 9,000 units of good production
b) the materials and labour costs of producing the additional units
c) the revised gross and operating profit for the SP2000
d) a revised calculation of the net assets based on the revised operating profit

DATA

HeetMe Ltd is considering purchasing a new machine to reduce the labour time taken to produce the SP3000. The machine would cost £300,000. The labour time would be reduced from five hours to two hours without compromising quality and the failure rates will remain at zero.

The discount factors you will need for 2.3 (a) and (b) are shown below.

Year	*Discount factor 5%*
0	1.000
1	0.952
2	0.907
3	0.864
4	0.823
5	0.784

Task 2.3

a) Calculate the discounted lifecycle cost of the machine based upon the following:

   i) purchase price of £300,000
   ii) annual running costs of £30,000 for the next 5 years
   iii) a residual value of £50,000 at the end of the 5 years

b) Calculate the discounted labour savings based upon annual production of 5,000 SP3000, a three hour saving per unit and a labour rate of £7 per hour.

c) Recommend whether the investment in the new machine will be financially beneficial.

UNIT 8

PRACTICE EXAM 2

GRIPPIT LTD

These tasks were set by the AAT in June 2008

Time allowed: 3 hours plus 15 minutes' reading time

INSTRUCTIONS

This exam paper is in TWO sections.

You must show competence in BOTH sections. So, try to complete EVERY task in BOTH sections.

Section 1 contains 3 tasks and Section 2 contains 3 tasks.

You should spend about 90 minutes on Section 1 and about 90 minutes on Section 2.

You should include all your workings and essential calculations in your answers.

Both sections are based on the information below about Grippit Ltd.

SECTION 1 (Suggested time allowance: 90 minutes)

DATA

Grippit Ltd processes old tyres into a product called Crumb. The Crumb is used in a variety of applications from road surfaces to brake linings. Grippit Ltd processes the tyres in the Crumbing Division and then either sells Crumb to other companies or uses Crumb in the manufacture of rubberised asphalt in the Road Division.

You work as an Accounting Technician reporting to the Finance Director.

The Crumbing Division operates a standard cost system in which:

- purchases of material are recorded at nil cost, as they are delivered free of charge from major tyre companies
- direct labour costs are variable
- production overheads are fixed and absorbed on a unit basis

The budgeted activity and actual results for the month of May 2008 are as follows:

		Budget		*Actual*
Production (tonnes)		200		210
Direct labour	600 hours	£4,800	600 hours	£5,100
Fixed overheads		£90,000		£95,000
Total cost		£94,800		£100,100

Task 1.1

a) Calculate the following for May:

i) standard labour rate per hour
ii) standard labour hours for actual production
iii) budgeted cost per tonne of Crumb
iv) budgeted overhead absorption rate per tonne
v) overheads absorbed into actual production
vi) total standard cost of actual production

b) Calculate the following variances for May:

i) direct labour rate variance
ii) direct labour efficiency variance
iii) fixed overhead expenditure variance
iv) fixed overhead volume variance

c) Using the variances you have calculated in Task 1.1b), prepare an operating statement for May which reconciles the standard cost of total actual production with the actual cost of total actual production.

ADDITIONAL DATA

The Production Director has reviewed the variances and has given you the following information.

- A pay rise of 25p per hour was awarded after the standard had been set.
- A software upgrade was purchased for the production machinery which cost £120,000 for a 2-year licence. The cost is being amortised (depreciated) on a straight-line basis.
- The software upgrade should increase labour efficiency by 10%, reducing the standard labour time to 2.7 hours per tonne.

d) Using the information provided by the Production Director, draft a report for the Finance Director explaining the variances you calculated in 1.1 b) above.

DATA

The Road Division, which manufactures rubberised asphalt, operates a standard costing system in which:

- Crumb material is transferred from the Crumbing Division at a standard cost of £474 per tonne
- purchases of asphalt material are recorded at standard cost
- direct material costs and direct labour costs are variable
- production overheads are fixed

The standard cost card for the coming month is being prepared and you have been given the following information.

- 50 tonnes of Crumb materials will be transferred from the Crumbing Division.
- 200 tonnes of asphalt material will be purchased at a cost of £150 per tonne.
- Labour required to produce 250 tonnes of output is 800 hours.
- Labour cost is £10 per hour.
- Fixed running costs of the machine are £150,000 per month.
- Budgeted production is 250 tonnes per month.
- Fixed production overheads are absorbed on the basis of tonnes.

Task 1.2

Prepare a standard cost card for the production of 250 tonnes of rubberised asphalt.

DATA

The Production Director has asked for your help. She has been given an equation and information to estimate the cost of asphalt for the coming three months.

The equation is $Y = a + bX$, where

- X is the time period in months
- The value for X in May 2008 is 25
- Y is the cost of asphalt
- the constant "**a**" is 125 and constant "**b**" is 2

The cost of asphalt is set on the first day of each month and is not changed during the month. The cost of asphalt in May 2008 was £175 per tonne.

Task 1.3

a) Calculate the expected price of asphalt per tonne for June and July 2008.

b) Convert the asphalt prices per tonne for June and July to index numbers using May 2008 as the base.

SECTION 2 (Suggested time allowance: 90 minutes)

DATA

Another division of Grippit, called Voltair, has developed a domestic wind turbine. A colleague has prepared forecast information based upon two scenarios. The forecast profit and loss account and balance sheet for both scenarios are shown below.

- Scenario 1 is to set the price at £1,250 per unit with sales of 10 000 units each year.
- Scenario 2 is to set the price at £1,000 per unit with sales of 14 000 units each year.

Forecast profit and loss account	*Scenario 1*	*Scenario 2*
	£'000	£'000
Turnover	12,500	14,000
Cost of production		
Direct (raw) materials	3,000	4,200
Direct labour	2,000	2,800
Fixed production overheads	3,000	3,000
Total cost of sales	8,000	10,000
Gross profit	4,500	4,000
Selling and distribution costs	1,000	1,000
Administration costs	750	750
Operating profit	2,750	2,250
Interest payable	600	600
Net profit	2,150	1,650

Extracts from the forecast balance sheet		
	£'000	£'000
Fixed assets	20,000	20,000
Current assets	5,000	5,500
Current liabilities	4,600	5,800
Long-term borrowing	12,000	11,300
Net assets	8,400	8,400
Represented by:		
Share capital	5,650	6,150
Profit and loss account	2,750	2,250
Net assets	8,400	8,400

Task 2.1

a) Calculate the following performance indicators for each scenario:

i) gross profit margin
ii) net profit margin
iii) direct materials cost per unit
iv) direct labour cost per unit
v) fixed production cost per unit
vi) gearing ratio
vii) interest cover

b) Draft a report for the Finance Director covering the following:

i) an explanation of why the gross profit margin is different in each scenario. Your answer should refer to the following:

– sales price per unit
– materials, labour and fixed cost per unit

ii) an assessment of the level of gearing and interest cover and whether it is a problem for the business

DATA

The Managing Director has been in talks with a Romanian manufacturer who could produce the wind turbines. You have been asked to analyse the information in order to evaluate whether Voltair should contract out the manufacture of the turbines.

If the turbines are manufactured in Romania the costs and savings would be as follows:

- The cost of each turbine would be £650 including transport costs to the UK.
- The material and labour costs would be saved.
- The fixed production costs consist of £1.95 million of specific costs which would be avoided, and £1.05 million of allocated overheads which would not be avoided.

Task 2.2

a) Calculate the following information for the demand level of 10,000 turbines per annum:

i) full production cost per turbine manufactured by Voltair, using your relevant answers from task 2.1 (a)
ii) Voltair's unavoidable fixed production cost per turbine if contracted out
iii) Voltair's avoidable production cost per turbine if contracted out

b) Calculate the following information for the demand level of 14,000 turbines per annum:

   i) full production cost per turbine manufactured by Voltair, using your relevant answers from task 2.1 (a)

   ii) Voltair's unavoidable fixed production cost per turbine if contracted out

   iii) Voltair's avoidable production cost per turbine if contracted out

c) Using your calculations in 2.2 (a) and (b) above, draft a report for the Managing Director covering the following:

   i) a recommendation on whether or not to contract out, based upon demand of 10,000 turbines

   ii) a recommendation on whether or not to contract out, based upon demand of 14,000 turbines

   iii) THREE other considerations which need to be taken into account

Task 2.3

A junior colleague is not certain of the difference between lifecycle costing and target costing.

a) Briefly explain the terms:

   i) lifecycle costing
   ii) target costing

b) Grippit Limited is developing a new product to monitor energy consumption. There are currently several other companies manufacturing similar products which sell for a price of £25 each. Grippit Ltd wishes to make a margin of 30%.

   Calculate the target cost of the new product.

UNIT 8

PRACTICE EXAM 3

TEESRUS LTD

These tasks were set by the AAT in December 2007

Time allowed: 3 hours plus 15 minutes' reading time

INSTRUCTIONS

This exam paper is in TWO sections.

You must show competence in BOTH sections. So, try to complete EVERY task in BOTH sections.

Section 1 contains 3 tasks and Section 2 contains 3 tasks.

You should spend about 80 minutes on Section 1 and 100 minutes on Section 2.

You should include all your workings and essential calculations in your answers.

Both Sections 1 and 2 are based on the business described below.

SECTION 1 (Suggested time allowance: 80 minutes)

DATA

TeesRus Ltd makes and packs tea bags. You work as an accounting technician reporting to the finance director. The company has two production divisions. In the bagging division tea is put into bags. In the packing division bags are put into boxes.

The packing division operates a standard costing system in which:

- purchases of packing materials (cardboard) are recorded at standard cost
- direct material costs and direct labour costs are variable
- production overheads are fixed
- tea bags are transferred from the bagging division at standard cost.

The packing division takes tea bags from the bagging division and packs them into boxes of 100 tea bags. The standard cost card for each pack of 100 tea bags is shown below.

Product: Box of 100 tea bags	**Quantity**	**Unit price £**	**Total cost £**
Direct materials (tea bags)	100 tea bags	0.033 per tea bag	3.30
Direct packing materials (cardboard)	50 grams	2.00 per kilogram	0.10
Direct labour	0.02 hours	10.00 per hour	0.20
Fixed overheads	0.02 hours	50.00 per hour	1.00
Standard cost			4.60

Actual and budgeted data for the packing division for November 2007 are shown below:

- Budgeted production for the month was 80,000 boxes of 100 tea bags.
- Actual production for the month was 84,000 boxes of 100 tea bags.
- Opening stock of tea bags was nil.
- 8,500,000 tea bags were transferred to the packing division from the bagging division at a cost of £280,500 or £0.033 per tea bag.
- Closing stock consisted of 50,000 tea bags.
- 1,800 direct labour hours were worked at a cost of £9.50 per hour.
- 4,200 kilograms of packing material (cardboard) was purchased and used at a cost of £8,800.
- Fixed production overheads incurred in the period were £85,000.

A colleague has correctly calculated the following variances:

- Direct material (tea bag) price variance as nil.
- Direct packing materials (cardboard) usage variance as nil.
- Direct labour rate variance as £900 favourable.
- Direct labour efficiency variance as £1,200 adverse.
- Fixed overhead efficiency variance as £6,000 adverse.

Task 1.1

a) Calculate the following information for November:

  i) budgeted production overheads
  ii) actual number of tea bags used in production
  iii) standard usage of tea bags for actual production.

b) Calculate the following variances for November:

  i) direct materials (tea bag) usage variance
  ii) direct packing materials (cardboard) price variance
  iii) fixed overhead expenditure variance
  iv) fixed overhead capacity variance.

c) Calculate the following:

  i) the total standard cost of actual production
  ii) the total actual cost of actual production.

d) Using your calculations in 1.1 b) and 1.1 c), and the variances calculated by your colleague, prepare an operating statement for November which reconciles the total standard cost of actual production with the total actual cost of actual production.

ADDITIONAL DATA

The production director has reviewed the variances and has given you the following information.

- A pay rise for staff is still outstanding.
- 2 new operators are still being trained.
- 3 machines are reaching the end of their operational life.

Task 1.1, continued

e) Draft a report for the Finance Director giving one reason for each of the following variances:

   i) direct materials (tea bag) usage variance
   ii) direct labour rate variance
   iii) direct labour efficiency variance.

ADDITIONAL DATA

The bagging division operates a standard costing system in which:

- purchases of materials are recorded at standard cost
- direct material costs and direct labour costs are variable
- production overheads are fixed

The standard cost card for the coming months is being prepared and you have been provided with the following information.

- Loose tea is expected to cost £5 per kilogram
- 1,000 tea bags require 3 kilograms of loose tea
- Tea bags cost 0.6 pence per bag
- One machine can package 5,000 bags per hour and requires one operator who costs £10 per hour
- Budgeted labour hours are 4,000 per month
- Fixed production overheads are £200,000 per month
- Budgeted production is 20,000 batches of 1,000 tea bags per month
- Fixed production overheads are absorbed on the basis of direct labour hours

Task 1.2

Prepare a standard cost card for the production of 1,000 tea bags.

ADDITIONAL DATA

The tea is imported from India and the historical cost per kilogram is shown below.

	June 07 £	July 07 £	Aug 07 £	Sept 07 £	Oct 07 £	Nov 07 £
Cost per kg of tea	4.95	4.97	4.99	5.05	5.08	5.10

Task 1.3

a) Convert the costs per kilogram for June and November to index numbers using January 2007 as the base year. The price per kilogram at January 2007 was £4.80.

b) It is expected that the index number for tea for January 2008 will be 108.25. Calculate the expected cost per kilogram for January 2008.

c) Calculate the percentage increase in the price of tea from January 2007 to January 2008.

SECTION 2 (Suggested time allowance: 100 minutes)

DATA

A division of TeesRus Ltd operates a tea plantation in Kenya. The plantation produces tea for sale to the tea bagging division and other wholesalers. The tea crop has been lower than expected due to bad weather. The actual and budgeted nformation is produced below.

You have also been given the following information:

- The poor tea crop has meant that harvesting took longer as the pickers could not pick as quickly.
- The tea pickers and tea processor operators are employed as and when needed on temporary contracts.
- The seeds and fertilisers are used at the start of the growing season.

	Actual £	Budgeted £
Turnover	787,500	1,125,000
Cost of sales:		
tea pickers	132,000	150,000
tea processor operators	35,000	50,000
depreciation of tea machines	60,000	60,000
seeds and fertiliser	75,000	75,000
Total cost of sales	**302,000**	**335,000**
Gross profit	**485,500**	**790,000**
Administration costs	150,000	150,000
Distribution costs	300,000	350,000
Operating profit	**35,500**	**290,000**
Amount of tea in kilograms harvested and sold	1,750,000	2,500,000
Number of harvest days	100	100
Number of tea pickers	440	500
Daily cost of a tea picker	£3	£3
Net assets	£935,500	£1,190,000

Task 2.1

a) Calculate the following performance indicators for the actual and budgeted information.

i) Cost of tea pickers as a percentage of turnover.
ii) Cost of tea processor operators as a percentage of turnover.
iii) Cost of seeds and fertilisers as a percentage of turnover.
iv) Gross profit margin.
v) Operating profit margin.
vi) Return on net assets.
vii) Net asset turnover.

b) Draft a report for the finance director giving an explanation of why the following ratios have changed.

i) Gross profit margin.
ii) Operating profit margin.

Note: Your answer should include comments on all elements of the profit and loss account.

ADDITIONAL DATA

The company currently has eight Pickmaster machines, which are coming to the end of their useful life. The company is considering replacing all eight machines with either new Pickmaster machines or new Pickmaster2 machines.

Each new Pickmaster machine costs £20,000 and requires 10 operators per day for the 100 days of the harvest. The machine will have a life of 10 years and a depreciation charge of £2,000 per year.

A new Pickmaster2 machine requires only 1 operator per day for the 100 days. This machine costs £90,000 to purchase and will have a life of 10 years. The depreciation charge will be £9,000 per year.

Other budgeted information for 2008 is as follows:

- The forecast harvest will last 100 days and produce 2.5 million kilograms of tea.
- The selling price of tea will be 45 pence per kilogram.
- Budgeted turnover is £1,125,000.
- Tea picker costs will be £150,000.
- Tea processor operators currently earn £6 per day.
- Seed and fertiliser costs will be £75,000.
- Administration costs will be £150,000 if the Pickmaster machines are purchased.
- Administration costs will be £135,000 if the Pickmaster2 machines are purchased.
- Distribution costs will be £350,000.
- The net assets at the end of the period will be £935,500 plus the budgeted operating profit.
- Disposing of the old machines will incur no profit, loss or any depreciation charge during 2008.

Task 2.2

a) Prepare TWO budgeted profit and loss accounts and net asset workings assuming that the business purchases either 8 Pickmaster or 8 Pickmaster2 machines.

b) Recalculate the following indicators for each option:

i) gross profit margin
ii) operating profit margin
iii) return on net assets

c) Prepare a report for the managing director to include the following:

i) comments on the indicators calculated in part b) above
ii) two other considerations
iii) a recommendation whether to purchase the Pickmaster or Pickmaster2 machines

Task 2.3

a) Briefly explain the term lifecycle costing.
b) Briefly explain why discounted cash flow techniques should be used in a lifecycle costing analysis.

UNIT 8

PRACTICE EXAM 4

FOODDRINK LTD

These tasks were set by the AAT in June 2007

Time allowed: 3 hours plus 15 minutes' reading time

INSTRUCTIONS

This exam paper is in TWO sections.

You must show competence in BOTH sections. So, try to complete EVERY task in BOTH sections.

Section 1 contains 2 tasks and Section 2 contains 2 tasks.

You should spend about 80 minutes on Section 1 and about 100 minutes on Section 2.

You should include all your workings and essential calculations in your answers.

Both sections are based on the information below about Fooddrink Ltd.

SECTION 1 (Suggested time allowance: 80 minutes)

DATA

Fooddrink Ltd manufactures and distributes nutritional supplements. One of its main products is IQ, a special vitamin supplement which claims to increase the concentration levels of individuals and helps them think carefully, especially when taking an exam. The supplement makes students read questions very carefully and show all their workings.

You work as an accounting technician reporting to the finance director.

The company operates an integrated standard cost system in which:

- purchases of materials are recorded at standard cost
- direct material costs and direct labour costs are variable
- production overheads are fixed and absorbed on a unit basis.

The budgeted activity and actual results for May 2007 are as follows:

		Budget		**Actual**
Production (units)		9,000		9,900
Direct materials	450 kgs	£5,400	594 kgs	£6,534
Direct labour	300 hours	£4,500	325 hours	£4,225
Fixed overheads		£18,000		£19,000
Total cost		£27,900		£29,759

Task 1.1

a) Calculate the following for May:

i) standard price of materials per kilogram
ii) standard usage of materials for actual production
iii) standard labour rate per hour
iv) standard labour hours for actual production
v) budgeted overhead absorption rate per unit
vi) overheads absorbed into actual production

b) Calculate the following variances for May:

i) direct material price variance
ii) direct material usage variance
iii) direct labour rate variance
iv) direct labour efficiency variance
v) fixed overhead expenditure variance
vi) fixed overhead volume variance

c) Using the variances you have calculated in Task 1.1b), prepare an operating statement for May which reconciles the standard cost of total actual production with the actual cost of total actual production.

d) Briefly explain how the treatment of fixed costs in an absorption costing system differs from that in a marginal costing system. Your answer should refer to the effect on fixed overhead variances and the stock valuation.

e) Explain how the fixed overhead volume variance can be analysed further. You do not need to do any calculations.

ADDITIONAL DATA

The material which is derived from soft fruit is either imported or purchased from UK farmers. The price of the material fluctuates month by month depending on the time of year. The cost information for the 4 months ending August 2006 is given below.

	May 06	June 06	July 06	August 06
Cost per 1,000 kg of vitamin	£1,000	£900	£700	£800

The underlying cost does not change during the period May to August. The change in cost over the 4 months is due only to the seasonal variations which are given below.

	May 06	June 06	July 06	August 06
Seasonal variations	£200	£100	-£100	£0

Task 1.2

a) Calculate the underlying cost per 1,000 kilograms for the period May to August 2006.

b) Indications are that the underlying cost per 1,000 kilograms for the period May 2007 to August 2007 will be £850. Calculate the percentage increase in the underlying cost from 2006 to 2007.

c) Calculate the forecast cost per 1,000 kilograms for the period May 2007 to August 2007 using the underlying cost and the seasonal variations given above.

SECTION 2 (Suggested time allowance: 100 minutes)

DATA

A division of Fooddrink Ltd is developing a new supplement and a colleague has prepared forecast information based upon two scenarios. The forecast profit and loss account and balance sheet for both scenarios is shown below.

- Scenario 1 is to set the price at £10 per unit with sales of 120,000 units each year.
- Scenario 2 is to set the price at £5 per unit with sales of 360,000 units each year.

	Scenario 1	**Scenario 2**
	£'000	**£'000**
Budgeted profit and loss account		
Turnover	1,200	1,800
Cost of production		
Direct (raw) materials	300	900
Direct labour	120	360
Fixed production overheads	360	360
Total cost of sales	780	1,620
Gross profit	**420**	**180**
Selling and distribution costs	74	122
Administration costs	100	100
Operating profit	**246**	**(42)**
Budgeted balance sheet		
Fixed assets		
Machinery	1,600	1,600
Current assets		
Stocks of raw materials	50	50
Trade debtors	150	150
Current liabilities		
Trade creditors	75	75
Net current assets	**125**	**125**
Long-term borrowing	754	1,042
Net assets	**971**	**683**
Represented by:		
Share capital	725	725
Profit and loss account	246	(42)
Net assets	**971**	**683**

Task 2.1

a) Calculate the following performance indicators for both scenarios:

i) gross profit margin
ii) operating profit margin
iii) direct materials as a percentage of turnover
iv) direct materials cost per unit
v) return on net assets
vi) stock turnover in days
vii) debtors' payment period in days
viii) gearing

b) Draft a report for the finance director giving an explanation of why the following ratios have changed:

i) gross profit margin
ii) operating profit margin
iii) direct materials as a percentage of turnover

ADDITIONAL DATA

You have found that your colleague has made a few mistakes with the figures for Scenario 2. The profit and loss account and balance sheet amendments for Scenario 2 are listed below.

- The raw material price per unit will fall to £1.50 per unit.
- The closing stock of raw materials will be £90,000.
- Trade debtors will be £225,000.
- Trade creditors will be £45,000.
- Short-term borrowing will be £145,000.
- Long-term borrowing will be £682,000.

c) Recalculate the following information:

i) gross profit
ii) operating profit
iii) net assets

d) Recalculate the following ratios:

i) gross profit margin
ii) operating profit margin
iii) return on net assets

e) Redraft your report for the finance director commenting on the ratios you recalculated in d) above and recommend whether the price of the product should be set at £10 or £5.

Task 2.2

The operations director has heard of the terms 'lifecycle costing' and 'target costing' and wonders whether the techniques can be used to aid future decisions. The company is about to start two projects. One is the design of a new cooler drinks bottle and the other is the design of a new production process for the manufacturing division. The new cooler drinks bottle will compete in an extremely competitive market.

a) Explain the terms:

   i) lifecycle costing
   ii) target costing

b) Explain which technique should be used for each project.

UNIT 8

PRACTICE EXAM 5

BETHERE AIRLINES

These tasks were set by the AAT in December 2006

Time allowed: 3 hours plus 15 minutes' reading time

PRACTICE EXAM

INSTRUCTIONS

This examination paper is in TWO sections.

You must show competence in BOTH sections.

You should therefore attempt and aim to complete EVERY task in EACH section.

All essential workings should be included within your answers, where appropriate.

Both sections are based on the information below about BeThere Airlines. Data provided in Section 1 may also be needed for Section 2.

SECTION 1 (Suggested time allowance: 80 minutes)

DATA

You are employed as an accounting technician at BeThere Airlines, a company that operates flights across Europe. The company has several divisions including a catering division operating from Manchester. The catering division produces meals daily for the flights. Currently all meals produced are used only on BeThere flights.

The company operates an integrated standard cost system in which:

- purchases of materials are recorded at standard cost
- direct material costs and direct labour costs are variable
- production overheads are fixed and absorbed using direct labour hours.

The budgeted activity and actual results for November 2006 are as follows:

		Budget		Actual
Production (meals)		112,000		117,600
Direct materials	56,000 kgs	£224,000	61,740 kgs	£185,220
Direct labour	28,000 hours	£252,000	27,930 hours	£279,300
Fixed overheads		£84,000		£82,000
Total cost		£560,000		£546,520

Task 1.1

a) Calculate the following information for November:

i) standard price of materials per kilogram
ii) standard usage of materials per meal
iii) standard labour rate per hour
iv) standard labour hours per meal
v) budgeted overhead absorption rate per hour
vi) overheads absorbed into actual production
vii) the total standard cost of actual production

b) Calculate the following variances for November:

i) direct material price variance
ii) direct material usage variance
iii) direct labour rate variance
iv) direct labour efficiency variance
v) fixed overhead expenditure variance
vi) fixed overhead volume variance
vii) fixed overhead capacity variance
viii) fixed overhead efficiency variance

c) Prepare a report to the managing director giving ONE possible reason for each of the following variances you calculated in Task 1.1b).

i) direct material price variance
ii) direct material usage variance
iii) direct labour rate variance
iv) direct labour efficiency variance

ADDITIONAL DATA

The airline operations director has asked for your help. He has been given an equation and information to estimate aviation fuel costs for the coming three months.

The equation is Y = a + bX where:

- X is the time period in months
- Y is the cost of aviation fuel
- the value for X in November 2006 is 11
- the constant 'a' is 0.998 and the constant 'b' is 0.002.

The cost of aviation fuel is set on the first day of each month and is not changed during the month. The cost of fuel in November 2006 was £1.020 per litre.

Task 1.2

a) Calculate the expected price of fuel for December 2006, and January and February 2007.

b) The operations director has been asked to provide a standard cost for the aviation fuel to be used to monitor the cost variance. Explain how a standard cost can be set for the coming quarter and any problems you foresee in setting the standard for aviation fuel costs.

c) Explain what is meant by the 'ideal standard'. How might using the ideal standard affect motivation?

SECTION 2 (Suggested time allowance: 100 minutes)

ADDITIONAL DATA

BeThere Airlines is reviewing its catering division and has provided the following information for the previous three months. The division has no administration or distribution costs. All costs are treated as costs of sales. All production has to be used in that day.

Catering Division

Cost report for the three-month period

	September	*October*	*November*
	£	£	£
Turnover	690,000	697,200	672,000
Cost of production			
Direct materials	185,000	185,100	185,220
Direct labour	274,313	275,975	279,300
Fixed production overheads	82,000	82,000	82,000
Total cost of sales	541,313	543,075	546,520
Profit	148,687	154,125	125,480
Catering Division balance sheet			
Fixed assets			
Land and buildings	800,000	795,000	790,000
Machinery	480,000	460,000	420,000
Current assets			
Stocks of raw materials	231,000	251,500	307,800
Amounts due from Airlines Division	690,000	697,200	672,000
Current liabilities			
Trade creditors	190,000	185,000	185,100
Net current assets	731,000	763,700	794,700
Long-term liabilities	800,000	800,000	800,000
Net assets	1,211,000	1,218,700	1,204,700
	Units	Units	Units
Capacity (meals per month)	125,000	125,000	125,000
Meals ordered by Flights Division	115,000	117,000	112,000
Budgeted meals	115,000	117,000	112,000
Meals produced	115,500	116,200	117,600

Task 2.1

a) Calculate the following performance indicators for each month, expressing each answer to two decimal places:

   i) Profit margin
   ii) Direct material cost as a percentage of turnover
   iii) Direct labour cost as a percentage of turnover
   iv) Return on capital employed (ROCE)
   v) Meals produced as a percentage of orders
   vi) Meals produced as a percentage of capacity

b) Draft a brief report to the managing director commenting on the performance of the division in November. You should base your report on your calculations in Task 2.1 a).

ADDITIONAL DATA

The operations director is reviewing various alternatives to determine whether it is possible to reduce monthly costs.

She is considering whether to invest in a new machine which:

- will mechanise part of the process and reduce the labour cost per meal from the current rate of £2.375 to £1.50
- could either be purchased for £3 million or rented for £50,000 per month
- is expected to have a life of 10 years and a scrap value of £900,000.

If the company purchases the machine, the division's net assets will increase by £1 million plus the profit for the period.

If the company rents the machine, the division's net assets will only increase by the profit for the period.

The operations director's performance is measured on ROCE, which she would like to see improved.

Task 2.2

a) Prepare a forecast profit and loss account and net asset calculation (a full balance sheet is not required) for both options (renting and purchasing) for one month.

   Note: Assume that the number of meals produced and sold will be 120,000 per month at a cost of £6 per meal. The material cost will remain as standard at £2 per meal, and monthly overheads will stay at £82,000 before any additional costs of the new machine. Ignore the time value of money.

b) Calculate the profit margin and the ROCE for both options.

c) What action would you recommend to the operations director?

Task 2.3

a) The operations director has heard of the term 'lifecycle costing' and wonders whether it can be used to aid the decision on whether to invest in a new machine.

b) Calculate the lifecycle cost of the TWO options outlined in the Additional Data on page 146.

Notes: Assume under both options that:

- the maintenance cost of the machine is £50,000 per annum
- decommissioning costs will be £100,000
- the machine will be used for 10 years

Ignore the time value of money and any opportunity costs when calculating the lifecycle cost.

UNIT 9

PRACTICE EXAM 6

GEEZER SCIENTIFIC

These tasks were set by the AAT in December 2008

Time allowed: 3 hours plus 15 minutes' reading time

INSTRUCTIONS

This exam paper is in TWO sections.

You must show competence in both sections. So, try to complete EVERY task in BOTH sections.

Section 1 contains 4 tasks and Section 2 contains 3 tasks.

You should spend about 100 minutes on Section 1 and about 80 minutes on Section 2. Please use the answer booklet provided.

You should include all your workings and essential calculations in your answers.

SECTION 1 (Suggested time allowance: 100 minutes)

DATA

Geezer Scientific, a company with two operating divisions, employs you as the budget accountant. The Pipstrelle division manufactures and sells the Pipstrelle. This is a precision measuring instrument for use in chemical laboratories. The other division is Equipment servicing, which maintains and repairs laboratory equipment. The company's financial year runs from 1 December to 30 November.

The tasks in Section 1 relate to the Pipstrelle division. You have been asked to prepare an operating budget for this division for the year ending 30 November 2009. You have obtained the operating statement for the year ended 30 November 2008.

Pipstrelle division
Operating statement for the year to 30 November 2008

		£
Turnover	382,000 units	4,393,000
Cost		
Opening stock	4000 units	35,200
Materials		1,650,600
Basic labour	117,600 hours	987,840
Labour overtime	1,456 hours	18,344
Variable overheard	119,056 hours	190,489
Fixed overheard		740,000
		3,622,473
Less closing finished stock	15,000 units	136,919
Total		3,485,554
Profit		907,446

Task 1.1

Calculate the following from the Operating Statement for the year to 30 November 2008:

a) average selling price
b) number of Pipstrelle instruments produced
c) average material cost of each Pipstrelle
d) average hourly pay rate for basic hours
e) average hourly pay rate for overtime
f) variable overhead cost per hour
g) profit percentage of turnover.

Note:

Where appropriate, you should round your answers to two decimal places.

DATA

You have been given further information about the production of Pipstrelles.

- Each Pipstrelle instrument is assembled from materials that are delivered each day by the suppliers. Material stocks are minimal and can be ignored for planning purposes.
- There are three stages in the production of the instruments. These are assembly, testing and dismantling rejects:

  i) It takes 12 minutes of labour time to assemble each instrument.

  ii) Testing each instrument takes a further three minutes. The quality standards are high: 15% of all assembled instruments are rejected at the testing stage because of faulty materials.

  iii) It takes three minutes to dismantle each rejected instrument.
- The suppliers replace faulty materials **free of charge**.
- Paid absence (sick leave and holidays) is charged to variable overheads. Variable overheads are all labour related.

The Board of Directors has agreed the following planning assumptions for the year to 30 November 2009:

- The Pipstrelle selling price will be reduced to £11 with effect from 1 December 2008.
- The number of instruments sold will be 25% higher than in the year to 30 November 2008.
- The closing stock of finished instruments at 30 November 2008 was higher than normal in anticipation of increased demand after the price cut. It can be reduced to 5,000 units at 30 November 2009.
- Material costs will increase by £0.10 per instrument.
- The average production staffing will be equivalent to 75 full time employees, each working 1,680 direct hours per year at basic rate.
- Any additional production hours required will be worked as overtime.

- Average pay rates for both basic hours and overtime will be 5% higher than in the year to 30 November 2008.
- The variable overhead rate per labour hour will also increase by 5%.
- Fixed overheads for the year will be £750,000.
- Strict quality control will be maintained and the level of rejections will not change.

Task 1.2

Draft the operating budget for the year ending 30 November 2009 for consideration by the Board of Directors. Present the budget clearly in the following stages:

a) sales volume

b) number of saleable instruments to be produced

c) cost of materials for the year

d) number of units to be assembled allowing for rejections at the testing stage

e) labour hours required in the year for:

   i) assembly
   ii) testing
   iii) dismantling rejects
   iv) total

f) annual cost of labour, including overtime

g) overhead costs for the year: variable, fixed and total

h) total cost of production for the year and per instrument (to two decimal places)

i) profit per instrument and profit percentage to selling price (ignore opening and closing stocks).

DATA

After your draft budget is circulated to the Board members, Myra Benjamin, the Quality Control Manager, contacts you. She explains that her department is struggling to cope with current production volumes.

'There are only twelve testing machines in my department', she says, 'I rotate the staff to cover absence but even with overtime we cannot carry out more than 425,000 tests a year.' She then explains that she can subcontract some of the testing. She has been quoted a price of £1.40 per test for this work, including transportation to and from the subcontractor's premises. Orders must be placed in multiples of 10,000 tests. Myra needs your help to make a recommendation for the Board of Directors.

Task 1.3

Calculate the additional cost that will be incurred through subcontracting, as follows:

a) number of tests to be subcontracted

b) additional cost of subcontracting these tests instead of carrying them out in overtime: per test and in total

c) revised cost per instrument, profit per instrument and profit percentage of selling price of the total planned production.

Task 1.4

Write a brief email to Myra explaining your findings.

a) Advise her:

   i) how the cost of subcontracting compares with doing the work in-house
   ii) whether the instruments that are subcontracted for testing are profitable.

b) Suggest one alternative strategy she could consider to overcome the capacity problem and explain whether it is likely to be cheaper than sub-contracting.

SECTION 2 (Suggested time allowance: 80 minutes)

DATA

The Equipment servicing division has been operating for three years and has grown rapidly. Because sales volumes were difficult to predict, the budget for the year to 30 November 2008 was prepared on the basis of the minimum and maximum likely level of sales. You have been asked to report on the division's performance for the year.

Equipment servicing division

Budgeted operating statement for the year to 30 November 2008

	Minimum sales level	*Maximum sales level*
Sales volume – chargeable hours	200,000	250,000
	£	£
Turnover	4,000,000	5,000,000
Costs		
Materials	100,000	125,000
Labour (basic hours)	1,470,000	1,470,000
Labour overtime	315,000	945,000
Energy	195,000	215,000
Equipment hire	250,000	275,000
Rent and rates	225,000	300,000
Administration	380,000	385,000
Collection and delivery	50,000	62,500
Depreciation	410,000	410,000
Total	3,395,000	4,187,500
Profit	605,000	812,500
Profit % turnover	15.1	16.3

Differences between the two budgets are entirely due to the number of chargeable hours of work. The budgets were prepared on the following assumptions:

- Customers are charged for the time spent servicing their equipment (chargeable hours).
- Material costs and collection and delivery costs are variable.
- 175,000 of the chargeable hours can be worked in normal time (basic hourly rate). Up to this point no overtime costs will be incurred.
- Further hours are worked as overtime at a premium rate.
- Rent and rates is a stepped variable cost dependent on the number of workshops rented. The annual cost of each workshop is £75,000. The number of chargeable hours that can be worked in each workshop each year is 70,000.
- Depreciation is a fixed cost.
- Other costs are semi-variable.

Task 2.1

Calculate the following information from the budget:

a) turnover per chargeable hour

b) variable cost per chargeable hour of:

   i) materials
   ii) energy
   iii) equipment hire
   iv) administration
   v) collection and delivery

c) labour cost per chargeable hour of hours worked in overtime

d) number of workshops required at the maximum sales level

e) annual fixed cost of:

   i) energy
   ii) equipment hire
   iii) administration.

DATA

The actual results for the year are now available.

Equipment servicing division

Actual operating statement for the year to 30 November 2008

Sales volume – chargeable hours	240,000
	£
Turnover	4,560,000
Costs	
Materials	123,500
Labour (basic hours)	1,390,000
Labour overtime	955,000
Energy	208,000
Equipment hire	297,200
Rent and rates	281,700
Administration	389,900
Collection and delivery	71,400
Depreciation	398,800
Total	4,115,500
Profit	444,500
Profit % of turnover	9.7

Task 2.2

Prepare an operating statement for the year to 30 November 2008, based on the layout shown above, that includes:

- the actual results
- the budget flexed to 240,000 chargeable hours
- the resulting variances.

Clearly indicate whether each variance is favourable or adverse.

Task 2.3

Write a brief report for the Board of Directors in which you:

a) summarise the performance of the division, identifying the main variances that have caused profitability to fall to 9.7% of turnover

b) suggest possible reasons why labour (basic hours), which is a fixed cost, is below budget and why this might not benefit the overall performance of the division

c) describe a statistical method of projecting sales that could be used to improve the budgeting process for the year ended 30 November 2009.

UNIT 9

PRACTICE EXAM 7

KEEPKOOL LTD

These tasks were set by the AAT in June 2008

Time allowed: 3 hours plus 15 minutes' reading time

PRACTICE EXAM

INSTRUCTIONS

This exam paper is in TWO sections.

You must show competence in both sections. So, try to complete EVERY task in BOTH sections.

Section 1 contains 3 tasks and Section 2 contains 2 tasks.

You should spend about 100 minutes on Section 1 and about 80 minutes on Section 2.

Please use the answer booklet provided.

You should include all your workings and essential calculations in your answers.

SECTION 1 (Suggested time allowance: 100 minutes)

DATA

You are employed as a Management Accountant by KeepKool Ltd.

The company only makes one product - air conditioning units. You have been asked to prepare sales and production budgets for the year ending 30 June 2009.

You have the following information to help you to prepare these budgets.

Forecast sales volumes (units)

- Sales volume for the four quarters of the year ending 30 June 2008 were:
  - quarter one (Q1) 15,000 units
  - quarter two (Q2) 5,000 units
  - quarter three (Q3) 5,000 units
  - quarter four (Q4) 20,000 units
- Sales for each quarter in the year ending 30 June 2009 are expected to be 2% higher than the corresponding quarter of the previous year

Stocks of finished goods

- Opening stock at the beginning of quarter one (Q1) will be 306 units.
- Stock at the end of each quarter must be equal to 2% of forecast sales in the following quarter.
- 1 in every 200 units is rejected by quality control. These have no scrap value.

Materials

- The units are made from three components, A, B and C.
- Each unit uses one of each component.
- The cost of the components is £180 for each A, £255 for each B and £140 for each C component.
- There are no opening or closing stocks of component parts.

Labour

- Each unit takes 1.5 labour hours to produce.
- KeepKool Ltd employs 25 production staff who each work a standard 480-hour quarter.
- The basic labour rate is £12 per hour and overtime is paid at 150% (basic pay plus an overtime premium equal to half basic pay per hour).
- Any overtime premium is charged to the cost of direct labour.
- In order to meet the peak production targets in Q1 and Q4, 15 agency staff will be recruited. They will be paid through the agency at £20 per hour.
- The agency staff will also work a standard 480-hour quarter but will not work any overtime.

Overheads

- Overheads are charged to the cost of production at the rate of £5 per labour hour including any idle time. There is a fixed overhead cost per quarter of £180,000.

Task 1.1

Prepare the following information for Q1, Q2 and Q3 in the year to June 2009 (round up your calculations to the next whole number, where applicable):

a) forecast sales of air-conditioning units
b) production budget in units
c) cost of materials budget
d) labour hours budget, identifying any expected overtime or idle time
e) cost of labour budget including agency staff and overtime
f) total cost of production budget

DATA

The board of directors is unhappy with the number of agency workers that have to be employed. They have asked you whether they may be able to reduce the need for agency staff. To do this you are asked to consider the possibility of only using employees and, if this is not achievable, how many agency staff you may still need.

You have the following additional information:

- The opening stock position for Q1 remains the same. However, there no longer needs to be any restriction on the amount of closing stock for each quarter.

- Overtime for permanent staff is preferred to the use of agency staff but this is limited to 120 hours per person per quarter.

- There are no restrictions on storage facilities

- Agency staff are available to cover any shortfall in production.

- 1 in every 200 units will still be rejected.

Task 1.2

Prepare THREE tables, showing calculations for all FOUR quarters of the year ending 30 June 2009, of the following:

a) the maximum number of units that can be produced in a quarter without using agency staff

b) the revised production budget (in units) showing where excess production or stock shortages occur and the number, if any, of any agency staff still needed to meet the full sales requirement

c) a revised labour budget

DATA

You are asked to report back to the directors with the results of your recalculations. They specifically want to know what will happen if they restrict the use of agency staff.

Task 1.3

From the results of your recalculations in task 1.2, write a report to the board of directors explaining:

a) the extent to which agency staff can be restricted and the implications this has for staff costs
b) TWO other ways to overcome any restrictions on production that you have identified in task 1.2.

SECTION 2 (Suggested time allowance: 80 minutes)

DATA

Kleanpacks Ltd makes an industrial liquid cleaner. You are the company's accountant.

The following is a copy of the original budgets and actual performance of the company for the last 12 months. Sales volumes were uncertain and the budgets were based on minimum and maximum levels of expected sales.

Draft budgets and actual results

	Draft budgets				*Actual*	
Sales volume (litres)	2,000,000		3,000,000		2,600,000	
	£'000	£'000	£'000	£'000	£'000	£'000
Turnover		£10,000		15,000		14,300
Material	1,600		2,400		1,950	
Labour	1,800		2,700		2,392	
Power	1,300		1,950		1,768	
Storage	870		1,030		992	
Transport	1,040		1,560		1,410	
Maintenance	770		770		790	
Depreciation	970		970		960	
Admin expenses	650		650		658	
		9,000		12,030		10,920
Operating profit		1,000		2,970		3,380

Assumptions made when preparing the original budget:

- Materials, labour and power are variable costs.
- Storage is a semi-variable cost.
- Transport is a stepped cost. For every £130,000 spent on transport, the company can carry 250,000 litres.
- Maintenance, depreciation and administrative expenses are fixed costs.
- There were no opening or closing stocks.
- There were no purchases or sales of fixed assets during the year.
- Any differences between the two budgets are due to the different volumes specified.

Task 2.1

a) Calculate the following budgeted prices and costs:

  i) selling price per litre
  ii) cost of material per litre
  iii) cost of labour per litre
  iv) storage variable cost per litre
  v) storage fixed cost per year

b) Prepare an operating statement to show the flexed budget for the actual turnover, the actual results and the resulting variances for the last 12 months.

c) Suggest ONE possible reason for each of the following variances:

  i) turnover
  ii) materials
  iii) labour
  iv) power
  v) storage
  vi) transport

DATA

The draft budgets were prepared by your department based on the results of the previous two years. Jan Barry, the Managing Director of Kleanpacks Ltd, is concerned that there is a lack of involvement of the departmental managers in the budgeting process that is leading to poor performances. She has asked you whether other types of budgeting might be more suitable for the company and to explain how these would help to involve the production and sales departments in preparing the forecasts.

Task 2.2

Write an email to Jan Barry that:

a) briefly explains how the company's budgeting procedures could be improved by using:

  i) departmental budgets
  ii) rolling budgets
  iii) computer generated models

b) explains TWO methods of motivating managers to be more involved in preparing the budgets.

UNIT 9

PRACTICE EXAM 8

KARTONS LTD

These tasks were set by the AAT in December 2007

Time allowed: 3 hours plus 15 minutes' reading time

INSTRUCTIONS

This exam paper is in TWO sections.

You must show competence in both sections. So, try to complete EVERY task in BOTH sections.

Section 1 contains 2 tasks and Section 2 contains 2 tasks.

You should spend about 100 minutes on Section 1 and about 80 minutes on Section 2.

You should include all your workings and essential calculations in your answers.

SECTION 1 (Suggested time allowance: 100 minutes)

DATA

You are employed as an accounting technician by Kartons Ltd.

The company makes packaging for the drinks industry. It makes two products, a 250ml carton and a 500ml carton. Both cartons use the same types of material and labour but in different quantities. You have been asked to prepare a production budget for both products for the four-week period ending 25 January 2008.

You have the following information to help you to prepare these budgets.

Forecast sales volumes (units)

- The company operates a five-day week for both production and sales.
- The company divides its operations into four-week periods.
- Sales for the period are forecast to be 250,000 units of the 250ml carton and 100,000 units of the 500ml carton.
- Sales for the next period to 23 February 2008 will be 4% higher than the period ending 25 January 2008.

Finished goods stocks

- Stocks at the beginning of the period were 62,500 of the 250ml cartons and 25,000 of the 500ml cartons.
- The stock of both cartons at the end of each period must be equal to 5 days forecast sales in the following period.

Materials

- The 250ml carton uses 40 square centimetres of material.
- The 500ml carton uses 50 square centimetres of material.
- The cost of the material is £55 per square metre (10,000 square centimetres).
- 2% of material is lost as wastage during production.
- At the beginning of the period, the opening material stock will be 132 square metres.
- At the end of the period, the closing material stock will be 145 square metres.

Labour

- Kartons Ltd employs 10 production employees who work a standard 35-hour week.
- 250ml cartons: 200 can be produced in one labour hour.
- 500ml cartons: 160 can be produced in one labour hour.
- The basic labour rate is £8 per hour and overtime is paid at 150% (basic pay plus an overtime premium equal to half basic pay per hour).
- Any overtime premium is charged to the cost of direct labour.
- Overtime costs should be allocated between the products on the basis of the average hourly rate.

Overheads

- Overheads are charged to the cost of production at the rate of £15 per labour hour.

Task 1.1

Prepare a budget for the four weeks to 25 January 2008 that includes the following (round up the quantities you calculate to the nearest whole number, where applicable):

Note: 1 square metre = 10,000 square centimetres

a) production in units for each of the 250ml and the 500ml cartons
b) the quantities of material required for the production of 250ml cartons and of 500ml cartons
c) material purchases in square metres
d) cost of material purchases
e) the labour hours required for the production of 250ml cartons and of 500ml cartons in the four-week period
f) basic labour hours and overtime
g) cost of direct labour
h) cost of production for each type of carton

ADDITIONAL DATA

Market research has shown that the demand for the 250ml carton will be greater than expected. The board of directors has asked you to revise the production budget to take into account an expected increase in unit sales of 8% over the original forecast for the four weeks to 25 January 2008.

You are given the following additional information.

- The increase in sales for the next period is still expected to be 4%.
- The wastage rate cannot be improved.
- The forecast for 500ml cartons has not changed.

Task 1.2

Recalculate the following budget data for the period ending 25 January 2008:

a) production units of 250ml cartons
b) material purchases in square metres
c) basic labour hours and overtime

ADDITIONAL DATA

The production director is concerned about his ability to increase production to meet the new sales forecast. He tells you that orders have already been placed for materials and he cannot acquire more than 1,500 square metres in time for January production. Also he only has 10 staff and he cannot expect them to work more than 50 hours overtime each during the period.

Task 1.3

Write a memo to the board of directors explaining the implications of the revised sales forecast. You should:

a) state whether your revised production unit budget can be achieved with existing resources

b) i) suggest THREE possible measures to overcome any shortage of resources in the period
   ii) explain what impact EACH of these measures could have on future production.

SECTION 2 (Suggested time allowance: 80 minutes)

ADDITIONAL DATA

You are the accountant for Miramar Ltd. The company makes a special type of binoculars for birdwatchers.

The following is a copy of the original budget and actual performance of the company for the last 12 months. You have been asked to prepare a flexible budget so that comparisons with the actual performance will be more useful.

Draft operating statement

	Original budget		*Actual*	
Sales volume units	50,000		60,000	
	£'000	£'000	£'000	£'000
Turnover		**15,000**		**16,500**
Material A	2,500		3,132	
Material B	990		1,557	
Material C	1,365		1,764	
Labour	2,700		2,980	
Energy	1,340		1,550	
Maintenance	745		987	
Rent and rates	940		945	
Administrative expenses	850		800	
Total expenses		**11,430**		**13,715**
Operating profit/(loss)		**3,570**		**2,785**

Assumptions made when preparing the original budget:

- Material and labour costs are variable.
- Energy is a semi-variable cost. The variable cost per unit produced is £18.
- Maintenance is a stepped variable cost. For every £149,000 spent on maintenance, the company can produce 10,000 binoculars.
- Both rent and rates, and administrative expenses, are fixed costs.
- There were no opening or closing stocks.
- There were no purchases or sales of fixed assets during the year

Task 2.1

a) Calculate the following budgeted prices and costs:

   i) selling price per unit

   ii) cost of material per unit for:

   – material A
   – material B
   – material C

   iii) cost of labour per unit

   iv) energy fixed cost for the year

b) Calculate the following actua prices and costs:

   i) selling price per unit

   ii) cost of material per unit for:

   – material A
   – material B
   – material C

   iii) cost of labour per unit

c) Prepare an operating statement to show the flexed budget for the actual turnover, the contribution, the actual results and the resulting variances for the last 12 months.

ADDITIONAL DATA

Gill Johns, the managing director of Miramar Ltd, has asked for a brief commentary on the variances that have arisen.

Task 2.2

Write a memo to Gill Johns in which you:

a) identify any variances in excess of £50,000 and suggest what action is required to investigate them

b) advise whether the change in selling price from that assumed in the budget appears to have been beneficial to Miramar.

UNIT 9

PRACTICE EXAM 9

BRIGHTER COVERS LTD

These tasks were set by the AAT in June 2007

Time allowed: 3 hours plus 15 minutes' reading time

INSTRUCTIONS

This exam paper is in TWO sections.

You must show competence in both sections. So, try to complete EVERY task in BOTH sections.

Section 1 contains 2 tasks and Section 2 contains 2 tasks.

You should spend about 100 minutes on Section 1 and about 80 minutes on Section 2.

You should include all your workings and essential calculations in your answers.

SECTION 1 (Suggested time allowance: 100 minutes)

DATA

Brighter Covers Ltd makes mobile phone covers. It produces two versions, a standard model and a luxury model.

You are employed as an accounting technician by the company and have been asked to prepare budgets for the two products for the next period for both sales and production.

You are given the following information to help you to prepare these budgets for the period ending 31 August 2007.

Forecast sales volumes (units)

- The company operates a five-day week for both production and sales.
- There are five weeks in each of the July and August accounting periods.
- Sales for the July 2007 period are forecast to be 67,500 units for the standard model and 32,500 for the luxury model.
- Sales are forecast to increase at a rate of 2% per period for both models.
- The sales price per unit is £3 for the standard model and £10 for the luxury model.

Stocks

- Opening stock at the beginning of the August 2007 period is 5,303 units of the standard product and 2,507 units of the luxury product.
- The finished stock of both models at the end of August is planned to be equal to 2 days sales of each product during August.
- There are no stocks of raw materials or work in progress at the start of each period.

Materials

- The luxury model uses a better quality material than the standard model.
- Each model uses 20 grams of material.

- The cost of the material is £50 per kg for the standard model and £250 per kg for the luxury model.
- 4% of material is lost during the process of manufacture. This material has no value.

Labour

- Brighter Covers employs 36 production employees who each work a standard 35-hour week.
- 24 employees work on the standard model and 12 employees work on the luxury model.
- 15 units of either the standard or the luxury model can be made in 1 labour hour.
- The basic labour rate is £10 per hour and overtime is paid at 150% (basic pay plus an overtime premium equal to half basic pay per hour).
- Any overtime premium is charged to the cost of direct labour.

Production overheads

- Overheads are charged to production at the rate of £12 per labour hour.

Task 1.1

Prepare the following information for the period to 31 August 2007 (rounding up the quantities you calculate to the nearest whole number):

a) sales forecast, in units, for each model
b) production budget, in units, for each model
c) material purchases budget in grams
d) cost of material purchases budget
e) direct labour hours budget
f) cost of direct labour budget
g) the budgeted operating statement for each model and for the whole company.

ADDITIONAL DATA

The luxury model has suddenly become very popular and demand is expected to be far more than originally forecast. The finance director, Tom Farrier, has asked you to revise the production budget to reflect the increase in the budgeted sales volumes. He also asks you to calculate the effect of employing 10 extra people to avoid the potential increase in overtime due to this increase in sales.

You are given the following additional information.

- The sales of the luxury model in August are now expected to be 40% more than originally forecast.
- Sales of the standard model remain as originally forecast.
- The extra staff will be employed only on making the luxury model.
- There is no restriction on the amount of materials available for making the luxury model.
- There is no restriction on overtime to be worked.

Task 1.2

a) Prepare, for the luxury model ONLY, the following for the period to 31 August 2007 (rounding up the quantities you calculate to the nearest whole number):

i) the revised production budget
ii) the revised material purchases budget
iii) the revised direct labour hours budget to include the 10 extra staff
iv) a revised budgeted operating statement for the luxury model.

b) In the form of an email to Tom Farrier, explain:

i) TWO implications for material stocks and purchases that arise from the increased production
ii) ONE other way in which the cost of direct labour could have been reduced.

SECTION 2 (Suggested time allowance: 80 minutes)

ADDITIONAL DATA

You are the accountant for QuikMaid Ltd. The company is a specialist retailer that sells a blender machine.

The following is a copy of the original budget and the actual performance of the company's current financial year. The original budget is based on the forecast level of sales produced at the end of the company's last financial year.

Draft budget and actual results

	Budget		**Actual**	
Sales volume	400,000		500,000	
Production volume	400,000		502,000	
	£'000	£'000	£'000	£'000
Turnover		14,000		20,000
Purchases	4,800		6,500	
Wages	2,600		3,350	
Warehousing costs	720		800	
Distribution costs	60		90	
Insurance	12		10	
Rent and rates	15		18	
Other administration	28		33	
Depreciation	50		50	
Total expenses		8,285		10,851
Less closing stock		–		40
Cost of sales		8,285		10,811
Operating profit		5,715		9,189

Warehousing costs are semi-variable.

- The budgeted fixed cost for warehousing is £40,000.
- The actual fixed cost for warehousing was £50,000.

Assumptions made when preparing the original budget

- There were no opening or closing stocks.
- Distribution cost is a stepped cost varying with every 100,000 blenders sold.
- Insurance is considered a fixed cost.
- There were no purchases or sales of fixed assets during the year.

Task 2.1

a) Calculate the following budgeted data:

   i) selling price per unit
   ii) cost of purchases per unit
   iii) variable cost of wages per unit
   iv) variable cost of warehousing per unit
   v) distribution costs per 100,000 blenders.

b) Calculate the following actual data:

   i) selling price per unit
   ii) cost of purchases per unit
   iii) variable cost of wages per unit
   iv) variable cost of warehousing per unit
   v) distribution costs per 100,000 blenders.

c) Prepare a marginal (or variable) cost operating statement to show:

   i) a flexed budget for the actual turnover of 500,000 units
   ii) the budgeted and actual marginal costs associated with that turnover
   iii) the budgeted and actual contribution
   iv) the budgeted and actual operating profit
   v) any resulting variances between the budgeted and actual results for the company's last financial year.

ADDITIONAL DATA

Clare Sands, the managing director of Quikmaid Ltd, has asked you to comment on the results for the last financial year based on a marginal costing approach. She also wants to know how to ensure a better budget forecast in future and how managers could be motivated to achieve this improvement.

Task 2.2

Write a report to Clare Sands that gives an analysis of the actual results and deals with the issues she has raised. This report should:

a) analyse the significance of EACH of the variances and explain how EACH could have arisen

b) explain TWO procedures that could be introduced in order to achieve a better sales budget forecast

c) explain THREE steps that Quikmaid Ltd can take to motivate managers to achieve budgets.

UNIT 9

PRACTICE EXAM 10

KANDO LTD

These tasks were set by the AAT in December 2006

Time allowed: 3 hours plus 15 minutes' reading time

INSTRUCTIONS

This examination paper is in TWO sections.

You must show competence in BOTH sections.

You should therefore attempt and aim to complete EVERY task in EACH section.

You should spend about 90 minutes on Section 1 and 90 minutes on Section 2.

Include all essential workings within your answers, where appropriate.

SECTION 1 (Suggested time allowance: 90 minutes)

DATA

You are the management accountant for Kando Ltd.

The company supplies products to the security industry. It is introducing a new product, the Keyfit, and you have been asked to prepare a sales and production budget for the next four periods.

You are given the following information to help you to prepare these budgets for the four periods ending 30 November 2007.

Forecast sales volumes (units)

- The company operates a five-day week for both production and sales.
- The company divides its operations into twelve-week periods.
- Period 1: sales are forecast to be 50,000 units.
- Period 2: sales are forecast to increase at a rate of 8% compared to the previous period.
- Periods 3, 4 and 5: sales are forecast to increase by 5% each period (compared to the previous period).

Stocks

- There is no finished stock at the beginning of period 1.
- The finished stock of Keyfits at the end of each period must be equal to 4 weeks forecast sales of Keyfits in the following period.
- 3% of finished stock is rejected by quality control as faulty when the product is completed. These items have no scrap value.
- There are no stocks of raw materials or work in progress at the start of period 1.

Materials

- Each Keyfit uses 2 kgs of material.
- The cost of the material is £4 per kg.

Labour

- Kando employs 400 production employees who work a standard 35-hour week.
- Each Keyfit takes three labour hours to produce.
- The basic labour rate is £10 per hour and overtime is paid at one and a half times the normal hourly rate.
- Any overtime premium is charged to the cost of direct labour.

Task 1.1

Prepare the following information for each of the four periods to 30 November 2007 (rounding up the quantities you calculate to the nearest whole number where applicable):

a) sales forecast for each of the four periods
b) production budget in units for each period of the sales forecasts
c) material purchases budget in kilograms
d) cost of material purchases budget
e) direct labour hours budget
f) cost of direct labour budget

ADDITIONAL DATA

Due to a shortage in raw materials, the board of directors has asked you to revise the production budget to reduce finished goods stocks to a level that still allows the budgeted sales volumes to be met.

You have been given the following additional information:

- Due to global demand, the total amount of material available for each period is restricted to120,000 kgs.
- The rate of faulty production cannot be improved.

Task 1.2

a) Calculate the revised material purchases and production budgets in units to meet the restricted volumes for the four periods.

b) Calculate how the restriction will affect budgeted stock levels and the production of stock units needed to meet the new forecasts.

c) Write a memo to the board of directors about the possibility of reducing the production of stocks of Keyfits. In your memo, explain:

   i) the implications for the company of the calculations you have made in a) and b)

   ii) TWO of the following techniques that are useful when forecasting sales and production of new products: strategic considerations, external analysis and internal analysis

   iii) TWO factors that you should take into account when considering the lifecycle of this new product.

SECTION 2 (Suggested time allowance: 90 minutes)

DATA

You are the management accountant for SeeWell Ltd. The company makes one type of musical equipment.

The following is a copy of the original budgets and actual performance of the company's last financial year. The original budgets are based on the forecast levels of sales volume produced at the end of the company's last accounting year and reflected the uncertainty of the economic situation.

SeeWell Ltd
Draft budgets and actual results

	Draft budgets				Actual	
Sales volume units	80,000		100,000		60,000	
		£'000		£'000		£'000
Turnover		6,000		7,500		4,320
Production volume units	80,000		100,000		60,000	
	£'000	£'000	£'000	£'000	£'000	£'000
Materials	1,200		1,500		1,000	
Labour	2,300		2,700		1,680	
Light, heat and power	1,080		1,340		800	
Insurance, rent and rates	760		840		650	
Depreciation	500		500		500	
Total expenses		5,840		6,880		4,630
Operating profit/(loss)		160		620		(310)

Assumptions made when preparing the original budget:

- There were no opening or closing stocks.
- There were no purchases or sales of fixed assets during the year.
- Any differences between the two budgets arise entirely from the different volumes.

Task 2.1

a) Calculate the following budgeted data:

i) selling price per unit
ii) cost of material per unit
iii) variable cost of labour per unit
iv) total labour fixed cost
v) variable cost of light, heat and power per unit
vi) total light, heat and power fixed cost
vii) variable cost of insurance, rent and rates per unit
viii) total insurance, rent and rates fixed cost

b) Prepare an operating statement to show the flexed budget for the actual production, the actual results and the resulting variances for the year ended 30 November 2006.

ADDITIONAL DATA

Victoria Andrews, the managing director of SeeWell Ltd, wants to know why there has been an actual loss and what factors, including economic factors, need to be taken into account to ensure a better budget forecast in future. She also needs you to explain what is the significance of the variances that have arisen and which control techniques the company should implement. You have been given the following additional information:

- Fixed costs have not changed.
- The world economy is currently subject to high prices and high demand for raw materials and other commodities.

Task 2.2

a) Calculate the actual:

i) selling price per unit
ii) cost of material per unit
iii) variable cost per unit for labour
iv) variable cost per unit for light, heat and power
v) variable cost per unit for insurance, rent and rates

b) Write a memo to Victoria Andrews which gives an analysis of the actual results and deals with the issues she has raised. This memo should explain:

i) THREE suggestions for the reasons for the actual loss and the significance of the variances that have arisen

ii) THREE general economic factors that SeeWell Ltd should take into account to ensure a better budget forecast

iii) the advantages of introducing flexible budgets and TWO other control techniques that could be introduced by SeeWell Ltd to avoid such losses occurring in the future.

ANSWERS

answers to chapter 1: INTRODUCTION TO MANAGEMENT ACCOUNTING

1 Financial accounting is predominantly concerned with the collection and classification of historic data in order to prepare the annual, or sometimes six monthly, financial statements of the business. These statements include a profit and loss account, balance sheet and a cash flow statement. These financial statements are prepared for users outside of the business such as:

- the current shareholders
- prospective investors
- providers of loan capital
- debtors and creditors
- the government

The aim of the financial statements is that they can be used by those external to the organisation to judge the performance of the management as a whole and in particular how successfully the directors of a company have carried out their stewardship function.

The financial statements must be prepared according to both legal requirements and the extensive requirements of accounting standards and must be presented in statutory formats. If the organisation is a company the financial statements must generally also be audited by an external auditor.

Management accounting, however, is all about providing the management of an organisation with the information that it needs to carry out its functions properly. The three main functions of management are planning, control and decision making. Therefore the purpose of management accounting information is to provide information that is relevant to these three functions.

This will require the provision of both historic information and estimates of future figures in a format which is useful to the relevant members of the management team. Most importantly the information must be provided regularly and on a timely basis, particularly for the purposes of control. Management accounting information can also take the form of one-off reports or information for decision making purposes.

2 i) The three main purposes of management accounting are **planning**, **control** and **decision making**.

ii) If production levels decrease then total variable costs will **decrease**.

iii) The stores department in a manufacturing organisation is an example of a **service** cost centre.

iv) Costs which cannot be directly attributed to a unit of production are known as **indirect** costs.

v) When service cost centre costs are divided between the production cost centres this is known as **apportionment** of costs.

vi) The range of activity levels over which a fixed cost is anticipated to remain fixed is known as the **relevant** range.

3

		True/false
i)	Management accounts must be audited by an external auditor	False
ii)	As production levels fall fixed costs per unit will rise	True
iii)	A semi-variable cost is one which is fixed for a certain range of activity and then increases and is fixed again for a further range of activity	False
iv)	As production levels rise the variable costs per unit will remain constant	True
v)	The salary of the production manager is an indirect cost	True
vi)	Absorption of overheads is the process of allocating overheads to relevant cost centres	False

4

	Activity level	
	16,000 units	*22,000 units*
Total cost	£54,400	£68,200
Cost per unit	£3.40	£3.10

Therefore this is not a variable cost – if it were a true variable cost then the cost per unit would be the same at each activity level.

5

Cost I	Variable cost
Cost II	Semi-variable or stepped cost
Cost III	Fixed cost
Cost IV	Variable cost

6

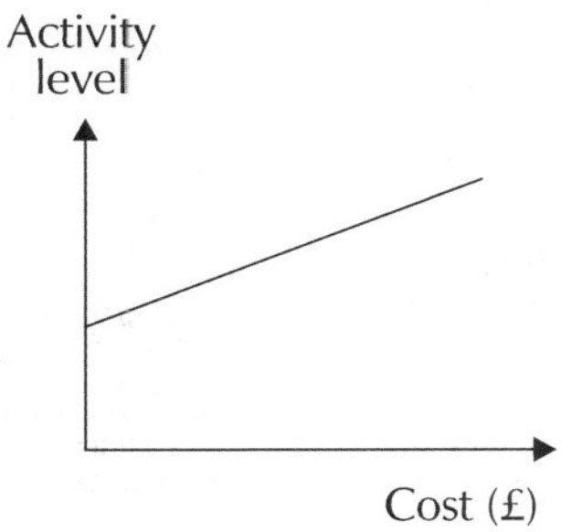

iii) semi-variable cost

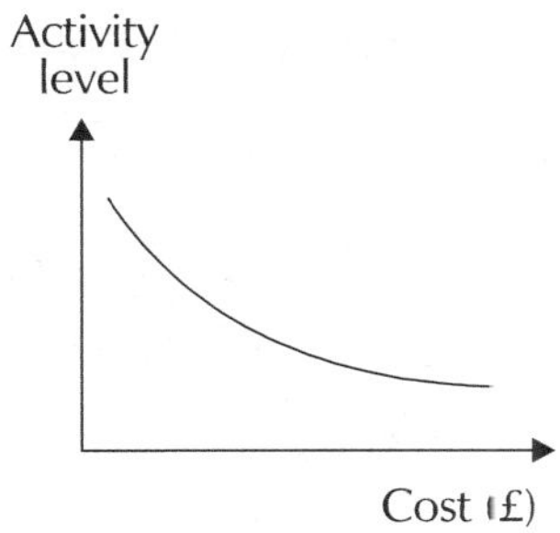

v) fixed cost per unit

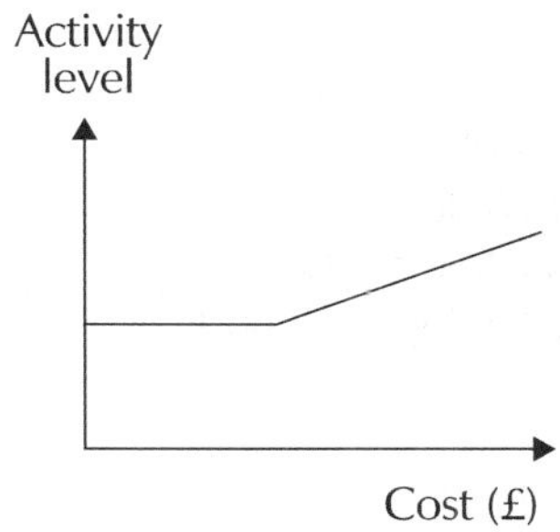

viii) production workers' wages

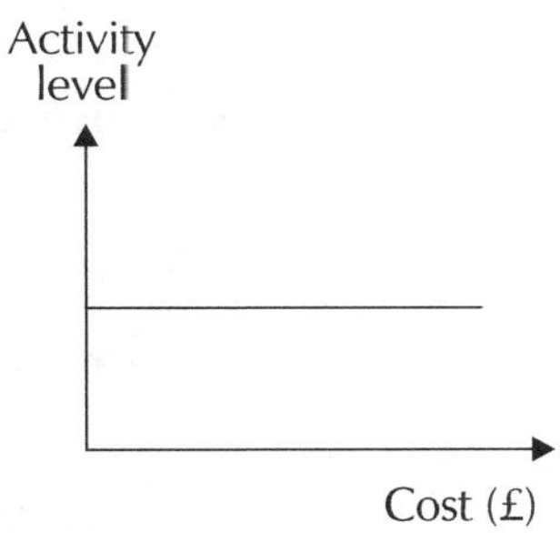

ii) total fixed cost

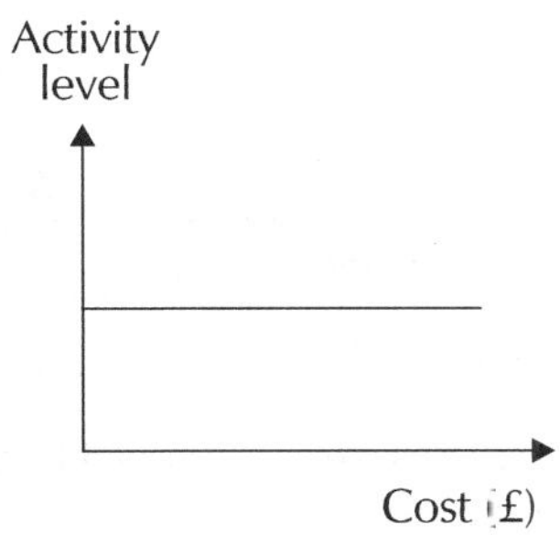

vi) variable cost per unit

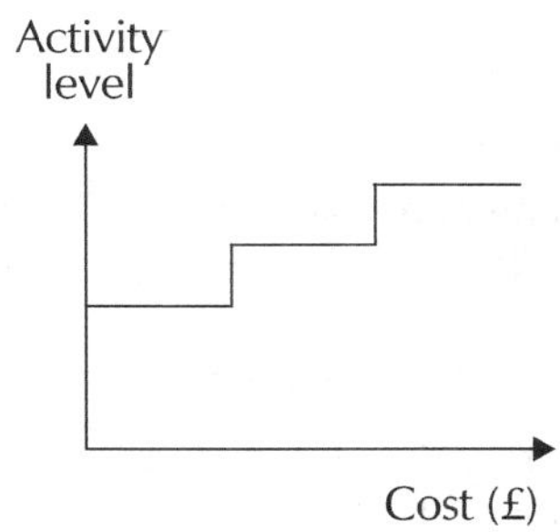

iv) stepped cost

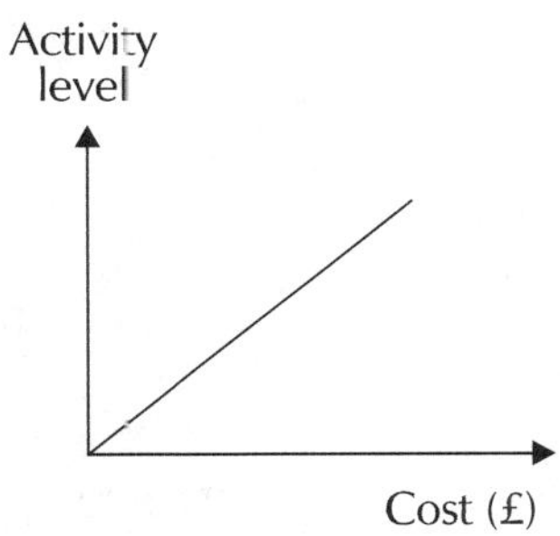

i) total variable cost

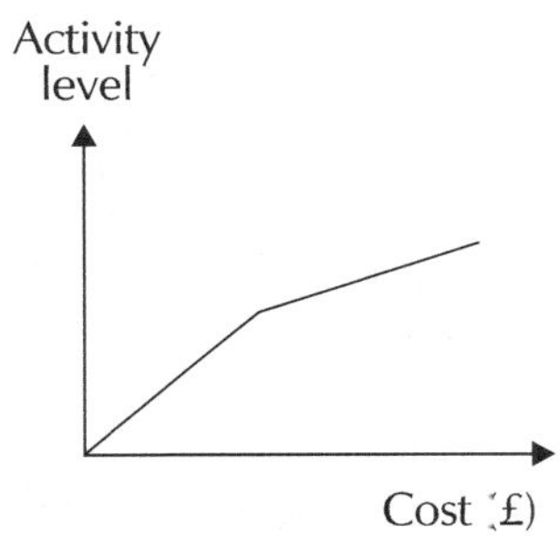

vii) materials cost with discount

Note: The graphs for ii) and vi) are interchangeable.

7

	Activity level		
	8,000 units	*12,000 units*	*15,000 units*
	£	£	£
Variable costs			
£32,000/10,000 x 8,000	25,600		
£32,000/10,000 x 12,000		38,400	
£32,000/10,000 x 15,000			48,000
Fixed costs	25,000	25,000	25,000
	50,600	63,400	73,000
Cost per unit	£6.325	£5.283	£4.867

8

		Cost behaviour
i)	Maintenance department costs which are made up of £25,000 of salaries and an average of £500 cost per call out	Semi-variable
ii)	Machinery depreciation based upon machine hours used	Variable
iii)	Salary costs of nursery school teachers where one teacher is required for every six children in the nursery	Stepped
iv)	Rent for a building that houses the factory, stores and maintenance departments	Fixed

9 i)

	Activity level		
	1,000 units	*1,500 units*	*2,000 units*
	£	£	£
Direct materials			
6kgs x £4.80 x units	28,800	43,200	57,600
Direct labour			
4 hours x £7.00 x units	28,000	42,000	56,000
Building costs – fixed	18,000	18,000	18,000
Leased machines	1,200	1,800	2,400
Stores costs			
£3,000 + £3.00 x units	6,000	7,500	9,000
	82,000	112,500	143,000
Cost per unit	£82.00	£75.00	£71.50

ii) The cost per unit is decreasing as production quantities increase. This is due to the fact that not all of the costs are variable. The buildings costs are fixed and part of the stores (inventories) costs are also fixed. For these elements of total cost as the production quantity increases so the cost per unit decreases. This in turn reduces the total overall unit cost as the quantity increases.

10 i) **Absorption costing**

Apportionment of overheads

	Cutting	*Finishing*	*Stores*
	£	£	£
Allocated overhead	380,000	280,000	120,000
Stores overhead apportioned 80:20	96,000	24,000	(120,000)
Overhead absorption rate	476,000	304,000	
	476,000	304,000	–

		Cutting	Finishing
Hours worked	50,000 x 3	150,000	
	50,000 x 2		100,000
Overhead absorption rate		476,000 / 150,000	304,000 / 100,000
		£3.17 per labour hour	£3.04 per labour hour

Unit cost – absorption costing

		£
Direct materials		16.00
Labour	– cutting 3 hours x £7.50	22.50
	finishing 2 hours x £6.80	13.60
Overheads	– cutting 3 hours x £3.17	9.51
	finishing 2 hours x £3.04	6.08
Unit cost		67.69

ii) **Marginal costing**

Unit cost – marginal costing

	£
Direct materials	16.00
Labour – cutting 3 hours x £7.50	22.50
finishing 2 hours x £6.80	13.60
Cutting £380,000 x 60%/50,000	4.56
Finishing £280,000 x 60%/50,000	3.36
Stores £120,000 x 60%/50,000	1.44
Unit cost	61.46

11 a) i) The fixed production overhead absorbed by the products would be 16,500 units produced x £2.50 (W1) = £41,250.

ii) Budgeted annual fixed production overhead = £150,000

	£
Actual quarterly fixed production o/hd = budgeted quarterly prod'n o/hd	37,500
Production o/hd absorbed into production (see (i) above)	41,250
Over absorption of fixed production o/hd	3,750

iii) **Profit for the quarter, using absorption costing**

	£	£	£
Sales (13,500 × £12)			162,000
Costs of production (no opening stocks)			
Value of stocks produced (16,500 × £8.50)(W2)		140,250	
Less value of closing stocks (3,000 units × full production cost of £8.50)(W2)		(25,500)	
		114,750	
Sales etc costs			
Variable (13,500 × £1)(W1)	13,500		
Fixed (¼ of £90,000)	22,500		
		36,000	
Total cost of sales		150,750	
Less over-absorbed production overhead		3,750	
			147,000
Profit			15,000

b) **Profit statement using marginal costing**

	£	£
Sales		162,000
Variable costs of production (16,500 × £6)(W1)	99,000	
Less value of closing stocks (3,000 × £6)(W1)	18,000	
Variable production cost of sales	81,000	
Variable sales etc costs (13,500 × £1)(W1)	13,500	
Total variable cost of sales (13,500 × £7)		94,500
Contribution (13,500 × £5)		67,500
Fixed costs: production	37,500	
sales etc	22,500	
		60,000
Profit		7,500

WORKINGS

1)

	Production costs	*Sales etc costs*
	£	£
Total costs of 60,000 units (fixed plus variable)	510,000	150,000
Total costs of 36,000 units (fixed plus variable)	366,000	126,000
Difference = variable costs of 24,000 units	144,000	24,000
Variable costs per unit	£6	£1

	Production costs	*Sales etc costs*
	£	£
Total costs of 60,000 units	510,000	150,000
Variable costs of 60,000 units	360,000	60,000
Fixed costs	150,000	90,000

2) The rate of absorption of fixed production overheads will therefore be:

$$\frac{£150{,}000}{60{,}000} = £2.50 \text{ per unit}$$

Total absorption costing production cost = £(6 + 2.50) = £8.50

12 a)

	£
Actual overheads incurred	496,500
Over-absorbed overheads	64,375
Overheads absorbed	560,875

Overhead absorption rate = £560,875/22,435 = £25 per hour

b) Change in stock = (8,500 – 6,750) litres = decrease of 1,750 litres

There was a reduction in stock during the period and so more overhead was charged against profit via opening stock than carried forward via closing stock. Marginal costing therefore shows the higher profit.

Absorption costing profit = marginal costing profit – (overhead absorbed in change in stock)

= £(27,400 – (1,750 × £2)) = £23,900

c) Overhead absorption rate = budgeted overheads/budgeted activity level

Budgeted number of machine hours = budgeted overheads ÷ overhead absorption rate
= £475,200/£32 = 14,850

13 a)

	HMG/012	*CFG/013*
	£	£
Equipment cost	175,000	120,000
Direct labour cost	130,000	66,000
Total direct cost	305,000	186,000
Gross profit percentage	50%	50%
Price	£457,500	£279,000

b) **Calculation of cost per unit of cost driver**

Activity	*Budgeted cost pool*	*Cost driver*	*Cost driver units pa*	*Cost per unit of cost driver*
	£			£
Design department	675,000	Design hours	25,000	27.00
Site engineers	370,000	Miles travelled	185,000	2.00
Purchasing department	105,000	Items purchased	15,000	7.00
Payroll department	75,000	Direct hours	300,000	0.25
Site management	750,000	Direct hours	300,000	2.50
Post-installation inspection	80,000	Items purchased	20,000	4.00

Schedule of activity-based overhead costs

Activity	*Cost per unit of cost driver*	HMG/012 *Cost driver units*	HMG/012 *ABC cost*	CFG/013 *Cost driver units*	CFG/013 *ABC cost*
	£		£		£
Design department	27.00	1,280	34,560	620	16,740
Site engineers	2.00	9,600*	19,200	900*	1,800
Purchasing department	7.00	650	4,550	410	2,870
Payroll department	0.25	10,000	2,500	6,000	1,500
Site management	2.50	10,000	25,000	6,000	15,000
Post installation inspection	4.00	650	2,600	410	1,640
Activity-based overhead			88,410		39,550

* Miles travelled = distance × visits

c) **MEMO**

To: Alice Devereaux
From: Accounts assistant
Cc: Mark Langton
Date: xx/xx/xx
Subject: **Profitability of jobs HMG/012 and CFG/013**

As requested, I have investigated jobs HMG/012 and CFG/013. Set out below is a statement which contains the projected profit for those two jobs.

	HMG/012	*CFG/013*
	£	£
Price	457,500	279,000
Equipment cost	175,000	120,000
Direct labour cost	130,000	66,000
Total direct cost	305,000	186,000
Gross profit	152,500	93,000
Activity-based overhead	88,410	39,550
Projected profit	64,090	53,450
Profit as a % of selling price	14.0%	19.2%
Profit as a % of total cost	16.3%	23.7%

Both jobs would be profitable at the suggested prices. The government contract is less profitable than the furniture store, however, because it is carrying a higher overhead cost. This higher overhead cost is caused by the extra complexity of the government contract and the distance of the government offices from our offices. It may therefore be necessary to increase the quoted price for the government contract to provide an adequate level of profit.

Please contact me if you require further information.

14 **FILE NOTE**

To: Drampton's finance director
From: Financial analyst
Date: xx/xx/xx
Subject: **Little Ltd – treatment of fixed overheads**

Following our recent discussions, I set out below calculations showing the reclassification of fixed overheads between the two units manufactured by Little Ltd, using activity-based costing.

a) **Reallocation of Little Ltd's budgeted total fixed annual overheads between server and PC production**

***Step 1.* Calculation of cost per cost driver**

	Budgeted total annual overheads	*Cost driver*	*Number of cost drivers*	*Cost per cost driver*
	£			£
Set-up costs	10,000	Number of set-ups	5	2,000.00
Rent and power (production area)	120,000	Number of wks' production	50	2,400.00
Rent (stores area)	50,000	Floor area of stores (m^2)	800	62.50
Salaries of store issue staff	40,000	No of issues of stock	10,000	4.00
	220,000			

***Step 2.* Reallocation of overheads based on costs per cost driver**

Server	(i) *Number of cost drivers*	(ii) *Cost per cost driver*	(i) × (ii) *Allocated overheads*
		£	
Set-up costs	5	2,000.00	10,000.00
Rent & power (production area)	10	2,400.00	24,000.00
Rent (stores area)	400	62.50	25,000.00
Salaries of store issue staff	2,000	4.00	8,000.00
			67,000.00

PC	(i) *Number of cost drivers*	(ii) *Cost per cost driver*	(i) × (ii) *Allocated overheads*
		£	
Set-up costs	0	2,000.00	–
Rent and power (production area)	40	2,400.00	96,000
Rent (stores area)	400	62.50	25,000
Salaries of store issue staff	8,000	4.00	32,000
			153,000

b) **Revised unit fixed overheads for each of the two types of computer**

Type of computer	*Allocated overheads*	*Annual budgeted volume*	*Unit fixed overheads*
	£'000	Units	£
Server	67	5	13,400.00
PC	153	5,000	30.60

15 A net present value is the net total of all of the present values of the cash inflows and outflows involved in a project. The purpose of calculating present values in project appraisal is to take account of the time value of money. For example, due to investment opportunities, the value of £100 in one year's time is less than the value of £100 now.

If the net present value of the cash flows of an investment is positive then the project should be accepted as this means that even after having taken account of the time value of money the cash inflows are greater than the cash outflows.

answers to chapter 2: COLLECTION OF DATA

1

		Primary/secondary
i)	Retail Price Index	Secondary
ii)	Stock Exchange share price listings	Secondary
iii)	Analysis of sales of a company by product	Primary
iv)	Trade Association inter-firm comparisons	Secondary
v)	A company's aged debtor listing	Primary

2 i) The Retail Price Index is an indication of the level of **inflation** in the UK.

ii) Quantitative data can be either **financial** or **non-financial** data.

iii) The National Statistics are published in 13 separate **themes**.

iv) A good alternative to pure random sampling are **quasi-random** sampling methods.

v) When sampling the name given to all items that are to be considered is the **population**.

3

		True/false
i)	An analysis of purchase invoices to determine the average trade terms from suppliers is an example of secondary data	False
ii)	The number of days holiday taken per year by qualified staff in a firm of solicitors is non-financial quantitative data	True
iii)	A survey showing favourite holiday destinations is an example of qualitative data	True
iv)	Quota sampling is an example of random sampling	False

4 The quantitative information that can be found from the purchase invoices of a business include:

- unit costs for materials
- cost of services
- trade and settlement discounts offered
- quantity of goods purchased
- payment terms

Such information can be used for a variety of purposes:

- valuing stock
- valuing the unit cost of production
- producing profit figures
- determining the amount of creditors
- comparison to budgeted costs
- estimating future costs
- choosing suppliers
- negotiating credit terms

5

		Source
i)	Local planning applications	Local council offices
ii)	The previous year's financial statements for a company	Companies House
iii)	Previous month's discounts allowed	Internal accounting records
iv)	Industry average profit margin	Trade association
v)	Information about a competitor's success	Financial press
vi)	Average sick days of employees per month	Personnel department

6 The government appreciates the importance of statistics regarding the state of the nation both fo[r] its own purposes and for those of businesses and the public and thus launched the new Nationa[l] Statistics in June 2000. A Statistics Commission was established together with the appointment o[f] a National Statistician who has overall responsibility for all National Statistics output.

The statistics available are divided into 13 separate themes covering distinct areas of national life[.] The themes are:

- agriculture, fishing and forestry
- commerce, energy and industry
- crime and justice
- economy
- education and training
- health and care
- labour market
- natural and built environment
- population and migration

- social and welfare
- transport, travel and tourism

Each of these themes can be accessed via the internet or by registering with the National Statistics office.

No business can operate in a vacuum and on many occasions it is likely that information about the economy, the population, social trends etc will be required. For example if a private health care organisation were considering investing in a new private hospital in an area they might wish to access information under the following themes:

- economy – the state of the economy in general and in this particular area
- health and care – information concerning health care in general in that area
- labour market – for potential staff in the area
- population and migration – moves into or out of the area
- social and welfare – information about the population in the area

7 i) **Random sampling** is the method of sampling that will give the best results as it is completely free from bias as to the items included in the sample. The entire population must be known and each item of the population is assigned a sequential number. The items to be sampled are then chosen using random number tables or a random number generator.

In order for random sampling to be used every item of the population must be known and numbered. An example where this could be used is if a check was to be made on the accuracy of calculations on sales invoices for the quarter from January to March. Each sales invoice has a sequential number therefore the first invoice sent out in January would be assigned the number 01, the second invoice sent out 02 etc. The invoices to be checked would then be chosen by random numbers.

ii) **Systematic sampling** is an approximation to random sampling where the first item in the sample is chosen by generating a random number and thereafter every nth item is chosen.

This method could be used for the invoice check considered above. The first invoice would be chosen by a random number and this may be invoice number 054131. Thereafter it is decided to check every 20th invoice so the next to be checked is invoice number 054151, then 054171 etc.

iii) **Stratified sampling** can be used where the population is split into a number of different groups. The size of the population in each group is determined and the size of sample from each group is then based upon the proportionate size of the group to the whole population.

For example if the sales invoices to be checked for accuracy had been prepared by three different divisions of the company the number of invoices sent out in the quarter by each division would determine the relative sizes of the samples taken from each division. Once the sizes of the divisional sample were determined, they would each then be chosen using random or systematic sampling.

8 i) As the entire population will be known, being all the purchase invoices processed in the period, and can be sequentially numbered, then the most appropriate method of sampling would be either random sampling or systematic sampling.

ii) In the case of the train customer sample it would not be possible to carry out random sampling as the entire population cannot be known or numbered.

As the types of passengers that travel on the railway are likely to be fairly diverse, in order to canvas the views of all types of commuter quota sampling may be most appropriate. For example the sample might be required to include a set number of business commuters, non-business commuters, men, women, commuters under 30, commuters between 30 and 60, commuters over 60 etc in order to gain a wide range of views.

iii) A sample of batches from production over a period needs to be tested to ascertain the number of defectives in each batch. As it will not necessarily be known in advance how many batches will be produced in the period, a pure random method may not be possible. Thus a form of systematic sampling may be used such that every, say, 3rd batch produced over the period is tested.

9 a) i) **Simple random sampling**

A simple random sample is one in which every member of the population has an equa chance of being included. A sampling frame of the entire adult population of the Northern sales territory would have to be drawn up if this method were to be used. Such a sampling frame would probably be constructed by combining the electoral registers fo the areas in question. Each person on the electoral register would then need to be allocated a number and a sample of 10,000 (500,000 x 2%) would be selected using random number tables or a random number generator on a computer.

ii) **Cluster sampling**

Cluster sampling involves selecting one definable subsection of the population as the sample, that subsection is taken to be representative of the population in question. In the Northern sales territory, where a sample of 10,000 is required, the regions might be split into groups (or clusters) of size 10,000 each. Northia would, for instance, contain 9 clusters while Wester would contain only one. In total there would be 50 clusters from which one would be selected randomly by numbering them and using random numbe tables as in (i). Every member of the selected cluster would then be surveyed. A more representative cluster sample could be obtained at greater cost by dividing the population into 500 geographic groups of 1,000 people each and then randoml selecting ten groups to be surveyed.

iii) **Stratified sampling**

It is possible that people's responses to the survey will depend on the region in whic they live and so, in order to obtain a representative sample, it is important to ensure tha all regions contribute to the sample in proportion to their population sizes. This i achieved by dividing the total population into strata (the regions in this case), samplin separately in the six strata (regions) and then pooling the samples. Regional sample must be proportional to regional sizes so, for instance, Northia's population of 90,00 would require a sample of 2% of 90,000 which is 1,800 people. The members of this sample would be selected randomly from the population of Northia by numbering and using random numbers as outlined in (i). The other sample sizes required would be as follows.

Wester	2% of 10,000 =	200
Southam	2% of 140,000=	2,800
Eastis	2% of 40,000 =	800
Midshire	2% of 120,000=	2,400
Centrasia	2% of 100,000=	2,000

The total of the six smaller samples is 10,000.

iv) **Systematic sampling**

This method selects the sample by choosing every nth person from a list of the population, having first made a random start at some point between 0 and fifty on the list (we require a sample of 2% of the population so every fiftieth (500,000 / 2% of 500,000) name will be chosen). Assuming that the territory does not have a single list of the adult population but does have electoral registers spanning the entire area, these could constitute a single list provided agreement could be reached on the order they were to be taken. A computer could randomly select one number between 0 and 50 and the person on the list in that position could be the random start. Thereafter every fiftieth person would be selected, with counting running on from one electoral list to the next until the total sample of 10,000 was selected.

b) The method likely to give the most representative sample is stratified sampling since this method deliberately selects from the different groups in the population in a representative fashion. The groups used in this case would be geographic, however, and it may be that people's characteristics regarding sales intentions do not vary according to the region in which they live. It may be that the sample would be more representative were it stratified by age or by gender. It would be very difficult, perhaps impossible, to stratify in such a way, however. With the caveat therefore that the basis of stratification needs to be relevant to the subject of the survey, stratification can be expected to give the most representative sample. Its disadvantages are that both the initial division of the sampling frame into strata and the process of numbering all population members, generating the required random numbers and identifying the corresponding people are difficult and time-consuming and therefore very costly.

The disadvantage of simple random sampling is that it is theoretically possible, although unlikely, to select highly unrepresentative samples. For example, every single sample member could live in Northia. Additional problems are that a sampling frame for the entire sales territory could be difficult to construct and, as for stratified sampling, the method of numbering and selecting by random numbers is cumbersome and costly.

In general, systematic sampling is just as likely to give unrepresentative samples as simple random sampling, but it has the added problems of bias if the sampling frame contains any cyclical patterns which correspond to the cycle of selection, such as every fiftieth person being elderly. The method we have suggested above would at least remove the danger of geographic imbalance, however. The combination of electoral registers into a single sampling frame would also be difficult.

Cluster sampling, although a relatively simple and cheap process by comparison with the other methods, is very open to bias. Indeed it would be surprising if one single geographic group could possibly be representative of the entire population. Even the selection of ten groups could easily prove to be very unrepresentative. There would also be some difficulty in dividing the population into clusters of exactly 10,000 each.

10 a) The major advantage of using personal interviews is that they are associated with high response rates. Other advantages are as follows.

i) The interviewer can clarify what the questions mean.

ii) The interviewer completes the questionnaire so it doesn't need to look especially attractive, responses can start being coded straight away and the questionnaire will be completed accurately and professionally.

iii) Answers may be entered immediately into a hand-held computer.

iv) Depending on the answers given to various questions, the interviewer need not bother the respondent with certain groups of questions.

There are however a number of disadvantages in using personal interviews. The main ones are that the method is costly and slow and is therefore associated with relatively small sample sizes. Other disadvantages are as follows.

i) People may be tempted to 'show off' or to try to give the responses that they think the interviewer favours.

ii) The interviewer may introduce bias by unintentionally letting his opinions show. This can be dealt with by training interviewers but this will only exacerbate the cost and time problem.

iii) In a personal interview, people may be reluctant to answer questions of an intimate nature.

iv) Generally speaking, it is not possible to schedule personal interviews at a time to suit the respondent. The respondent may be out or busy when the interviewer calls.

v) It is often impractical to use personal interviews if the survey covers a wide geographic area.

vi) The respondent may need time to reflect on certain questions or to look for information. The time available to the respondent and the interviewer is often too brief to allow this.

b) Postal surveys have more or less opposite advantages and disadvantages to personal interviews, and so will be dealt with next.

The major advantages of the use of postal questionnaires are that they are very easy, quick and cheap and hence relatively large samples can be used. Other advantages are as follows.

i) There is no possibility of interviewer bias and people are less inclined to give what they perceive to be the desired responses.

ii) People are less reluctant to answer questions of an intimate nature.

iii) The respondent can complete the questionnaire at a convenient time and can take as long to reflect on questions or to find information as he needs, subject to sending the questionnaire back in time.

iv) There are fewer problems in locating respondents than there are when using personal interviews.

v) The survey can spread over an area of any size provided that it is covered by the postal service.

The disadvantages of using postal surveys tend to mirror the advantages of personal interviews. The main disadvantage is that low response rates are very common and it is not possible to know whether the views of non-respondents are similar to those of respondents. There are consequently great difficulties in judging the reliability of these surveys. Other disadvantages are as follows.

i) A great deal of thought and effort goes into making the questionnaire look attractive and approachable.

ii) Ideally the questionnaire should be short and simple but it will often have to involve complex formulations like 'if "yes", answer questions 8 and 9, otherwise go straight to question 10'. Interviewers are capable of dealing with these types of question more easily than are postal questionnaires.

iii) Questions should be short and simple but, since there is no possibility of clarifying them, they often have to be long and complicated in order to be as clear as possible.

iv) Postal questionnaires are often filled in very badly and many respondents give up and fail to complete them.

v) Respondents who do not walk past post boxes in their day-to-day routine need to make an effort to go out of their way to return the form.

c) The advantages of telephone surveys fall somewhere between those of personal interviews and postal surveys. For example, telephone surveys will generally achieve higher response rates than postal surveys but lower response rates than personal interviews. They are not as cheap or as quick as postal surveys but they are quite a bit cheaper and easier than personal interviews. Their advantages are as follows.

i) They have reasonable response rates.

ii) The interviewer can clarify questions and can omit any irrelevant questions.

iii) The appearance of the questionnaire does not matter. Responses can be coded immediately. This type of survey is the best method for immediate data entry into a computer.

iv) There is less interviewer bias than there is with personal interviews.

v) They are reasonably quick and cheap to carry out provided the questionnaire is kept short. They are therefore associated with larger samples than personal interviews but smaller samples than postal surveys.

vi) The survey can encompass any area provided that it is covered by the telephone network.

The main disadvantage is that there are still quite a lot of people who do not have telephones and this can lead to unrepresentative samples being selected. Other disadvantages are as follows.

i) As with personal interviews, there can be a tendency to 'show off', intimate questions can cause problems, the respondent cannot generally select a convenient time for the interview and the respondent does not have time to reflect or to gather information.

ii) If the respondent is not at home, this is less of a problem than it is with personal interviews since it is simple enough to phone again.

iii) It is not possible to show any forms of identification to the respondent. This is thought to contribute to the response level for this type of survey being lower than that of personal interviews.

answers to chapter 3: TIME SERIES ANALYSIS AND INDEXATION

1 i) The trend of a set of figures in a time series analysis is the underlying movement of the figures over time. For example sales may be erratic each month but in general terms are gradually rising therefore the trend would be a steady increase in sales.

ii) Cyclical variations are due to the fact that most economies will tend to have periods of growth and periods of recession. It is considered that such economic cycles typically take place over a seven to nine year period. Such long term economic cycles will cause alterations in the pattern of sales and costs and this is reflected in the cyclical variations. If the economy is growing then sales are likely to be increasing more rapidly but if the economy is in recession then sales growth may slow down or even reverse.

iii) Seasonal variations stem from the fact the many businesses will experience some sort of regular growth reduction pattern due to the seasonality of their business (not necessarily relating to the actual seasons, summer, winter etc). For example a restaurant that is open 7 nights a week may generally experience peak numbers of customers on Friday and Saturday nights with lows on Monday and Tuesday.

iv) Random variations are the other unforseeable factors over which management have no control which will affect their sales or their production costs. For example in a manufacturing business if 30% of the workforce are affected by flu over a two-week period then production will probably drop. These random variations are totally unpredictable.

2

		3-month moving total	*3-month moving average*
	£	£	£
March	104,500		
April	110,300	327,600	109,200
May	112,800	332,500	110,833
June	109,400	339,800	113,267
July	117,600	343,000	114,333
August	116,000	352,800	117,600
September	119,200	357,500	119,167
October	122,300	362,000	120,667
November	120,500	362,100	120,700
December	119,300		

3 i)

			5-day moving average TREND	Seasonal variation (actual – trend)
		£	£	£
Week 1	Day 1	600		
	Day 2	700		
	Day 3	1,000	1,000	–
	Day 4	1,200	1,016	+184
	Day 5	1,500	1,026	+474
Week 2	Day 1	680	1,076	–396
	Day 2	750	1,116	–366
	Day 3	1,250	1,188	+ 62
	Day 4	1,400	1,216	+184
	Day 5	1,860	1,272	+588
Week 3	Day 1	820	1,410	–590
	Day 2	1,030	1,550	–520
	Day 3	1,940	1,678	+262
	Day 4	2,100	1,714	+386
	Day 5	2,500	1,772	+728
Week 4	Day 1	1,000	1,696	–696
	Day 2	1,320	1,734	–414
	Day 3	1,560	1,768	–208
	Day 4	2,290		
	Day 5	2,670		

ii) Seasonal variations

	Day 1	*Day 2*	*Day 3*	*Day 4*	*Day 5*
	£	£	£	£	£
Week 1			–	+184	+474
Week 2	–396	–366	+62	+184	+588
Week 3	–590	–520	+262	+386	+728
Week 4	–696	–414	–208		
	–1,682	–1,300	+116	+754	+1,790
Average	–561	–433	+29	+251	+597
Difference 117/5	+24	+23	+23	+23	+24
	–537	–410	+52	+274	+621

(Note that day 3 has four figures even though the seasonal variation in week 1 was zero, therefore it must be averaged over four figures.)

iii) The trend shows how the daily takings have increased each day over the four week period and the seasonal variations show how the takings on some days of the week are generally lower or higher than on other days of the week. As the restaurant has only just opened and the time series figures are for the first four weeks of operations the trend figure may not be a good indication of the future trend of the business. The takings appear to be increasing rapidly but this may be due to the fact that the restaurant is new and that customers are trying it out. Only if this trend continues in the longer term will it be a reliable basis for future predictions.

The same criticism of the daily seasonal variation can also be made. However, this does at least appear on the whole to be showing the same pattern each week, other than on day 3 when out of the four figures the variation is zero in the first week, negative for two weeks and then positive in week 4.

In general in order to be able to use the trend of figures and seasonal variations a more stable and longer term set of results is necessary.

4 i)

			4-quarter moving average	*Centred moving average TREND*	*Seasonal variations*
		£	£	£	£
2005	Quarter 3	50,600			
	Quarter 4	52,800			
			51,900		
2006	Quarter 1	55,600		51,975	+3,625
			52,050		
	Quarter 2	48,600		52,188	–3,588
			52,325		
	Quarter 3	51,200		52,625	–1,425
			52,925		
	Quarter 4	53,900		53,075	+825
			53,225		
2007	Quarter 1	58,000		53,450	+4,550
			53,675		
	Quarter 2	49,800		53,763	–3,963
			53,850		
	Quarter 3	53,000		54,113	–1,113
			54,375		
	Quarter 4	54,600		54,488	+112
			54,600		
2008	Quarter 1	60,100		54,750	+5,350
			54,900		
	Quarter 2	50,700		54,975	–4,275
			55,050		
	Quarter 3	54,200			
	Quarter 4	55,200			

ii) Seasonal variations

	Quarter 1	Quarter 2	Quarter 3	Quarter 4
	£	£	£	£
2006	+3,625	–3,588	–1,425	+825
2007	+4,550	–3,963	–1,113	+112
2008	+5,350	–4,275		
	+13,525	–11,826	–2,538	+937
Average	+4,508	–3,942	–1,269	+469
Difference 234/4	+59	+59	+58	+58
	+4,567	–3,883	–1,211	+527

iii)

	A	B	C	D	E
1	2005	Q3	50,600		
2					
3		Q4	52,800		
4				=(C1+C3 +C5+C7)/4	
5	2006	Q1	55,600		=(D4+D6)/2
6				=(C3+C5 +C7+C9)/4	
7		Q2	48,600		=(D6+D8)/2
8				=(C5+C7 +C9+C11)/4	
9		Q3	51,200		=(D8+D10)/2
10				=(C7+C9 +C11+C13)/4	
11		Q4	53,900		=(D10+D12)/2
12				=(C9+C11 +C13+C15)/4	
13	2007	Q1	58,000		=(D12+D14)/2
14				=(C11+C13 +C15+C17)/4	
15		Q2	49,800		=(D14+D16)/2
16				=(C13+C15 +C17+C19)/4	
17		Q3	53,000		=(D16+D18)/2
18				=(C15+C17 +C19+C21)/4	
19		Q4	54,600		=(D18+D20)/2
20				=(C17+C19 +C21+C23)/4	
21	2008	Q1	60,100		=(D20+D22)/2
22				=(C19+C21 +C23+C25)/4	

5 Predicted sales

		£
Quarter 1	£418,500 + £21,500	440,000
Quarter 2	£420,400 + £30,400	450,800
Quarter 3	£422,500 – £16,700	405,800
Quarter 4	£423,800 – £35,200	388,600

6 i)

	Actual costs	*RPI*		*Costs at January prices*
	£			£
January	129,600	171.1	129,600	129,600
February	129,700	172.0	129,700 x 171.1/172.0	129,021
March	130,400	172.2	130,400 x 171.1/172.2	129,567
April	131,600	173.0	131,600 x 171.1/173.0	130,155
May	130,500	174.1	130,500 x 171.1/174.1	128,251
June	131,600	174.3	131,600 x 171.1/174.3	129,184

ii) The unadjusted figures show that costs are generally increasing each month. However when adjusted to January prices using the RPI it can be seen that, other than in April, costs are in fact below the January level.

iii)

		RPI		*June prices*
	£			£
January	129,600	171.1	129,600 x 174.3/171.1	132,024
February	129,700	172.0	129,700 x 174.3/172.0	131,434
March	130,400	172.2	130,400 x 174.3/172.2	131,990
April	131,600	173.0	131,600 x 174.3/173.0	132,589
May	130,500	174.1	130,500 x 174.3/174.1	130,650
June	131,600	174.3	131,600 x 174.3/174.3	131,600

iv) The price adjusted figures show that costs have fallen in real terms over the six month period.

v) Yes

7 i)

		Sales £		Index
2007	Quarter 1	126,500		100.0
	Quarter 2	130,500	130,500/126,500 x 100	103.2
	Quarter 3	131,400	131,400/126,500 x 100	103.9
	Quarter 4	132,500	132,500/126,500 x 100	104.7
2008	Quarter 1	133,100	133,100/126,500 x 100	105.2
	Quarter 2	135,600	135,600/126,500 x 100	107.2
	Quarter 3	136,500	136,500/126,500 x 100	107.9
	Quarter 4	137,100	137,100/126,500 x 100	108.4

ii) The index shows that sales are growing at a steady rate each quarter.

iii)

		Sales £		Sales at 2006 quarter 4 prices £
2007	Quarter 1	126,500	126,500 x 149.1/135.4	139,299
	Quarter 2	130,500	130,500 x 149.1/138.2	140,793
	Quarter 3	131,400	131,400 x 149.1/141.7	138,262
	Quarter 4	132,500	132,500 x 149.1/142.3	138,832
2008	Quarter 1	133,100	133,100 x 149.1/144.4	137,432
	Quarter 2	135,600	135,600 x 149.1/146.2	138,290
	Quarter 3	136,500	136,500 x 149.1/147.5	137,981
	Quarter 4	137,100		137,100

iv)

		Sales at 2006 Quarter 4 prices £		Index
2007	Quarter 1	139,299		100.0
	Quarter 2	140,793	140,793/139,299 x 100	101.1
	Quarter 3	138,262	138,262/139,299 x 100	99.3
	Quarter 4	138,832	138,832/139,299 x 100	99.7
2008	Quarter 1	137,432	137,432/139,299 x 100	98.7
	Quarter 2	138,290	138,290/139,299 x 100	99.3
	Quarter 3	137,981	137,981/139,299 x 100	99.1
	Quarter 4	137,100	137,100/139,299 x 100	98.4

v) The index based upon the price-adjusted figures shows that other than in quarter 2 2007 the real sales have actually fallen below the 2007 quarter 1 figures. This is in contrast to the index in ii) based upon the unadjusted sales figures which showed fairly significant increases in sales in each quarter.

8 a) Updated standard cost = £3.50 x 145/115 = £4.41

b)

Planned cost	=	100,000/10 = £10,000
Actual cost	=	100,000/11.2 = £8,929
Difference	=	£1,071

9 a)

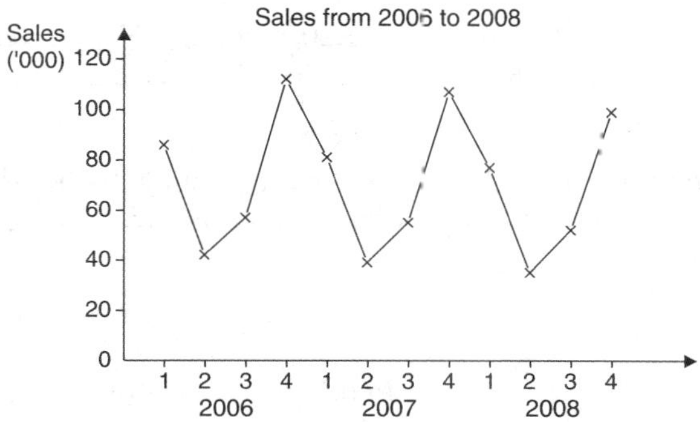

There are very marked seasonal fluctuations, with the fourth quarter of each year showing the highest sales and the second quarter the lowest sales. There does appear to be a steadily falling trend, with each peak and each trough slightly lower than the previous one.

b)

Year	*Quarter*	*Data* £'000	*4-quarter total* £'000	*Moving average of 4-quarter total* £'000	*Trend* £'000
2006	1	86			
	2	42	297	74.25	
	3	57	292	73.00	73.625
	4	112	289	72.25	72.625
2007	1	81	287	71.75	72.000
	2	39	282	70.50	71.125
	3	55	278	69.50	70.000
	4	107	274	68.50	69.000
2008	1	77	271	67.75	68.125
	2	35	263	65.75	66.750
	3	52			
	4	99			

c) **2008**

Quarter	*Data* £'000	*Adjustment* £'000	*Adjusted data* £'000
1	77	–9	68
2	35	+32	67
3	52	+16	68
4	99	–39	60

d) We can forecast sales by extrapolating the trend and then making seasonal adjustments.

Over the period from 2006, quarter 3 to 2008, quarter 2 (a duration of seven quarters, not eight) the trend fell by 73.625 – 66.75 = 6.875, giving an average fall per quarter of 6.875/7 = 0.982.

Forecasts can then be prepared as follows, extrapolating the trend at this rate from the value for 2008, quarter 2. Forecasts have been rounded to avoid giving a false impression of great precision.

2009

Quarter	*Trend* £'000	*Adjustment* £'000	*Forecast* £'000
1	*63.804	+9	73
2	62.822	–32	31
3	61.840	–16	46
4F	60.858	+39	100

* 66.750 – (3 × 0.982)

These forecasts should **not be assumed to be reliable**. Although the decline in the trend has been steady, and the pattern of seasonal variations consistent, from 2006 to 2008, it is always dangerous to extrapolate into the future. The trend or seasonal patterns may break down, or random variations may have a substantial effect.

10 a)

Year	*Revenue*	*Sales*	*Moving total of 4-quarters' sales*	*Moving average of 4-quarters' sales*	*Mid-point of two mowing averages Trend*	*Variation*
2006	1	200				
	2	110	870	217.5		
	3	320	884	221.0	219	+101
	4	240	892	223.0	222	+18
2007	1	214	906	226.5	225	–11
	2	118	926	231.5	229	–111
	3	334	932	233.0	232	+102
	4	260	938	234.5	234	+26
2008	1	220	944	236.0	235	–15
	2	124	962	240.5	238	–114
	3	340				
	4	278				

b)

	Quarter				
Year	*1*	*2*	*3*	*4*	*Total*
2006			+101	+18	
2007	–11	–111	+102	+26	
2008	–15	–114			
	–26	–225	+203	+44	–4
Unadjusted average	–13.0	–112.5	+101.5	+22.0	–2
Adjustment	+0.5	+0.5	+0.5	+0.5	+2
Adjusted average	–12.5	–112.0	+102.0	+22.5	0

answers to chapter 4: STANDARD COSTING

1 i) Total materials cost variance

	£
Standard cost of actual production 2,800 units x 5 kg x £4.00	56,000
Actual cost	60,480
Total cost variance	4,480 (A)

ii) Materials price variance

	£
Actual quantity at standard cost 14,400 kg x £4.00	57,600
Actual cost	60,480
Price variance	2,880 (A)

iii) Materials usage variance

	£
Standard quantity at standard cost 2,800 units x 5 kg x £4.00	56,000
Actual quantity at standard cost 14,400 kg x £4.00	57,600
Usage variance	1,600 (A)

2 i) Total materials cost variance

	£
Standard cost for actual production 11,400 units x 4 kg x £3	136,800
Actual cost	150,480
Total cost variance	13,680 (A)

ii) Materials price variance

	£
Actual quantity at standard cost 44,800 kg x £3	134,400
Actual cost	150,480
Price variance	16,080 (A)

iii) Materials usage variance

	£
Standard quantity at standard cost 11,400 units x 4kg x £3	136,800
Actual quantity at standard cost 44,800 kg x £3	134,400
Usage variance	2,400 (F)

3 i) Total labour cost variance

	£
Standard cost for actual production 12,100 units x 4.5 hours x £7.30	397,485
Actual cost	410,200
Total cost variance	12,715 (A)

ii) Labour rate variance

	£
Actual hours at standard rate 54,900 x £7.30	400,770
Actual hours at actual cost	410,200
Rate variance	9,430 (A)

iii) Labour efficiency variance

	£
Standard hours at standard rate 12,100 units x 4.5 hours x £7.30	397,485
Actual hours at standard rate 54,900 x £7.30	400,770
Efficiency variance	3,285 (A)

4 i) Total labour cost variance

	£
Standard cost for actual production 11,400 x 3 hours x £9	307,800
Actual cost	316,400
Total variance	8,600 (A)

ii) Labour rate variance

	£
Actual hours at standard rate 34,700 hours x £9	312,300
Actual cost	316,400
Rate variance	4,100 (A)

iii) Labour efficiency variance

	£
Standard hours at standard rate 11,400 units x 3 hours x £9	307,800
Actual hours at standard rate 34,700 hours x £9	312,300
Efficiency variance	4,500 (A)

5 i) Fixed overhead expenditure variance

	£
Budgeted overhead £7 x 10,000 units	70,000
Actual overhead	75,000
Expenditure variance	5,000 (A)

ii) Fixed overhead volume variance

	£
Actual production @ OAR 11,500 x £7	80,500
Budgeted production @ OAR 10,000 x £7	70,000
Volume variance	10,500 (F)

6 a) i) Fixed overhead expenditure variance

	£
Budgeted fixed overhead 50,000 units x 6 hours x £7.60	2,280,000
Actual fixed overhead	2,200,000
Expenditure variance	80,000 (A)

ii) Fixed overhead volume variance

	£
Standard hours for actual production @ OAR 52,000 units x 6 hours x £7.60	2,371,200
Standard hours for budgeted production @ OAR 50,000 units x 6 hours x £7.60	2,280,000
Volume variance	91,200 (F)

b) Fixed overhead efficiency variance

	£
Standard hours for actual production @ OAR 52,000 x 6 hours x £7.60	2,371,200
Actual hours @ OAR 310,000 x £7.60	2,356,000
Efficiency variance	15,200 (F)

Fixed overhead capacity variance

	£
Actual hours @ OAR 310,000 x £7.60	2,356,000
Budgeted hours @ OAR 50,000 x 6 x £7.60	2,280,000
Capacity variance	76,000 (F)

7 i)

	£
Budgeted fixed overhead	
14,000 units x 4 hours x £3.60	201,600

ii) Fixed overhead expenditure variance

	£
Budgeted fixed overhead	201,600
Actual fixed overhead	203,000
Expenditure variance	1,400 (A)

iii) Fixed overhead volume variance

	£
Standard hours for actual production @ OAR	
13,200 units x 4 hours x £3.60	190,080
Standard hours for budgeted production @ OAR	
14,000 units x 4 hours x £3.60	201,600
Volume variance	11,520 (A)

iv) Fixed overhead efficiency variance

	£
Standard hours for actual production @ OAR	
13,200 x 4 hours x £3.60	190,080
Actual hours @ OAR 50,000 x £3.60	180,000
Efficiency variance	10,080 (F)

v) Fixed overhead capacity variance

	£
Actual hours @ OAR 50,000 x £3.60	180,000
Budgeted hours @ OAR 14,000 x 4 x £3.60	201,600
Capacity variance	21,600 (A)

8 i) Materials price variance

	£
Actual quantity at standard cost 5,800 x £2.80	16,240
Actual cost	17,100
	860 (A)

Materials usage variance

	£
Standard quantity at standard cost 1,240 x 4.8 x £2.80	16,666
Actual quantity at standard cost 5,800 x £2.80	16,240
	426 (F)

ii) Labour rate variance

	£
Actual hours at standard cost 3,280 x £8.50	27,880
Actual cost	27,060
	820 (F)

Labour efficiency variance

	£
Standard hours at standard cost 1,240 x 2.5 x £8.50	26,350
Actual hours at standard cost 3,280 x £8.50	27,880
	1,530 (A)

iii) Fixed overhead expenditure variance

	£
Budgeted fixed overhead 1,100 x 2.5 x £1.60	4,400
Actual fixed overhead	4,650
	250 (A)

Fixed overhead efficiency variance

	£
Standard hours for actual production @ OAR	
1,240 x 2.5 x £1.60	4,960
Actual hours @ OAR 3,280 x £1.60	5,248
	288 (A)

Fixed overhead capacity variance

	£
Actual hours @ OAR 3,280 x £1.60	5,248
Budgeted hours @ OAR 1,100 x 2.5 x £1.60	4,400
	848 (F)

iv) **Reconciliation of standard cost of actual production to actual cost**

	Variances		
	Adverse	*Favourable*	
	£	£	£
Standard cost of actual production 1,240 x £38.69			47,976
Variances:			
Materials price	860		
Materials usage		426	
Labour rate		820	
Labour efficiency	1,530		
Fixed overhead expenditure	250		
Fixed overhead efficiency	288		
Fixed overhead capacity		848	
	2,928	2,094	
Add: adverse variances			2,928
Less: favourable variances			(2,094)
Actual cost of production (17,100 + 27,060 + 4,650)			48,810

9 a) **Standard cost per unit**

		£	£
Materials			
A	1.2 kg × £11 =	13.20	
B	4.7 kg × £6 =	28.20	
			41.40
Labour			
1.5 hours × £8			12.00
Prime cost			53.40
Overheads			
1.5 hours × £30			45.00
Standard cost per unit			98.40

b)

215,000 hrs should cost (× £8)	1,720,000	
but did cost	1,700,000	
Labour rate variance	20,000	(F)
126,000 units should take (×1.5 hrs)	189,000	hrs
but did take	215,000	hrs
	26,000	hrs (A)
× standard rate per hour	× £8	
Labour efficiency variance	£208,000	(A)

c) **Material A**

	£	
150,000 kg should cost (× £11)	1,650,000	
but did cost	1,650,000	
Price variance	0	
126,000 units should use (× 1.2 kgs)	151,200	kgs
but did use	150,000	kgs
	1,200	kgs (F)
× standard cost per kg	× £11	
Usage variance	£13,200	(F)

Material B

	£	
590,000 kgs should cost (×£6)	3,540,000	
but did cost	3,600,000	
Price variance	60,000	(A)
126,000 units should use (× 4.7 kgs)	592,200	kgs
but did use	590,000	kgs
	2,200	kgs (F)
× standard cost per kg	× £6	
Usage variance	£13,200	(F)

Note: (F) denotes favourable variance, (A) denotes adverse variance.

10 a) Budgeted fixed overhead absorption rate = £22,260 ÷ 8,400 hours = £2.65 per labour hour

Standard labour hours per unit of component RYX = 8,400 hours ÷ 1,200 units = 7 hours per unit

Standard fixed overhead absorbed per unit = 7 hours x £2.65 per hour = £18.55

	£
Fixed production overhead incurred	25,536
Fixed production overhead absorbed (1,100 × £18.55)	20,405
Fixed production overhead cost variance	5,131 (A)

i) Budgeted expenditure	22,260
Actual expenditure	25,536
Fixed production overhead expenditure variance	3,276 (A)

ii) 1,100 units should have taken (× 7 hrs)	7,700 hrs
but did take	7,980 hrs
	280 hrs (A)
× standard rate per hour	× £2.65
Fixed production overhead volume efficiency variance	£742 (A)

iii)	Budgeted hours of work	8,400 hrs
	Actual hours of work	7,980 hrs
		420 hrs (A)
	× standard rate per hour	× £2.65
	Fixed production overhead volume capacity variance	£1,113 (A)

b) **Reconciliation of fixed overhead variances**

	£
Expenditure variance	3,276 (A)
Volume efficiency variance	742 (A)
Volume capacity variance	1,113 (A)
Cost variance	5,131 (A)

11 a)

i)		£
	Budgeted fixed overhead expenditure (4,100 × 40 × £12.50)	2,050,000
	Actual fixed overhead expenditure	2,195,000
	Fixed overhead **expenditure variance**	145,000 (A)
ii)		£
	Actual production at standard rate (3,850 × 40 × £12.50)	1,925,000
	Budgeted production at standard rate (4,100 × 40 × £12.50)	2,050,000
	Fixed overhead **volume variance**	125,000 (A)
iii)	Budgeted hours (4,100 × 40)	164,000 hrs
	Actual hours	159,000 hrs
	Fixed overhead capacity variance in hours	5,000 hrs (A)
	× standard rate per hour	× £12.50
	Fixed overhead **capacity variance**	£62,500 (A)
iv)	3,850 units should have taken (× 40 hrs)	154,000 hrs
	but did take	159,000 hrs
	Fixed overhead efficiency variance in hours	5,000 hrs (A)
	× standard rate per hour	× £12.50
	Fixed overhead **efficiency variance**	£62,500 (A)

b) **REPORT**

To: Production Director
From: Assistant Management Accountant
Date: xx/xx/xx
Subject: **Performance of Division Omega** – 4 weeks ended 1 April

Set out below is a **reconciliation of the standard cost of production to the actual cost of production** in Division Omega for the four-week period ended 1 April.

			£
Standard cost of production (3,850 units × £975)			3,753,750
Variances	(F)	(A)	
	£	£	
Material price		45,000	
Material usage		76,250	
Labour rate		32,500	
Labour efficiency		37,500	
Fixed overhead expenditure		145,000	
Fixed overhead capacity		62,500	
Fixed overhead efficiency		62,500	
	–	461,250	461,250 (A)
Actual cost of production (W)			4,215,000

Working

	£
Materials	795,000
Labour	1,225,000
Fixed overheads	2,195,000
Actual cost of production	4,215,000

c) **MEMORANDUM**

To: Production Director
From: Assistant Management Accountant
Date: xx/xx/xx
Subject: **Fixed overhead variances**

This memorandum provides information on fixed overhead variances. In particular it covers the similarities between fixed overhead variances and other cost variances, the meaning of the various fixed overhead variances and the ways in which such variances can be of assistance in the planning and the controlling of the division.

Similarities between fixed overhead variances and other variances

The fixed overhead expenditure variance is the difference between the budgeted fixed overhead expenditure and actual fixed overhead expenditure. It is therefore similar to the material price and labour rate variances in that it shows the effect on costs and hence profit of paying more or less than anticipated for resources used.

Material usage and labour efficiency variances show the effect on costs and hence profit of having used more or less resource than should have been used for the actual volume of production. Fixed overheads should remain constant within the relevant range of production, however; they should not change simply because budgeted and actual production volumes differ. Fixed overhead variances similar to material usage and labour efficiency variances (reflecting the difference between the actual fixed overhead expenditure and the fixed overhead expenditure which should have been incurred at the actual volume of production) cannot therefore occur.

The meaning of fixed overhead variances

Whereas labour and material total variances show the effect on costs and hence profit of the difference between what the actual production volume should have cost and what it did cost (in terms of labour or material), if an organisation uses standard absorption costing (as we do), the fixed overhead total variance is the difference between actual fixed overhead expenditure and the fixed overhead absorbed (the under- or over-absorbed overhead).

The total under or over absorption is made up of the fixed overhead expenditure variance and the fixed overhead volume variance. The volume variance shows that part of the under- or over-absorbed overhead which is due to any difference between budgeted production volume and actual production volume.

The volume variance can be further broken down into an efficiency variance and a capacity variance. The capacity variance shows how much of the under- or over-absorbed overhead is due to working the labour force or plant more or less than planned whereas the efficiency variance shows the effect of the efficiency of the labour force or plant.

The volume variance and its two subdivisions, the efficiency variance and the capacity variance, measure the extent of under or over absorption due to production volume being different to that planned. Material usage and labour efficiency variances, on the other hand, measure the effect of usage being different from that expected for the actual volume achieved.

Fixed overhead variances and planning and control

The fixed overhead volume variance and its subdivisions are perhaps misleading as variances for management control, because unlike expenditure variances or variable cost efficiency variances, they are not a true reflection of the extra or lower cash spending by an organisation as a result of the variance occurring. However, the fixed overhead efficiency and capacity variances are of some relevance for planning and control. They provide some measure of the difference between budgeted production volume and actual production volume, and management should obviously be interested in whether budgeted output was achieved, and if not, why not. A favourable efficiency variance might indicate an efficient workforce whereas an unfavourable capacity variance might indicate plant breakdowns or strikes. The existence of a fixed overhead volume variance can therefore be important; it is only the monetary value given to it that can be misleading.

The fixed overhead expenditure variance highlights the effect on costs and hence profit of changes to the level of overheads. For overhead expenditure variances to have any practical value as a planning or control measure, the variance for each overhead cost centre needs to be calculated, and reported to the manager responsible. Within each overhead cost centre the manager should be able to analyse the total variance into indirect material cost variances, indirect labour cost variances and excess or favourable spending on other items, such as depreciation, postage, telephone charges and so on. Managers can then, for example, consider other suppliers, reconsider pricing structures of products and the like.

answers to chapter 5: STANDARD COSTING – FURTHER ASPECTS

1 The standard cost of the direct labour for a product will be made up of:

- the amount of time being spent on each unit of the product
- the hourly wage rate for the employees working on the product

Factors that should be taken into account when setting the standard for the amount of labour time include:

- the level of skill or training of the labour used on the product
- any anticipated changes in the grade of labour used on the product
- any anticipated changes in work methods or productivity levels
- the effect on productivity of any bonus scheme to be introduced

The hourly rate for the direct labour used on the product can be found from the payroll records. However consideration should be given to:

- anticipated pay rises
- any anticipated changes in the grade of labour to be used
- the effect of any bonus scheme on the labour rate
- whether any overtime is anticipated and should be built into the hourly rate

2 There are two main problems with using ideal standards in business:

Planning – if ideal standards are used for planning purposes it is likely that the results will be inaccurate as the standard does not reflect the reality of the working conditions. Therefore if a labour cost standard is set with no allowance for any inefficiency or idle time in the operations the reality is that the operations will take longer or will require more employees than planned for.

Control – if ideal standards are compared to actual costs then this will always result in adverse variances as the reality is that there will be some inefficiencies and wastage. This can be demotivational to managers and employees who will feel that in reality these standards can never be met and therefore they may stop trying to meet them. A further problem with these adverse variances is that they will be viewed as the norm and be ignored meaning that any corrective action that might be required is not taken.

3 i) A favourable materials price variance may be caused by:

- negotiation of a better price from a supplier
- negotiation of a trade or bulk purchase discount from a supplier
- purchase of a lower grade of materials

ii) A favourable materials usage variance may be caused by:

- use of a higher grade of material which led to less wastage
- use of more skilled labour leading to less wastage than normal
- new machinery which provides greater efficiency

iii) An adverse labour rate variance may be caused by:

- unexpected increase in labour costs
- use of a higher grade of labour than anticipated
- unexpectedly high levels of overtime

iv) An adverse labour efficiency variance may be caused by:

- use of a less skilled grade of labour
- use of a lower grade of material which takes longer to work on
- more idle time than budgeted for
- poor supervision of the workforce
- problems with machinery

4 i) The fixed overhead volume variance will occur when the actual production level is different from the budgeted production level. If actual production is greater than budget, then the volume variance will be favourable. The volume variance is caused by the absorption of the fixed overheads – therefore this variance only appears in absorption costing systems and not in marginal costing systems. If the absorption is done on the basis of labour hours then the variance will be caused by the standard labour hours worked for the actual level of production being different from the standard labour hours for budgeted production. Analysis of the volume variance into the efficiency and capacity variances can help to find reasons for the volume variance.

ii) The fixed overhead efficiency variance is caused by the efficiency of the workforce, if the absorption basis is that of labour hours. Therefore whatever caused the labour efficiency variance will also be the cause of the fixed overhead efficiency variance.

If the absorption basis is that of machine hours then the fixed overhead efficiency variance will reflect how efficiently the machinery has been used to produce the cost units

iii) The fixed overhead capacity variance, if the absorption basis is that of labour hours, measures whether more or less hours were worked than were budgeted. Therefore the cause of the capacity variance will be the underlying reason for more or less hours than budgeted being worked.

Similarly if the absorption basis is that of machine hours the capacity variance measures whether more or less machine hours were operated than were budgeted.

5 i)
- Favourable labour rate variance
- Adverse labour efficiency variance
- Adverse materials usage variance

ii)
- Adverse labour efficiency variance
- Adverse fixed overhead expenditure variance (due to additional costs of mending the machine)
- Adverse fixed overhead volume variance
- Adverse fixed overhead efficiency variance
- Adverse fixed overhead capacity variance

6 **New warehouse** – this will have the effect of simply reducing the fixed overhead expense (assuming the rent saved exceeds any new depreciation charge) and therefore is part of the favourable fixed overhead expenditure variance. The standard fixed overhead cost should be adjusted to reflect the rental saving.

New machines – the new machines use less power than the old ones therefore reducing the power costs element of the fixed overhead. The additional depreciation charge however will increase the fixed overhead expense. Once the reduction in power costs and increase in depreciation charge are known then the standard fixed overhead should be adjusted

Price increase – the price increase will be a cause of the adverse materials price variance. The price increase appears to be a permanent one as all suppliers have increased their prices so the standard materials cost should be altered.

Skilled labour – the use of the higher skilled labour will have been part of the cause of the favourable labour efficiency variance and the favourable materials efficiency variance. If the fixed overheads are absorbed on a labour hour basis then the efficiency of the skilled labour will also be a cause of the favourable fixed overhead efficiency variance. The additional expense of the skilled labour and the overtime that has been worked will have been causes of the adverse labour rate variance. The overtime may also have led to the favourable capacity variance as actual hours exceeded the budgeted hours. Unless the use of this grade of labour is likely to be a permanent policy then there should be no change to the standard labour rate or hours.

7 i) Total materials price variance

	£	
Standard cost for actual quantity 45,100 x £8	360,800	
Actual cost	397,400	
	36,600	(A)

ii) Planning variance caused by price increase

	£	
Standard cost for actual quantity 45,100 x £8	360,800	
Adjusted cost for actual quantity 45,100 x £8.50	383,350	
	22,550	(A)

Control variance caused by other factors

	£
Adjusted cost for actual quantity 45,100 x £8.50	383,350
Actual cost	397,400
	14,050 (A)

iii) The purchasing manager should not be held responsible for the entire price variance of £36,600 as the element caused by the price increase is not within his control. However the control element caused by other factors, the adverse variance of £14,050, is controllable by the purchasing manager and he should therefore be held responsible.

8 i) Total materials price variance

	£
Standard cost of actual quantity 10,600 x £6.50	68,900
Actual cost	73,140
	4,240 (A)

Planning variance due tc price increase

	£
Standard cost of actual quantity 10,600 x £6.50	68,900
Price adjusted cost of actual quantity 10,600 x £7.00	74,200
	5,300 (A)

Control variance due to other factors

	£
Price adjusted cost of actual quantity 10,600 x £7.00	74,200
Actual cost	73,140
	1,060 (F)

ii) The total materials cost variance is £4,240 adverse. However all of this is due to the price increase as the adverse variance caused by the price increase is higher at £5,300. The purchasing manager, instead of being blamed for this portion of the variance, should in fact be praised for the favourable variance caused by other factors.

9 Total materials price variance

	£	
Standard cost of actual quantity 92,000 x £7.00	644,000	
Actual cost	631,200	
	12,800	(F)

Planning variance due to season

	£	
Standard cost of actual quantity 92,000 x £7.00	644,000	
Seasonally adjusted price 92,000 x £7.00 x 0.94	605,360	
	38,640	(F)

Control variance due to other factors

	£	
Seasonally adjusted price 92,000 x £7.00 x 0.94	605,360	
Actual cost	631,200	
	25,840	(A)

10 Total materials cost variance

	£	
Standard cost of actual quantity 42,300 x £4.00	169,200	
Actual cost	194,580	
	25,380	(A)

Planning variance due to season

	£	
Standard cost of actual quantity 42,300 x £4.00	169,200	
Seasonally adjusted cost 42,300 x £4.00 x 1.18	199,656	
	30,456	(A)

Control variance due to other factors

	£	
Seasonally adjusted cost 42,300 x £4.00 x 1.18	199,656	
Actual cost	194,580	
	5,076	(F)

11 a) i) 1) **Standard marginal cost of a unit of Alpha**

	£
Material (36,000m ÷ 12,000) 3m × (£432,000 ÷ 36,000) £12 per m	36.00
Labour (72,000 hrs ÷ 12,000) 6 hrs × (£450,000 ÷ 72,000) £6.25 per hr	37.50
	73.50

2) **Standard cost of producing 10,000 units of Alpha**

	£
Material (£36 × 10,000)	360,000
Labour (£37.50 × 10,000)	375,000
Fixed overheads	396,000
	1,131,000

ii) 1)

	£
32,000 m should have cost (× £12)	384,000
but did cost	377,600
Material price variance	6,400 (F)

2)

10,000 units should have used (× 3 m)	30,000 m
but did use	32,000 m
Material usage variance in metres	2,000 m (A)
× standard cost per metre	× £12
Material usage variance in £	£24,000 (A)

3)

	£
70,000 hrs should have cost (× £6.25)	437,500
but did cost	422,800
Labour rate variance	14,700 (F)

4)

10,000 units should have taken (× 6 hrs)	60,000 hrs
but did take	70,000 hrs
Efficiency variance in hours	10,000 hrs (A)
× standard rate per hour	× £6.25
Labour efficiency variance in £	£62,500 (A)

5)

	£
Budgeted fixed overhead expenditure	396,000
Actual fixed overhead expenditure (£(330,000 + 75,000))	405,000
Fixed overhead expenditure variance	9,000 (A)

iii) **MEMO**

To: Managing Director
From: Assistant Management Accountant
Date: xx/xx/xx
Subject: The use of standard marginal costing at Finchley Ltd

As discussed at our earlier meetings, because all companies within the Hampstead Group use standard marginal costing, Finchley Ltd will need to adopt the system from 1 August 2008. This report is intended to demonstrate and describe the use of standard marginal costing in your company.

1) Set out below is a statement reconciling the standard cost of production for the three months ended 31 May 2008 with the actual cost of production for that period.

			£
Standard cost of output((see a) i) 2))			1,131,000
Variances	*(A)*	*(F)*	
	£	£	
Material price		6,400	
Material usage	24,000		
Labour rate		14,700	
Labour efficiency	62,500		
Fixed overhead expenditure	9,000		
	95,500	21,100	74,400 (A)
Actual cost of output			1,205,400

2) The total labour variance in the statement above (£47,800 (A)) differs from that in your absorption costing management report for the three months ended 31 May 2007 because the original report compares the actual cost of producing 10,000 units and the budgeted cost of producing 12,000 units. It therefore fails to compare like with like. The report above, however, compares actual costs of producing 10,000 units and what costs should have been given the actual output of 10,000 units. The total material variances in the two reports differ for this reason. There is very little point comparing a budgeted cost with an actual cost if the production level upon which the budgeted cost was based is not achieved.

   The fixed overhead expenditure variance in the statement above also differs from the fixed overhead variance reported in the absorption costing statement. This is because the absorption costing statement compares overhead absorbed whereas the marginal costing statement compares overhead expenditure.

3) There are other reasons why the marginal costing statement provides improved management information.

   i) It separates total variances into their components and so you will be able to determine whether, for example, the total material variance is the responsibility of the purchasing manager (price variance) or the production manager (usage variance).

ii) It avoids the use of under-or over-absorbed overhead, which is simply a bookkeeping exercise and does not reflect higher or lower cash spending.

iii) It allows management by exception.

iv) The original statement conveys the wrong message (that the overall variance was favourable).

I hope this information has proved useful. If I can be of further assistance or you have any questions, please do not hesitate to contact me.

b)

			£
Standard cost of output			1,131,000
Variances	*(A)*	*(F)*	
	£	£	
Labour rate due to machine breakdown (W1)		2,520	
Labour rate due to normal working (W1)		12,180	
Labour efficiency due to machine breakdown (W2)	75,000		
Labour efficiency due to normal working (W2)		12,500	
Material price due to change in price index (W3)		38,400	
Material price due to other reasons (W3)	32,000		
Material usage	24,000		
Fixed overhead expend ture	9,000		
	140,000	65,600	74,400 (A)
Actual cost of output			1,205,400

Workings

1)

	£
Total labour rate variance	14,700 (F)
Labour rate variance due to machine breakdown (12,000 × £14,700/70,000)	2,520 (F)
Labour rate variance due to normal working (balance)	12,180 (F)

2)

	£
Total labour efficiency variance	62,500 (A)
Labour efficiency variance due to machine breakdown (12,000 hrs × £6.25)	75,000 (A)
Labour efficiency variance due to normal production	12,500 (F)

3)

	£	£
Total material price variance		6,400 (F)
Variance due to price index change 32,000 m should have cost (× £12 × 420.03/466.70)	345,600	
but should originally have cost (× £12)	384,000	
		38,400 (F)
Variance due to other reasons		32,000 (A)

12 a) **MEMO**

To: Richard Jones, Managing Director
From: Accounting Technician
Date: xx/xx/xx
Subject: **Variations in kit prices**

i) 1) **UK cost per kit at the time the contract was agreed**

$54,243 ÷ $9.80 = £5,535

2) **UK cost of kits delivered**

	September	*October*	*November*
Kits delivered	2,000	2,100	2,050
Contract cost in $ (× $54,243)	$108,486,000	$113,910,300	$111,198,150
Exchange rate	$9.00	$10.00	$10.25
Contract cost in £($ cost/exchange rate)	£12,054,000	£11,391,030	£10,848,600

3) **Price variance due to exchange rate differences**

	September	*October*	*November*
	£	£	£
Contract cost of kits delivered should have been (from (2) ÷ $9.8)	11,070,000	11,623,500	11,346,750
but cost of kits delivered was (from (2))	12,054,000	11,391,030	10,848,600
Variance	984,000 (A)	232,470 (F)	498,150 (F)

4) Total variance = price variance + usage variance

If price variance is as in 3) above, usage variance is total variance minus price variance in 3).

Usage variance

	September £	October £	November £
Kits delivered should have cost (see (3))	11,070,000	11,623,500	11,346,750
but did cost (given)	12,059,535	11,385,495	10,848,600
	989,535 (A)	238,005 (F)	498,150 (F)
Less price variance (see (3))	984,000 (A)	232,470 (F)	498,150 (F)
	5,535 (A)	5,535 (F)	NIL

ii) The price variances due to exchange rate differences should be excluded from any standard costing report prepared for the production manager of Pronto Ltd because they are not controllable by him and so he can do nothing to influence their occurrence. They do need to be recognised and monitored, however.

b) i) 1) Budgeted overheads per machine (or track) hour = £840,000 ÷ 140 = £6,000 per hour

2) Budgeted number of cars produced per machine (or track) hour = 560/140 = 4 per hour

3) Standard hours of actual production = 500 cars ÷ 4 per hour = 125 hours

ii) 1) **Fixed overhead expenditure variance**

	£
Budgeted expenditure	840,000
Actual expenditure	842,000
	2,000 (A)

2) Fixed overhead absorption rate per unit = £6,000/4 = £1,500

Fixed overhead volume variance

	£
Budgeted production at standard rate (560 × £1,500)	840,000
Actual production at standard rate (500 × £1,500)	750,000
	90,000 (A)

3) **Fixed overhead efficiency variance**

500 cars should have taken (from b)i)3))	125 hrs
but did take	126 hrs
Variance in hours	1 hr (A)
× standard absorption rate per hour	× £6,000
	£6,000 (A)

4) **Fixed overhead capacity variance**

Budgeted hours of work	140 hrs
Actual hours of work	126 hrs
	14 hrs (A)
× standard absorption rate per hour	× £6,000
	£84,000 (A)

iii) **Reconciliation of fixed overheads incurred to fixed overheads absorbed**

	£	£	£
Fixed overheads incurred			842,000
Variances			
Expenditure		2,000 (A)	
Volume efficiency	6,000 (A)		
Volume capacity	84,000 (A)		
Volume		90,000 (A)	
			92,000 (A)
Fixed overheads absorbed (125 hrs × £6,000)			750,000

13 a) i) 1) Standard price of fuel = £497,664/1,244,160 litres = £0.40 per litre.

2) Standard litres of fuel per crossing = 1,244,160/6,480 = 192 litres
Standard litres of fuel for 5,760 crossings = 192 × 5,760 = 1,105,920 litres

3) Standard labour rate per hr = £699,840/93,312 hrs = £7.50 per hr

4) Standard labour hours per crossing = 93,312/6,480 = 14.4 hours
Std labour hrs for 5,760 crossings = 14.4 × 5,760 = 82,944 hrs

5) Standard fixed overhead cost per budgeted operating hour = £466,560/7,776 = £60 per hour

6) Standard operating hours per crossing = 7,776/6,480 = 1.2 hours
Std operating hrs for 5,760 crossings = 1.2 × 5,760 = 6,912 hrs

7) Standard fixed overhead cost absorbed by 5,760 crossings = 6,912 hours (vi) × £60 per hour (from (5)) = £414,720

ii) 1)

	£
1,232,800 litres should cost (× £0.40 a)i)1))	493,120
but did cost	567,088
Material price variance for fuel	73,968 (A)

2)

5,760 crossings should have used (a)i)2))	1,105,920	litres
but did use	1,232,800	litres
Usage variance in litres	126,880	litres (A)
× standard price per litre (a)i)1))	× £0.40	
Material usage variance for fuel	£50,752	(A)

3)

	£	
89,856 hours should have cost (× £7.50 a)i)3))	673,920	
but did cost	696,384	
Labour rate variance	22,464	(A)

4)

5,760 crossings should take (a)i)4))	82,944	hours
but did take	89,856	hours
Efficiency variance in hours	6,912	hours (A)
× standard rate per hour (a)i)3))	× £7.50	
Labour efficiency variance	£51,840	(A)

5)

	£	
Budgeted fixed overhead expenditure	466,560	
Actual fixed overhead expenditure	472,440	
Fixed overhead expenditure variance	5,880	(A)

6)

	£	
Actual number of crossings (5,760) at standard rate (a)i)7))	414,720	
Budgeted number of crossings at standard rate	466,560	
Fixed overhead volume variance	51,840	(A)

7)

Budgeted operating hours	7,776	
Actual operating hours	7,488	
Capacity variance in hours	288	(A)
× std fixed o/hd cost per operating hour (a)i)5))	× £60	
Fixed overhead capacity variance	£17,280	(A)

8)

5,760 crossings should take (a)i)6))	6,912	operating hours
but did take	7,488	operating hours
Efficiency variance in operating hours	576	operating hours (A)
× std fixed o/hd cost per op hr (a)i)5))	× £60	
Fixed overhead efficiency variance	£34,560	(A)

iii) **Statement reconciling the actual cost of operations to the standard cost of operations for year ended 30 November 2008**

Number of ferry crossings		5,760
	£	£
Actual cost of operations		1,735,912
Cost variances	*Adverse*	
Material price for fuel	73,968	
Material usage for fuel	50,752	
Labour rate	22,464	
Labour efficiency	51,840	
Fixed overhead expenditure	5,880	
Fixed overhead capacity	17,280	
Fixed overhead efficiency	34,560	
		256,744 (A)
Standard cost of operations		1,479,168*

* Check. 5,760/6,480 × £1,664,064 = £1,479,168

b) **MEMO**

To: Chief executive
From: Management accountant
Date: xx/xx/xx
Subject: Variances for the year ended 30 November 2008

This memo addresses some of your concerns about the large number of adverse variances arising during the year.

i) **Subdivision of the material price variance for fuel**

Standard price of fuel per litre (a)i)1)) = £0.40
Actual market price of fuel per litre = £0.40 × 1.2 = £0.48

	£	£
1,232,800 litres at standard price would have cost (× £0.40 (a)(i))		493,120
1,232,800 litres at actual market price would have cost (× £0.48)		591,744
Price variance due to difference between standard price and market price (part (1))		98,624 (A)
1,232,800 litres at actual market price should have cost (× £0.48)	591,744	
but did cost	567,088	
Price variance due to other reasons (part (2))		24,656 (F)
Total material price variance		73,968 (A)

ii) The fixed overhead efficiency variance is not controllable. This variance is caused by the difference between the standard and actual operating hours for the 5,760 crossings. Since this difference arose entirely because of weather conditions, the corresponding variance is not controllable.

iii) The part of the material price variance due to reasons other than the difference between the standard price and the market price for fuel is controllable. This amount was calculated in i) as £24,656 favourable. The adverse variance of £98,624 calculated in i) is non-controllable, but the remainder of the price variance has arisen due to controllable factors, since the price paid was different to the prevailing market price.

The labour rate variance is also controllable. It is not affected by the uncontrollable factors of the change in the market price for fuel and the adverse weather conditions.

14 a) i) 1) Actual number of meals served = 4 meals × 7 days × 648 guests
= 18,144 meals

2) Standard number of meals for actual number of guests = 3 meals × 7 days × 648 guests
= 13,608 meals

3) Actual hourly rate of pay = $5,280 ÷ 1,200 hours
= $ 4.40 per hour

4) Standard hours allowed for actual number of guests = (648 guests × 3 meals × 7 days) ÷ 12 meals per hour
= 1,134 hours

5) Standard fixed overhead per guest = budgeted overheads ÷ budgeted number of guests
= $38,340 ÷ 540 = $71 per guest

6) **Total standard cost for actual number of guests**

	$
Meal costs (13,608 meals × $3 per meal)	40,824
Catering staff costs (1,134 hours × $4 per hour)	4,536
Fixed overhead costs (648 × $71 per guest)	46,008
Total standard cost	91,368

ii) 1)

	$
18,144 meals should cost (× $3)	54,432
but did cost	49,896
Material price variance for meals served	4,536 (F)

2)

648 guests should have used (a)i)2))	13,608 meals
but did use (a)i)1))	18,144 meals
Usage variance in meals	4,536 meals (A)
× standard cost per meal	× $3
Material usage variance for meals served	$13,608 (A)

3)

	$
1,200 hrs worked should have cost (× $4/hr)	4,800
but did cost	5,280
Labour rate variance for catering staff	480 (A)

4)

Meals for 648 guests should have taken (a)i)4))	1,134 hours
but did take	1,200 hours
Labour efficiency variance in hours	66 hours (A)
× standard rate per hour	× $4
Labour efficiency variance for catering staff	$264 (A)

5)

	$
Budgeted fixed overhead expenditure	38,340
Actual fixed overhead expenditure	37,800
Fixed overhead expenditure variance	540 (F)

6)

Actual number of guests	648
Budgeted number of guests	540
Volume variance – number of guests	108 (F)
× standard fixed overhead per guest (a)i)5))	× $71
Fixed overhead volume variance	$7,668 (F)

iii) **Bare Foot Hotel complex**

Standard cost reconciliation for seven days ended 27 November 2008

Budgeted number of guests	540
Actual number of guests	648

	$		$	
Standard cost for 648 guests (a)i)6))			91,368	
Cost variances				
Material price variance (a)ii)1))	4,536	(F)		
Material usage variance (a)ii)2))	13,608	(A)		
			9,072	(A)
Catering labour rate variance (a)ii)3))	480	(A)		
Catering labour efficiency variance (a)ii)4))	264	(A)		
			744	(A)
Fixed overhead expenditure variance (a)ii)5))	540	(F)		
Fixed overhead volume variance (a)ii)6))	7,668	(F)		
			8,208	(F)
Actual cost for 648 guests			92,976	

Note: (A) denotes adverse variance, (F) denotes favourable variance.

b) **MEMO**

To: Alice Groves, general manager
From: Assistant management accountant
Date: xx.xx.xx
Subject: **Performance report** for seven days ended 27 November 2008

This memorandum deals with a number of issues arising from the standard cost reconciliation statement prepared for the seven days ended 27 November 2008.

i) **Subdivision of the catering labour efficiency variance**

The adverse catering labour efficiency variance of $264 can be divided into that part due to guests taking more meals than planned and that part due to other efficiency reasons.

Standard hours allowed for 648 guests taking 3 meals ((a)(i)(4))	1,134 hours
Standard hours allowed for 648 guests taking 4 meals	
= (648 guests × 4 meals × 7 days) ÷ 12 meals per hour	1,512 hours
Excess hours due to guests taking more meals than planned	378 hours (A)
× standard rate per hour	× $4
Efficiency variance due to guests taking more meals than planned	$1,512 (A)

Standard hours allowed for 648 guests taking 4 meals (from above)	1,512 hours
Actual hours worked	1,200 hours
Efficiency variance due to other reasons (in hours)	312 hours (F)
× standard rate per hour	× $4
Catering labour efficiency variance due to other reasons	$1,248 (F)

ii) **The meaning of the fixed overhead capacity and efficiency variances**

The fixed overhead absorption rate for our hotel is based on the budgeted overhead expenditure for the period, divided by the budgeted number of guests.

$$\text{Fixed overhead absorption rate} = \frac{\text{budgeted fixed overhead}}{\text{budgeted number of guests}}$$

If the actual overhead, or the actual number of guests, or both, are different from budget then over or under absorption of overhead may occur, so that there may be a fixed overhead variance.

A **volume variance** arises when the activity level is different from that budgeted, in our case if the actual number of guests is different from the budgeted number. In some organisations it may be possible to sub-divide the volume variance into two parts: the capacity variance and the efficiency variance.

The **capacity variance** arises when the utilisation of the available capacity is higher or lower than budgeted. It is usually calculated as the difference between budgeted and actual hours worked, multiplied by the fixed overhead absorption rate. Under or over utilisation of capacity can potentially lead to under– or over-absorbed overhead.

The **efficiency variance** arises when employees are working at a more or less efficient rate than standard to produce a given output. Producing output at a faster or slower rate could also potentially lead to under– or over-absorbed overhead.

iii) **Calculating the fixed overhead capacity and efficiency variances for the Bare Foot Hotel complex**

The above descriptions of the fixed overhead capacity and efficiency variances highlight the need to be able to measure hours of work so that the volume variance can be subdivided.

It is not feasible to do this for the Bare Foot Hotel complex. We do have a measure of hours worked within the catering activity, but a large proportion of overheads are incurred on entertainment, for which we have no record of hours worked.

The absence of an activity measure based on hours worked therefore makes it difficult and meaningless to subdivide the fixed overhead volume variance into its capacity and efficiency elements.

15 a) i) Actual cost of a telephone unit = total actual cost ÷ total actual units = £79,200 ÷ 1,200,000 = £0.066

ii) Actual hourly wage rate of operators = actual total cost of operators' wages ÷ actual hours worked = £877,800 ÷ 114,000 hours = £7.70

iii) Standard number of operator hours per call = 6 mins = 0.1 hr

Standard number of operator hours for 1,000,000 calls = 0.1 hr × 1,000,000 = 100,000 hours

iv) Fixed overheads are based on budgeted operator hours.

Budgeted number of calls = 900,000

Budgeted number of operator hours = 900,000 × 0.1 hour = 90,000

Fixed overhead absorption rate = £6.50 per hour

Budgeted cost of fixed overheads = 90,000 hours × £6.50 per hour
= £585,000

v) See iv) above

vi) Standard cost of actual operations = actual number of calls × standard cost per call = 1,000,000 × £1.42 = £1,042,000

b)

i) **Price variance for telephone calls**

	£	
1,200,000 units should have cost (× £0.07)	84,000	
but did cost	79,200	
	4,800	(F)

ii) **Usage variance for telephone calls**

1,000,000 calls should have used (× 1 unit)	1,000,000 units	
but did use	1,200,000 units	
Variance in units	200,000 units	(A)
× standard rate per unit	× £0.07	
	£14,000	(A)

iii) **Labour rate variance for the telephone operators**

	£	
114,000 hours should have cost (× £7.00)	798,000	
but did cost	877,800	
	79,800	(A)

iv) **Labour efficiency variance for the telephone operators**

1,000,000 calls should have taken (from a)iii))	100,000 hrs	
but did take	114,000 hrs	
Variance in hours	14,000 hrs	(A)
× standard rate per hour	× £7.00	
	£98,000	(A)

v) **Fixed overhead expenditure variance**

	£	
Budgeted expenditure (from a)iv))	585,000	
Actual expenditure	540,400	
	44,600	(F)

vi) **Fixed overhead volume variance**

	£	
Budgeted number of calls	900,000	
Actual number of calls	1,000,000	
Variance in calls	100,000	(F)
× standard fixed overhead per call	× £0.65	
	65,000	(F)

vii) **Fixed overhead capacity variance**

Budgeted operator hours (from a)v))	90,000 hrs	
Actual operator hours	114,000 hrs	
Variance in units	24,000 hrs	(F)
× standard absorption rate per hour	× £6.50	
	£156,000	(F)

viii) **Fixed overhead capacity variance**

Labour efficiency variance (as overheads are absorbed on a labour hour basis)(from b)iv))	14,000 hrs (A)
× standard absorption rate per hour	× £6.50
	£91,000 (A)

c) **Reconciliation statement – 3 months ended 31 May 2008**

			£
Standard cost of actual operations (from a)vi))			1,420,000
	£	£	
Variances	(F)	(A)	
Price for telephone calls	4,800		
Usage for telephone calls		14 000	
Labour rate		79 800	
Labour efficiency		98 000	
Fixed overhead expenditure	44,600		
Fixed overhead capacity	156,000		
Fixed overhead efficiency		91 000	
	205,400	282 800	77,400 (A)
Actual cost of actual operations			1,497,400

16 a) i) **Actual litres of material used** = actual total cost of materials/actual cost per litre = £23,985/£58.50 = 410 litres

ii) **Standard litres of material required for 40 barrels of X14** = standard litres per barrel × 40 = 10 litres × 40 = 400 litres

iii) **Average actual labour rate per hour** = actual total cost of labour/actual number of hours = £2,788/328 hours = £8.50

iv) **Standard labour hours required for 40 barrels of X14** = standard labour hours per barrel × 40 = 8 hours × 40 = 320 hours

v) **Budgeted number of machine hours** = budgeted production × budgeted number of hours per barrel = 45 barrels × 16 = 720 hours

vi) **Budgeted fixed overheads** = standard fixed overhead per barrel × budgeted production = £320 × 45 = £14,400 (or = budgeted number of machine hours for processing department × standard rate per machine hour = 720 hours × £20 = £14,400 or = (budgeted machine hours for processing department/factory budgeted machine hours) × factory budgeted fixed overheads = (720 hours/1,152 hours) × £23,040 = £14,400)

vii) **Actual fixed overheads** (for the processing department) = (budgeted machine hours for processing department/factory budgeted machine hours) × factory actual fixed overheads = (720 hours/1,152 hours) × £26,000 = £16,250

viii) **Standard machine hours produced** = actual production output × standard machine hours per barrel = 40 barrels × 16 machine hours = 640 standard machine hours

ix) **Standard absorption cost of actual production** = standard absorption cost per barrel × actual production = £984 × 40 barrels = £39,360

x) **Actual absorption cost of actual production** = actual cost of material + labour + fixed overheads = £(23,985 + 2,788 + 16,250) = £43,023

b)

i) **Material price variance**

	£	
410 litres (from a)i)) should have cost (× £60)	24,600	
but did cost	23,985	
	615	(F)

ii) **Material usage variance**

40 barrels should have used (× 10 litres) (from a)ii))	400	litres
but did use (from (a)(i))	410	litres
Variance in litres	10	litres (A)
× standard cost per litre	× £60	
	£600	(A)

iii) **Labour rate variance**

	£	
328 hours should have cost (× £8)	2,624	
but did cost	2,788	
	164	(A)

iv) **Labour efficiency variance**

40 barrels should have taken (× 8 hours) (from a)iv))	320	hours
but did take	328	hours
Variance in hours	8	hours (A)
× standard cost per hour	× £8	
	£64	(A)

v) **Fixed overhead expenditure variance**

	£	
Budgeted fixed overhead expenditure (from a)vi))	14,400	
Actual fixed overhead expenditure (from a)vii))	16,250	
	1,850	(A)

vi) **Fixed overhead volume variance**

	£	
Actual production at standard rate (40 barrels × £320)	12,800	
Budgeted production at standard rate (45 barrels × £320)	14,400	
	1,600	(A)

vii) **Fixed overhead efficiency variance**

40 barrels should take (× 16 hours) (from a)viii))	640	hours
but did take	656	hours
Variance in hours	16	hours (A)
× standard rate per hour	× £20	
	£320	(A)

viii) **Fixed overhead capacity variance**

Budgeted machine hours (from a)v))	720	
Actual machine hours	656	
Variance in hours	64	(A)
× standard absorption rate per hour	× £20	
	£1,280	(A)

c) **Reconciliation statement – five weeks ended 31 May 2008**

			£	
Standard absorption cost of actual production (from a) ix))			39,360	
	£	£		
	(F)	(A)		
Variances				
Material price	615			
Material usage		600		
Labour rate		164		
Labour efficiency		64		
Fixed overhead expenditure		1,850		
Fixed overhead efficiency		320		
Fixed overhead capacity		1,280		
	615	4,278	3,663	(A)
Actual absorption cost of actual production (from a) x))			43,023	

d) **MEMO**

To: Judith Green, production manager
From: Accounting technician
Date: xx.xx.xx
Subject: **Croxton Ltd – analysis of variances for 5 weeks ended 31 May 2008**

Following our recent meeting, I set out below some issues to consider in relation to our discussions.

i) **Revised standard material price per litre** = £60 x 133/140 = £57

ii) **Subdivision of material price variance**

	£	£
410 litres were expected to have cost (at the original standard of £60 per litre)	24,600	
but should then have been expected to have cost (at the revised standard of £57 per litre)	23,370	
Variance due to the change in the price index		1,230 (F)
410 litres should have cost, if the revised standard of £57 had been used	23,370	
but did cost	23,985	
Variance due to other reasons		615 (A)
Total material price variance		615 (F)

iii) **Reasons for the occurrence of the material price variance**

A favourable material price variance of £615 was reported for the five weeks ended 31 May 2008. The standard price used as the basis for this calculation was out of date, however, and was too high. If a more realistic standard had been used, the actual cost was in fact greater than the standard cost, not less than the standard cost. The purchasing department had therefore purchased material at a price greater than the realistic standard (although at a price lower than the out of date standard).

The purchasing department have therefore been inefficient, not efficient.

iv) **Implications of one scrapped barrel**

1) **Material usage variance**

The material usage variance shows that 10 litres more than standard were used. As the standard usage per barrel is 10 litres it is possible that the scrapped barrel is the reason for this adverse variance.

2) **Labour efficiency variance**

The labour efficiency variance shows that eight hours more than standard were worked. As a standard eight hours should be worked per barrel it is possible that the scrapped barrel is the reason for this adverse variance.

3) **Labour rate variance**

328 hours were actually worked during the five weeks. Overtime is paid on hours in excess of 320 hours, and hence an overtime premium of eight hours x £8 = £64 was paid in the period. Suppose the eight hours of overtime were worked because one barrel was scrapped (see (2) above). The total labour rate variance is £164 and so there is still £164 - £64 = £100 of the variance not explained by the scrapping of the barrel. This £100 would be due to other, unexplained reasons.

v) **Why the fixed overheads might not be controllable by the processing department**

1) The apportionment of both budgeted and fixed overheads to the department is done on the arbitrary basis of budgeted machine hours. Budgeted machine hours are determined by budgeted production volume, which is outside the control of the processing department.

2) The actual overheads apportioned to the processing department are a share of total fixed overheads. The processing department is unable to control the fixed overheads incurred in other parts of Croxton Ltd, however.

Note: Only one reason was required for v).

answers to chapter 6: PERFORMANCE INDICATORS

1

		November	December	January	February
i)		$\frac{98,200}{64,300}$	$\frac{107,300}{68,900}$	$\frac{90,200}{62,100}$	$\frac{92,000}{60,200}$
	Actual hours per unit	1.53 hours per unit	1.56 hours per unit	1.45 hours per unit	1.53 hours per unit
ii)		$\frac{64,300 \times 1.5}{98,200}$	$\frac{68,900 \times 1.5}{107,300}$	$\frac{62,100 \times 1.5}{90,200}$	$\frac{60,200 \times 1.5}{92,000}$
	Efficiency ratio	98.2%	96.3%	103.3%	98.2%
iii)		$\frac{98,200}{65,000 \times 1.5}$	$\frac{107,300}{65,000 \times 1.5}$	$\frac{90,200}{60,000 \times 1.5}$	$\frac{92,000}{62,000 \times 1.5}$
	Capacity ratio	100.7%	110.1%	100.2%	98.9%
iv)		$\frac{64,300}{65,000}$	$\frac{68,900}{65,000}$	$\frac{62,100}{60,000}$	$\frac{60,200}{62,000}$
	Activity ratio	98.9%	106.0%	103.5%	97.1%

2 Productivity is the quantity of output, either goods or services, in relation to the resources used to produce the output. Productivity measures how efficiently the resources of the organisation are being used.

An increase in productivity does not necessarily lead to an increase in profitability although in many cases it does. For example in a manufacturing business if the number of units produced per hour increases this is an increase in productivity. We now have more units of product to sell and if these can be sold at the same price as the current number of products then profit should increase. However if the additional units have to be sold at a lower price as there is not enough demand for these units then profitability may fall.

A further example would be an increase in units produced per hour with associated higher levels of materials wastage. This is an increase in productivity which will not necessarily lead to an increase in profit due to the additional costs of the materials wastage.

3 i) a taxi firm – number of fares per shift
– number of miles per shift

ii) a hospital – out-patients seen per day

iii) a motorbike courier service – miles per week
– number of packages per day

iv) a firm of accountants – chargeable hours as a percentage of total hours

v) a retail store – sales per employee
– sales per square metre of shop floor

vi) a maker of hand-made pottery – number of pots thrown per day
– number of pots painted per day

4

	£
Sales	1,447,600
Less: cost of materials	(736,500)
cost of services	(316,900)
Total value added	394,200.
Value added per employee	£394,200/15
	£26,280

5 a)

	January	February	March
i) Productivity per labour hour	$\frac{8,540}{8,635}$	$\frac{8,670}{7,820}$	$\frac{9,320}{9,280}$
	0.99 units per hour	1.11 units per hour	1.00 unit per hour
ii) Efficiency ratio	$\frac{8,540 \times 1.1}{8,635}$	$\frac{8,670 \times 1.1}{7,820}$	$\frac{9,320 \times 1.1}{9,280}$
	108.8%	122.0%	110.5%
iii) Capacity ratio	$\frac{8,635}{8,500 \times 1.1}$	$\frac{7,820}{8,200 \times 1.1}$	$\frac{9,280}{9,500 \times 1.1}$
	92.4%	86.7%	88.8%
iv) Activity ratio	$\frac{8,540}{8,500}$	$\frac{8,670}{8,200}$	$\frac{9,320}{9,500}$
	100.5%	105.7%	98.1%

v)	Cost per unit	$\frac{£657,100}{8,540}$	$\frac{£666,800}{8,670}$	$\frac{£740,300}{9,320}$
		£76.94 per unit	£76.91 per unit	£79.43 per unit

vi)	Value added per employee	£	£	£
	Sales	916,000	923,000	965,000
	Production costs	(552,300)	(568,500)	(629,500)
	Value added	363,700	354,500	335,500
	Value added per employee	£6,613	£6,445	£5,784

b) Both the productivity per hour and efficiency indicators show that in all three months the time taken to produce units is less than the standard time of 1.1 hours. Although the activity ratio shows that in all three months the actual activity level was fairly close to the budgeted level the capacity ratio indicates that the available hours of work were never exceeded. Production significantly increased in March but this appears to have caused a higher cost per unit and lower value added per employee.

6 a) i) Efficiency ratio $= \frac{\text{Standard hours for actual production}}{\text{Actual hours worked}} \times 100$

$= \frac{14,200 \times 3}{46,000} \times 100$

$= 92.61\%$

As the efficiency ratio is less than 100% this indicates that the workforce have not worked as efficiently as was anticipated. The actual hours worked are more than the standard hours for that level of production.

ii) Capacity ratio $= \frac{\text{Actual hours worked}}{\text{Budgeted hours}} \times 100$

$= \frac{46,000}{15,000 \times 3} \times 100$

$= 102.22\%$

The capacity ratio indicates whether as many hours have been worked as were budgeted for. In this instance the capacity ratio is greater than 100% meaning that the number of hours worked was more than those budgeted for.

iii) Production volume ratio $= \dfrac{\text{Actual output}}{\text{Budgeted output}} \times 100$

$= \dfrac{14{,}200}{15{,}000} \times 100$

$= 94.67\%$

The production volume ratio is an indicator of how the volume of actual production compares to the budgeted level of output. In this instance as the production volume ratio is below 100% this indicates that the actual level of output was below the budgeted level.

b) Production volume ratio = Efficiency ratio x Capacity ratio

= 92.61% x 102.22%

= 94.67%

c) Hours worked @ 95% efficiency $= \dfrac{14{,}200 \times 3}{0.95}$

= 44,842

Hours saved (46,000 – 44,842) = 1,158 hours

7 i) Cost per unit = £3,204,430/467,800 units

= £6.85 per unit

ii) Efficiency ratio $= \dfrac{\text{Standard hours for actual production}}{\text{Actual hours worked}} \times 100$

$= \dfrac{467{,}800 \times 1.5}{748{,}500} \times 100$

= 93.7%

iii) Capacity ratio $= \dfrac{\text{Actual hours worked}}{\text{Budgeted hours}} \times 100$

$= \dfrac{748{,}500}{428{,}000 \times 1.5} \times 100$

= 116.6%

iv) Activity ratio $= \dfrac{\text{Standard hours for actual production}}{\text{Budgeted hours}} \times 100$

$= \dfrac{467,800 \times 1.5}{428,000 \times 1.5} \times 100$

$= 109.3\%$

8 a) i) Gross profit margin $= \dfrac{\text{Gross profit}}{\text{Turnover}} \times 100$

$= \dfrac{1,007,200}{2,650,400} \times 100$

$= 38\%$

ii) Net profit margin $= \dfrac{\text{Operating profit}}{\text{Turnover}} \times 100$

$= \dfrac{336,600}{2,650,400} \times 100$

$= 12.7\%$

iii) Return on capital employed $= \dfrac{\text{Operating profit}}{\text{Capital employed}} \times 100$

$= \dfrac{336,600}{2,337,500} \times 100$

$= 14.4\%$

iv) Asset turnover $= \dfrac{\text{Turnover}}{\text{Capital employed}}$

$= \dfrac{2,650,400}{2,337,500}$

$= 1.13$

v) Fixed asset turnover $= \dfrac{\text{Turnover}}{\text{Fixed assets}}$

$= \dfrac{2,650,400}{1,920,400}$

$= 1.38$

vi) Current ratio $= \frac{\text{Current assets}}{\text{Current liabilities}}$

$= \frac{607,400}{190,300}$

$= 3.19 : 1$

vii) Quick ratio $= \frac{\text{Current assets} - \text{stock}}{\text{Current liabilities}}$

$= \frac{607,400 - 191,200}{190,300}$

$= 2.19 : 1$

viii) Debtors' collection period $= \frac{\text{Debtors}}{\text{Turnover}} \times 365$

$= \frac{399,400}{2,650,400} \times 365$

$=$ 55 days

ix) Stock turnover $= \frac{\text{Average stock}}{\text{Cost of sales}} \times 365$

$= \frac{(180,000 + 191,200)/2}{1,643,200} \times 365$

$=$ 41 days

x) Creditors' payment period $= \frac{\text{Creditors}}{\text{Purchases}} \times 365$

$= \frac{190,300}{1,654,400} \times 365$

$=$ 42 days

xi) Interest cover $= \frac{\text{Profit before interest}}{\text{Interest charge}}$

$= \frac{336,600}{36,000}$

$= 9.35$

xii) Gearing ratio $= \dfrac{\text{Long term loans}}{\text{Shareholders' funds}}$

$= \dfrac{600{,}000}{1{,}737{,}500}$

$= 34.5\%$

b) Increase in cash balance $= \dfrac{£1{,}654{,}400}{365} \times (60 - 42)$

$= £81{,}587$

9 a)

		July	Aug	Sept	Oct	Nov	Dec
i)	Gross profit margin	34%	34%	34%	32%	31%	31%
ii)	Net profit margin	12%	12%	12%	11%	10%	9%
iii)	Expenses to sales %	22%	22%	22%	21%	21%	22%
iv)	Return on capital employed (W1)	15.2%	14.6%	13.1%	11.6%	10.9%	10.0%
v)	Asset turnover (W2)	1.27	1.21	1.09	1.06	1.09	1.11

b) Sales revenue decreased from July to September and then increased significantly until the end of the year. However the increase in sales has been at the cost of the gross profit margin which has decreased from 34% to 31%. Although the expenses to sales percentage has remained reasonably constant over the period the net profit margin has fallen due to the decrease in gross profit margin.

Return on capital employed fell dramatically in the first four months of the period although this was due to a significant decrease in asset turnover in that period more than a decline in profitability. The fall in return on capital employed continues in the last three months of the year due to the fall in net profit margin; however the drop in return is not as bad as it might have been as the asset turnover is again improving.

Workings

1 Here, return on capital employed is calculated as

$$\text{ROCE} = \frac{\text{Profit before interest}}{\substack{\text{Capital employed} \\ \text{(shareholders funds+loans)}}} = \frac{(550-374-116)}{468+50} = 11.6\% \text{ for October, etc}$$

Alternatively, it may be computed as a return on equity:

$$\text{ROCE (RoE)} = \frac{\text{Profit after interest}}{\text{Shareholders' funds}} = \frac{(550-374-116-3)}{468} = 12.2\% \text{ for October, etc}$$

2 To be consistent with the ROCE definition used, asset turnover has been calculated as

$$\text{Asset turnover} = \frac{\text{Turnover}}{\text{Total capital employed}} = \frac{550}{468+50} = 1.06 \text{ for October, etc}$$

(assets - current liabilities)

10

		2006	*2007*	*2008*
i)	Gross profit margin	40.1%	39.1%	37.9%
ii)	Net profit margin	14.1%	13.0%	11.0%
iii)	Return on capital employed (Note: total CE used)	13.3%	11.9%	10.6%
iv)	Asset turnover	0.95	0.92	0.97
v)	Fixed asset turnover	1.29	1.20	1.16
vi)	Current ratio	3.9 : 1	3.5 : 1	2.55 : 1
vii)	Quick ratio	3.1 : 1	2.6 : 1	1.6 : 1
viii)	Debtors' collection period	40 days	46 days	48 days
ix)	Stock turnover	45 days	54 days	64 days
x)	Creditors' payment period	60 days	62 days	65 days

Profitability has fallen significantly over the three-year period. Return on capital employed has fallen by almost 3% and this is due solely to decreases in gross and net profit margins as asset turnover has remained fairly constant with a minor increase in 2008. Although both gross profit margin and net profit margin have fallen, the net profit margin has fallen proportionally a great deal more. This means that as well as the gross profit margin falling the expenses of the business are increasing.

There also seems to have been some loss of control regarding the working capital of the business The stock turnover period has increased dramatically, meaning that large amounts of funds are being tied up in stock holding. Debtors' days have also increased by eight days whereas the creditors' payment period has only increased by five days over the three-year period.

The overall working capital of the business does appear to be high, particularly the high cash balances at the end of 2006 and 2007. This has improved by 2008 but this may be as a result of the stock turnover increase rather than a conscious policy.

Workings

	2006	2007	2008
	£000	£000	£000
Profit and loss summary			
Sales	1,420	1,560	1,740
Cost of sales	(850)	(950)	(1,080)
Gross profit	570	610	660
Expenses	(370)	(407)	(469)
Profit before interest	200	203	191
Interest	–	(7)	(6)
Profit after interest	200	196	185
Balance sheet summary			
Fixed assets	1,100	1,300	1,500
Stock	105	140	190
Debtors	155	198	230
Cash	280	224	73
Creditors	(140)	(162)	(193)
	1,500	1,700	1,800
Long term loan	–	(100)	(100)
Capital and reserves	1,500	1,600	1,700

11 a)

		North	South	Central
i)	Gross profit margin	32.0%	30.0%	35.0%
ii)	Net profit margin	18.0%	11.1%	13.4%
iii)	Return on capital employed	16.0%	9.0%	14.0%
iv)	Asset turnover	0.89	0.81	1.04
v)	Stock turnover	0.6 months	1.1 months	1.0 months
vi)	Debtors' collection period	1.4 months	2.3 months	1.6 months
vii)	Creditors' payment period	2.1 months	1.3 months	1.9 months
viii)	Units per square metre	34.0 units	25.5 units	29.3 units
ix)	Units per employee	944 units	850 units	820 units
x)	Units per hour	2 units	1.8 units	1.8 units

b) In terms of profitability North is clearly the most profitable with the highest net profit margin and return on capital employed. However Central has a higher gross profit margin which may be due to production of a different product to North or due to higher local selling prices or lower purchasing prices for Central. Although Central's net profit margin is significantly lower than North's its return on capital employed is not so different due to a higher asset turnover in Central. South seems to have profitability problems with gross and net profit margins, asset turnover and return on capital employed significantly lower than those of the other two divisions.

North again appears to have the best working capital control with the lowest stock turnover and debtors collection period and the longest creditors payment period. Central's working capital control appears to be adequate but again there are questions to be asked at South with a relatively long debtors collection period and a month shorter creditors payment period.

Finally, whichever way productivity is measured, the productivity at North is significantly greater than at either of the other two divisions. Central makes the same number of units per hour as South but less per employee indicating that there could be room for improvement in employee productivity at Central.

Workings		*North*	*South*	*Central*
		£	£	£
Profit and loss				
Sales		870,000	560,000	640,000
COS:	o/stock	34,000	41,000	34,000
	purchases	590,000	380,000	420,000
	c/stock	(32,000)	(29,000)	(38,000)
		592,000	392,000	416,000
Gross profit		278,000	168,000	224,000
Expenses		(121,000)	(106,000)	(138,000)
Net profit		157,000	62,000	86,000
Balance sheet				
Debtors		100,100	107,300	87,600
Creditors		(103,400)	(42,600)	(66,700)
Other net assets		983,300	625,300	594,100
Capital		980,000	690,000	615,000

12 i) Gross profit = 380,000 x 0.48
= £182,400

ii) Sales = £425,000/0.34
= £1,250,000

iii) Gross profit = £85,000 x 0.40
= £34,000

Net profit = £85,000 x 0.115
= £9,775

Expenses = £34,000 – £9,775
= £24,225

iv) Capital employed = £100,000/0.116
= £862,069

v) Asset turnover = 0.10/0.08
= 1.25

vi)	Average stock	= (£158,000 + £182,000)/2 = £170,000
	Cost of sales	= £158,000 + £560,000 – £182,000 = £536,000
	Stock turnover	= £536,000/170,000 = 3.2 times
vii)	Sales	= £96,000/48 x 365 = £730,000

13 The decrease in gross profit margin could have been due to a number of factors:

- decrease in selling price
- increase in suppliers' prices
- loss of trade discount on purchases
- significant decrease in stock levels
- significant stock write-offs
- any combination of the above

14 a)

		Y/e 31 Dec 2008	*Y/e 31 Dec 2007*
i)	Gross profit margin	45.3%	42.4%
ii)	Net profit margin (Profit before tax/turnover)	16.6%	15.2%
iii)	Return on capital employed (Profit before tax/ capital + reserves + loan)	13.3%	12.5%
iv)	Asset turnover	0.80	0.82
v)	Fixed asset turnover	0.85	0.89
vi)	Current ratio	1.75 : 1	2.3 : 1
vii)	Quick ratio	1.2 : 1	1.6 : 1
viii)	Debtors' collection period	40 days	44 days
ix)	Stock turnover	31 days	36 days
x)	Creditors' payment period	51 days	51 days
xi)	Interest cover	11.0	9.6
xii)	Gearing ratio	25%	27.8%

b) Return on capital employed has increased over the two-year period and this is solely due to increased profitability as both the asset turnover and fixed asset turnover have decreased over the period. There has been a significant increase in gross profit margin in 2008 and, although net profit margin has also increased, it has not done so at the rate of the gross profit margin, indicating that expenses are in fact increasing at a faster rate than sales. This may be due to a large advertising campaign which has increased costs but allowed the gross profit margin to increase or some similar reason.

As well as an increase in sales and profitability there also appears to be general improvement in the working capital management. Both the current and quick ratios have fallen but are still at acceptable levels. The debtors collection period and stock turnover period have both been reduced by a few days and in combination with the increase in the creditors payment period by 10 days this will have a significant positive effect on the cash flows of the business.

The level of gearing does not appear to be a problem as the gearing ratios are quite low and the interest cover is quite high.

15 Ratio analysis can be a useful tool for providing information to management about the performance of a business or part of a business. However care must be taken with the analysis as there are a number of limitations that must be borne in mind:

Comparison of like with like – if ratios are to be compared then they must have been calculated in the same way and using comparable figures. When comparing ratios over time in an organisation, any change in accounting policies over the period may impact upon the ratios. If comparing the accounts of two different organisations, it is likely that they will have different accounting policies and ideally adjustments should be made to bring the accounting policies in line before calculating the ratios.

Inflation – if ratios are being compared over time on the basis of historical cost accounting figures then adjustment must be made using an appropriate index in order to restate all the figures in terms of a common price basis.

Representative figures – in many cases we are using year-end balance sheet amounts to calculate ratios and these may not necessarily be representative of the value throughout the year, for example when calculating stock turnover or the debtors collection period.

Year-end transactions – as year-end figures are used for the ratios just one significant accounting adjustment or transaction before the year-end can alter the position shown by the balance sheet and the resulting ratios. For example if a large cash payment were made to creditors just before the year end this would significantly improve the current ratio and reduce the creditors collection period calculated.

Age of fixed assets – if comparing one company with another using ratio analysis the figures may not be entirely comparable unless the fixed assets are of similar age. Older fixed assets will have a lower balance sheet value as they have been depreciated for longer and this can serve to improve figures such as asset turnover and return on capital employed.

16 a) **Performance indicators for Melosoven Ltd for quarter 4**

i)	Quarterly return on capital employed	(352/8,111) × 100%	4.3%
ii)	Operating profit margin	(352/4,759) × 100%	7.4%
iii)	Quarterly asset turnover	4,759/8,111	0.59 times

iv)	Average age of period-end debtors in days	(2,040/4,759) × 91	39 days
v)	Average age of period-end trade creditors in days	[2,362/(1,583 + 43)]× 91	132 days
vi)	Average age of period end materials stocks in days	(305/1,583) × 91	18 days
vii)	Average age of period-end finished goods stocks in days	(1,326/3,980) × 91	30 days

b) i) **Performance indicators for Melosoven Ltd for quarters 1 to 4**

	Q1	*Q2*	*Q3*	*Q4*
Return on capital employed	4.3%	1.2%	2.8%	4.3%
Operating profit margin	9.0%	2.6%	5.3%	7.4%
Quarterly asset turnover	0.54	0.55	0.52	0.59
Age of debtors in days	39	33	44	39
Age of trade creditors in days	192	167	158	132
Age of materials stocks in days	29	24	18	18
Age of finished goods stocks in days	51	41	28	30

ii) **BRIEFING NOTE**

To: Louise Simpson
From: Financial analyst
Date: xx/xx/xx
Subject: **Performance of Melosoven Ltd in quarters 1 to 4**

The above financial performance ratios expose a sharp drop in performance between quarter 1 and quarter 2. Quarters 3 and 4 showed an improvement and the key ratios (return on capital employed, operating profit margin and asset turnover) are returning to the levels achieved in quarter 1.

1) **Return on capital employed**. This ratio dropped from 4.3% to 1.2%. Between quarters 1 and 2, but has now returned to its earliest level.

2) **Operating profit margin**. This fell in quarter 2 and, although it improved in quarters 3 and 4, is not yet back to the level of quarter 1. The drop in profit margin in quarter 4 was the reason for the fal in ROCE.

3) **Quarterly asset turnover**. This was higher in quarter 4 than in any of the earlier quarters and is the reason that the return on capital employed is back to 4.3% in quarter 4 despite the profit margin being lower than in quarter 1.

4) **Age of debtors in days**. This ratio has remained comparatively stable during the year, and at 39 days is not excessively high.

5) **Age of trade creditors in days**. At the end of quarter 1 Melosoven was taking an average of 192 days (more than six months) to pay its trade creditors, which seems excessive. This figure has been progressively reduced during the year to 132 days (still more than 4 months, however) by the end of quarter 4.

6) **Age of materials stocks in days.** Material stocks have fallen from 29 days at the end of quarter 1 to stabilise at 18 days in quarters 3 and 4.

7) **Age of finished goods stocks in days.** Finished goods stocks have dropped from 51 days sales at the end of quarter 1 to 30 days at the end of the year. This is a significant improvement.

17 a)

To:	Angela Wade
From:	A Technician
Date:	xx.xx.xx
Subject:	**West Ltd and East Ltd – Performance Report**

i) **Return on capital employed (ROCE)**

The ROCE is a key financial ratio which shows the amount of profit which has been made in relation to the amount of resources invested. It also gives some idea of how efficiently the company has been operating.

$$\text{ROCE} = \frac{\text{Operating profit}}{\text{Net assets}}$$

$$\text{ROCE (West Ltd)} = \frac{3{,}068}{15{,}340} = 0.2 \times 100\% = 20\%$$

$$\text{ROCE (East Ltd)} = \frac{2{,}795}{6{,}500} = 0.43 \times 100\% = 43\%$$

ii) **Asset turnover**

The asset turnover is one of the main balance sheet ratios, and is a measure of how well the assets of a business are being used to generate sales.

$$\text{Asset turnover} = \frac{\text{Net turnover}}{\text{Net assets}}$$

$$\text{Asset turnover (West Ltd)} = \frac{17{,}910}{15{,}340} = 1.17 \text{ times}$$

$$\text{Asset turnover (East Ltd)} = \frac{17{,}424}{6{,}500} = 2.68 \text{ times}$$

iii) **Sales margin**

The sales margin ratio is a measure of overall profitability and it provides a measure of performance for management. Unsatisfactory sales margins are investigated by management, and are generally followed by control action. Increasing selling prices and reducing costs will have a direct effect on this ratio.

$$\text{Sales margin} = \frac{\text{Operating profit}}{\text{Net turnover}}$$

$$\text{Sales margin (West Ltd)} = \frac{3{,}068}{17{,}910} = 0.171 \text{ x } 100\% = 17.1\%$$

$$\text{Sales margin (East Ltd)} = \frac{2{,}795}{17{,}424} = 0.16 \text{ x } 100\% = 16\%$$

b) **Measure of customer service: faulty sales**

The percentage of faulty sales as a measure of the level of customer service is calculated as :

$$\frac{\text{Returns}}{\text{Gross sales}}$$

$$\text{West Ltd} = \frac{100}{20{,}000} = 0.005\% \text{ x } 100\% = 0.5\%$$

$$\text{East Ltd} = \frac{220}{22{,}000} = 0.01\% \text{ x } 100\% = 1\%$$

c) **Further measure of customer service**

Another possible measure of the level of customer service which could be derived from the accounting data is the number of days between order and delivery of goods.

This can be calculated as follows.

$$\textbf{Time between order and delivery} = \frac{\text{Orders received in year} - \text{net sales ('000 litres)}}{\text{Net sales ('000 litres)}} \times 365 \text{ days}$$

$$\text{West Ltd} = \frac{20{,}173 - 19{,}000}{19{,}900} \text{ x } 365 \text{ days} = 5 \text{ days}$$

$$\text{East Ltd} = \frac{22{,}854 - 21{,}780}{21{,}780} \text{ x } 365 \text{ days} = 18 \text{ days}$$

The amount of money which the subsidiaries invest in research and development, and training could also provide a measure of customer service.

d) **Limitations of financial ratios**

Financial ratios as a measure of performance are only concerned with the data recorded in the accounts. For example, East Ltd appears to be a much more efficient company than West Ltd based on its ROCE and asset turnover ratios. However, when calculations are made to measure customer service, West Ltd has far fewer days between order and delivery of goods, and half as many faulty sales (as a percentage of gross sales).

The financial ratios also treat research and development, and training costs as expenses which are written off to the profit and loss account. These expenses are likely to have an impact on the future profitability of the company, and are more of an investment than expense.

Both West Ltd and East Ltd use plant of similar size and technology. There is however, a large difference in the net book values of the plant, and hence a large difference in the net assets of each company.

East Ltd purchased its plant before West Ltd, and has a lower cost, and a higher depreciation to date than West Ltd. These differences arise mainly due to the fact that the accounts are prepared using historical cost accounting. The fact that East Ltd's net assets are so much lower than those of West Ltd, means that the ROCE of East Ltd will be much higher than that of West Ltd.

18 a)

i) Return on capital employed = (operating profit ÷ net assets) x 100%
= (£975,000/£4,875,000) x 100% = 20%

ii) Asset turnover = turnover/net assets = £3,900,000/£4,875,000 = 0.8

iii) Sales (operating profit) margin = (operating profit/turnover) x 100%
= (£975,000/£3,900,000) x 100%
= 25%

iv) Average age of debtors (in months) = (debtors/turnover) x 12
= (£325,000/£3,900,000) x 12
= 1 month

v) Average age of finished stock (in months) = (finished goods stock/cost of sales) x 12
= (£140,000/£840,000) x 12 = 2 months

b) **Briefing notes on the usefulness of performance indicators**

Prepared for Angela Frear

Prepared by Financial Analyst

Dated: xx.xx.xx

i) **Return on capital employed**

The return on capital employed can be misleading.

1) Profits should be related to average capital employed but we compute the ratio using year-end assets. Using year-end figures can distort trends and comparisons. If a new investment is undertaken near to a year end and financed, for example by an issue of shares, the capital employed will rise by the finance raised but profit will only have a month or two of the new investment's contribution.

2) The ROCE would be higher if costs such as marketing, research and development and training were not treated as revenue expenditure but were viewed as investment for the future and were capitalised.

ii) **Sales (operating profit) margin**

The sales (or operating profit) margin can be manipulated in a number of ways. The following activities would result in short-term improvements in the margin, but probably at the expense of the organisation's long-term viability.

1) Reducing expenditure on discretionary cost items such as research and development

2) Depreciating assets over a longer period of time, so that the depreciation charge is less

3) Choosing an alternative stock valuation method to increase the value of closing stock

iii) **Average delay in fulfilling orders**

	£
Orders during the year	4,550,000
Turnover during the year	3,900,000
Unfulfilled orders	650,000

Average delay = (£650,000/£3,900,000) × 12 months = 2 months

iv) **Measures of customer satisfaction**

As well as the delay in fulfilling orders, other measures of customer satisfaction include the following.

- Repeat business ((£3,120,000/£3,900,000) × 100% = 80%)
- Cost of customer support per £ of turnover (£400,000/£3,900,000 = 10p)
- Cost of customer support per customer (information not available)

v) **Measuring performance from an internal perspective**

A number of indicators may help to measure performance from an internal perspective.

- Training costs as a percentage of production costs ((£140,000/£930,000) × 100% = 15.05%)

- Reworked faulty production as a percentage of total production ((£37,200/£930,000) × 100% = 4%)

- Returns as a percentage of sales ((£100,000/£4m) × 100% = 2.5%)

The first indicator should be relatively high, the second and third as low as possible.

vi) **Measuring the innovation and learning perspective**

The innovation and learning perspective could be measured with one of the following indicators.

- Turnover from new products as a percentage of total turnover ((£1.56m/£3.9m) × 100% = 40%)

- Research and development expenditure as a percentage of cost of production ((£750,000/£930,000) × 100% = 81%)

- Research and development expenditure as a percentage of turnover ((£750,000/£3.9m) × 100% = 19.2%)

Note: A fuller answer has been given here than was required in the task for assessment purposes.

19 a)

i) Gross profit margin $= \frac{£221,760}{£633,600} \times 100\% = 35\%$

ii) Net profit margin $= \frac{£76,032}{£633,600} \times 100\% = 12\%$

iii) Return on capital employed $= \frac{£76,032}{£95,040} \times 100\% = 80\%$

iv) Asset turnover $= \frac{£633,600}{£95,040} = 6.7$ times

v) No. of passengers in the year $= \frac{\text{turnover}}{\text{fare per passenger}} = \frac{£633,600}{£1}$

$= 633,600$ passengers

vi) Total cost per mile $= \frac{£633,600 - £76,032}{356,400} = £1.56$

vii) No. of journeys in the year $= \frac{356,400 \text{ miles}}{18 \text{ miles per journey}} = 19,800$ journeys

No. of journeys per day $= \frac{19,800}{360} = 55$ journeys

viii) Maintenance cost per mile $= \frac{£28,512}{356,400} = £0.08$

ix) Passengers per day $= \frac{633,600 \text{ (from v))}}{360} = 1,760$ passengers

x) Passengers per journey $= \frac{1,760 \text{ (from(ix))}}{55 \text{ (from(vii))}} = 32$ passengers

xi) Number of drivers $= \frac{\text{wages paid}}{\text{wages per driver}} = \frac{£142,000}{£14,200}$

b) **MEMO**

To:	Chief executive
From:	Management accountant
Date:	xx.xx.xx
Subject:	**Performance of Travel Bus Ltd for the year to 30 November 2008**

This memo addresses a number of issues concerning the productivity and profitability of Travel Bus Ltd.

i) **Productivity and profitability**

Productivity is the quantity of service produced (output) in relation to the resources put in (input). It measures how efficiently resources are being used.

An increase in productivity does not always lead to increased profitability. For example the number of passengers carried per driver, a measure of productivity, could increase. The extra passengers may have been attracted by offering substantial fare reductions, however, and this could lead to reduced profitability.

Another example might be an increase in productivity in terms of the number of journeys per bus. This increase in 'output' arising from the increase in productivity may not be saleable: the buses may be running empty. The revenue gained might be less than the additional costs incurred, leading to reduced profitability.

ii) **Driver productivity**

A possible measure of driver productivity is the number of miles per driver.

	2007	*2008*
Miles per driver	$\frac{324,000}{8} = 40,500$	$\frac{356,400}{10} = 35,640$

The number of miles per driver has decreased between 2007 and 2008 and so, in terms of this measure of productivity, the drivers' claim that their productivity has increased is incorrect.

Even if the productivity had increased the drivers might still be unable to claim that this had resulted in improved profitability. As discussed above, the extra miles might have been travelled with too few fare-paying passengers, so profitability would not necessarily have improved.

iii) **Reason for improved profitability**

A major reason for the improved profitability was the Council's decision not to charge for parking. This reduced the overall cost of using the service for passengers, and demand therefore increased considerably. Since many of the costs incurred by Travel Bus Ltd are fixed, costs did not increase at the same rate as turnover, and profitability improved.

iv) **Performance indicators to measure the satisfaction of passenger needs**

1) The satisfaction of passenger needs could be monitored by the number of passengers per journey.

	2007	*2008*
Number of passengers per journey	30	32

Depending on the size of the buses, passenger needs may have been less satisfied during 2008 because of more crowding or the need to stand because no seats were available.

Another measure of the satisfaction of passenger needs is the number of journeys per day.

	2007	*2008*
Number of journeys per day	50	55

This increase probably led to reduced waiting times and so passenger needs may have been better satisfied in 2008.

2) A measure of the satisfaction of customer needs that cannot be derived from the existing data is cleanliness of the buses.

Monitoring the cleaning cost per day or per bus might give some indication of the effort put into keeping the buses clean.

Another measure of the satisfaction of customer needs **is punctuality** of the buses and their **adherence to published** timetables.

Monitoring the percentage of buses arriving and departing within five minutes of their published time would give an indication of performance in this area.

Note. Only one measure required by the task

v) **Monitoring the safety aspect of Travel Bus's operations**

1) The safety aspect of Travel Bus's operations could be monitored by the maintenance cost per mile.

	2007	*2008*
Maintenance cost per mile	£0.10	£0.08

This has reduced, which may indicate a reduction in attention to safety, especially as maintenance costs are likely to increase as buses become older. No new buses have been added to the fleet (cost value of buses has remained at £240,000); the buses are older and likely to require more maintenance.

On the other hand, some of this reduction in the cost per mile may have been caused by the spreading of the fixed element of maintenance costs over a higher number of miles in the year 2008.

Another indicator of attention to the safety aspect might be the average age of the buses. The depreciation charge for the year 2008 was £12,000 (£180,000 – £168,000). On a cost value of £240,000, assuming straight line depreciation and no residual value, this suggests a useful life of 20 years. Accumulated depreciation of £180,000 means that the buses were on average 15 years old by the end of 2006, and thus nearing the end of their useful lives.

2) A measure of the safety aspect that cannot be derived from the existing data is the number of accidents per year.

Another measure could be the percentage of maintenance cost that is incurred to prevent faults compared with the percentage incurred to correct faults. This would indicate whether faults were being prevented before they occurred, or whether maintenance was being carried out 'after the event', which could compromise safety.

Note. Only one measure required by the task.

20 a)

i)	Sales (or net profit) margin	**= (operating profit/turnover) x 100%** = (138/480) x 100% = 28.75%
ii)	Gross profit margin	**= (gross profit/turnover) x 100%** = (270/480) x 100% = 56.25%
iii)	Asset turnover	**= (turnover/net assets)** = (480/240) = 2 times
iv)	Return on capital employed	**= (operating profit/net assets) x 100%** = (138/240) x 100% = 57.5%
v)	Average age of stocks	**= (closing stock/cost of sales) x 12 months** = (140/210) x 12 months = 8 months
vi)	Average age of debtors	**= (debtors/sales) x 12 months** = (40/480) x 12 months = 1 month
vii)	Added value per employee	**= (turnover – cost of sales (as no bought-in services))/number of employees** = £(480 – 210)m/4,000 = £67,500
viii)	Average sales value per transaction	**= turnover/number of transactions** = £480m/60 million = £8
ix)	Sales per employee	**= turnover/number of employees** = £480m/4,000 = £120,000
x)	Transactions per employee	**= number of transactions/number of employees** = 60 million/4,000 = 15,000
xi)	Sales per square metre	**= turnover/square metres of floor space** = £480m/200,000 = £2,400

b) i) **Meaning of productivity and efficiency**

1) **Productivity**

Productivity is a measure of output relative to some sort of input.

- The output might be socks, cars, meals served in a restaurant, calls answered in a customer service department and so on.
- The input might be the workforce, machines or raw materials.

Productivity measures compare the output achieved from a certain amount of input. Here are some examples.

- Number of customers served per employee per day
- Number of components produced per machine per month
- Number of hotel rooms occupied as a percentage of rooms available.

Input or output or both can also be expressed in financial terms. So other measures of productivity include:

- Number of litres of chemical X produced per £ of labour
- Revenue per employee
- Revenue per £ of labour

Asset turnover (turnover/assets) is a commonly-used measure of productivity, with both input and output expressed in financial terms. It gives an indication of how well the assets of the business (the input) are being used to generate sales (the output).

2) **Efficiency**

Efficiency also looks at output relative to input, but it is not the same as productivity because the output is considered in terms of financial gain or value to the organisation. If the value of the output is greater than the value of the input, the operation is efficient. The greater the difference between the values of the input and output, the greater the efficiency.

In most organisations, the value generated is normally some sort of profit.

Return on capital employed is one of the major measures of efficiency in organisations with an objective to earn profit. It measures the efficiency with which managers have used resources under their control (capital employed) to generate profit.

ii) **Reasons for a difference in the net book value of the fixed assets of the two companies**

1) With rising prices, the older an asset, the lower its initial cost. Even with the same depreciation policies and rates, the older asset will have a lower net book value.

Both companies depreciate their leasehold buildings over fifty years (£500m/£10m for Alderton Ltd, £200m/£4m for Brandon Ltd). The average age of Alderton Ltd's buildings is 10 years (given that annual depreciation is £10m and total depreciation to date is £100m). The average age of Brandon Ltd's buildings is 46 years, however (given that annual depreciation is £4m and total depreciation to date is £184m).

2) If two assets have the same initial cost and the same depreciation policy and rate is applied to each, but one is older than the other, the older asset will have been

depreciated more and so will have a lower net book value. The net book value of Brandon Ltd's leasehold buildings is only 8% of the initial cost, whereas that of Alderton is 80% of initial cost.

3) The use of different depreciation rates will affect net book values. Brandon Ltd depreciates its fixtures and fittings over ten years (£80m/£8m), whereas Alderton Ltd depreciates over five years (£200m/£40m).

(**Note**. Only two required)

iii) **How the difference in net book value of Alderton's fixed assets affects return on capital employed**

1) Alderton Ltd has newer assets and hence their net book value is likely to be higher than for companies such a Brandon Ltd with older assets. This will increase net assets and hence reduce return on capital employed.

2) Even with the same depreciation policies, the depreciation charge on newer assets is likely to be higher than that on older assets because of the higher initial cost. A higher annual depreciation charge will reduce Alderton Ltd's profit and hence reduce return on capital employed.

3) Different depreciation rates will affect the depreciation charge against profit. Alderton Ltd depreciates its fixtures and fittings over a shorter period of time than Brandon Ltd, and so its annual depreciation charge will be higher, thereby reducing profit and return on capital employed.

(**Note**. Only two required)

iv) **Likely effect of first in, first out (FIFO) and last in, first out (LIFO) stock valuation policies on operating profits**

During the twelve months to 31 May 2008, the cost of purchases has been falling. Using a FIFO valuation basis, cost of sales will reflect the earlier, more expensive purchases while closing stock will reflect the more recent, cheaper purchases. The reverse is true if LIFO is used.

Alderton Ltd's operating profit is therefore lower than it would have been if it had used LIFO, and its closing stock valuation (and hence its net assets) is lower than it would have been.

The reverse situation applies to Brandon Ltd, which would have reported lower operating profit and lower net assets if it had used FIFO instead of LIFO.

v) **Limitations of using added value per employee as a measure of employee productivity**

Measures of employee productivity compare the output received from a certain amount of input from employees. In this instance the output is value added, which is sales value minus cost of purchased materials and bought-in services.

1) Improvements (or deteriorations) in value added may not be due to employees' efforts. Improvements to shop layouts or facilities may encourage more customers into the stores.

2) Some accounting policies influence the measure. For example, the stock valuation policy will affect cost of sales and hence value added.

vi) **Alternative measures of employee productivity**

The number of transactions per employee per day could be used to measure employee productivity as the number of transactions is a valid reflection of the level of employees' work effort. Sales revenue per employee per day could also be used.

answers to chapter 7: QUALITY

1 Quality could be described as the 'degree of excellence of the product or service' or 'how well the product or service serves its purpose'.

Quality is therefore judged by the customer. The product or service will only be perceived as having quality if it satisfies the customers' requirements. Therefore the product or service must have two main elements if it is to satisfy the customer and have quality:

- It must be fit for the purpose for which it has been acquired
- It must represent value for money to the customer

This does not mean that products or services need to be made more expensive by using better materials or more highly skilled staff. Provided that the product or service does what it is meant to do and is viewed as value for money to the customer then this product or service will have quality.

2 Prevention costs are the costs incurred with the aim of reducing substandard output to a minimum. They are the costs of actions taken to investigate, prevent or reduce defects in products or mistakes in services.

Examples of prevention costs are:

- improvements in product design or specification to reduce defective products
- improvements in systems designed to reduce mistakes in the provision of services
- design, development and maintenance of quality control or inspection equipment

Appraisal costs are the costs incurred in initially ascertaining how the product or service conforms to quality requirements. They are all of the costs associated with assessing the level of quality achieved.

Examples of appraisal costs are:

- inspection of goods and raw materials received
- inspection of production processes and work in progress
- inspection or performance testing of finished goods

Internal failure costs are the costs arising from inadequate quality identified before the goods or services are sold to the customer. Therefore they are costs arising within the organisation due to the failure to achieve the required level of quality.

Examples of internal failure costs are:

- investigation and analysis of failed units
- lost contribution on defective units scrapped or sold at a lower price than normal
- losses due to faults in raw materials purchased

External failure costs are costs arising from inadequate quality discovered after the goods or services have been sold to the customer.

Examples of external failure costs are:

- costs of running a customer service department
- product liability costs
- costs of replacing or repairing goods returned from customers

3		Type of cost
i)	lost contribution on defective products sold as seconds	Internal failure
ii)	cost of replacing faulty products	External failure
iii)	claims from customers relating to defective products	External failure
iv)	products scrapped due to faulty raw materials	Internal failure
v)	training for quality control staff	Prevention
vi)	maintenance of quality control equipment	Prevention
vii)	performance testing of finished goods	Appraisal
viii)	costs of customer after sales service department	External failure
ix)	costs of inspection of raw materials	Appraisal
x)	costs of production delays due to re-working defective products discovered in quality inspection	Internal failure

4 i) **New zipper design**

Prevention costs – will have increased due to the costs of the design

Appraisal costs – no effect

Internal failure costs – these should be reduced as the product is more reliable

External failure costs – these should be reduced as the new zipper has a longer lifespan and will reduce returns of products

ii) **Faulty jumpers**

Prevention costs – no obvious effect

Appraisal costs – these will probably increase as machines should be checked regularly to ensure that this problem is not repeated

Internal failure costs – these will increase due to investigation of the failure, repairs to the machines which may cause disruption to the production process and re-inspection costs

External failure costs – any damages claims received from customers and the loss of these customers for future sales

iii) **Flawed fabric**

Prevention costs – finding a new supplier for the fabric

Appraisal costs – these will increase with the costs of inspection procedures

Internal failure costs

- the lost contribution from having to sell the suits at a lower price
- reduction of costs as the benefits of the inspection controls are felt

External failure costs – these should reduce as fewer defective products will be sold to customers

5 Explicit costs of quality are the costs of quality that can be identified and valued from the cost accounting records. Implicit costs are other types of cost which are not recorded in the accounting records and which can often only be estimated.

Examples of explicit costs are:

- costs of repairing defective products
- costs of quality control inspections
- costs of repair of returned goods from customers

Examples of implicit costs are:

- the opportunity cost of lost sales to customers who are dissatisfied due to faulty goods and will not purchase from the organisation again
- loss of goodwill or reputation due to factors such as the widespread recall of one of an organisation's products
- costs of production disruption due to reworking of faulty products – these costs will be included in the production costs but cannot be separately identified

6 Number of estimated defective goods 10 million/1,000 x 3 = 30,000 units

	£
Appraisal costs – quality inspections	35,000
Internal failure costs – lost contribution on sales of seconds 4,000 x (£15 – £11)	16,000
External failure costs – replacement cost 30,000 x £10 x 70%	210,000
	261,000

There are also implicit costs of the lost sales to customers who have purchased faulty products.

7

	£
Appraisal costs	60,000
Internal failure costs – lost contribution 7,500 units x (£33 – £20)	97,500
Total quality cost	157,500

8

Cost of repair of returned goods 8,000,000/6,000 x 75% x £10	£10,000 – external failure cost
Advertising cost	£5,000 – external failure cost
Lost customers 8,000,000/6,000 x 25% = 333 units	Implicit cost, cannot be estimated – external failure cost

9

Quality inspection costs	£340,000	– appraisal cost – explicit
Lost contribution 5,200 units x (£200 – 108)	£478,400	– internal failure cost – implicit
Replacement of defective units 1,000,000/2,000 x 60% x £120	£36,000	– external failure cost – explicit
	£12,000	
Lost customers	–	– external failure cost – implicit

10 Under traditional costing methods the costs of a product are only recorded and analysed once production of the product has begun. However, it is recognised that a large proportion of the costs of a product are incurred before production has started in the early stages of the product life cycle. Life cycle costing recognises all of these pre-production costs of the product such as:

- design costs
- prototyping
- programming
- process design
- equipment acquisition

The aim of life cycle costing is to ensure that all the costs of the product are accumulated over the whole of its life cycle in order to ensure that all costs are covered by revenue from the product.

11 a) The four general headings making up the cost of quality are as follows.

i) Prevention costs
ii) Appraisal costs
iii) Internal failure costs
iv) External failure costs

b) Examples of types of cost likely to be found in each category are as follows.

i) Prevention costs. Maintenance of quality control and inspection equipment, training in quality control

ii) Appraisal costs. Inspection of goods inwards, inspection costs of in-house processing

iii) Internal failure costs. Losses from failure of purchased items, losses due to lower selling prices for sub-quality goods

iv) External failure costs. Costs of customer complaints section, cost of repairing products returned from customers

c) Implications for the existing costing system

i) If there are fixed price contracts with guaranteed levels of quality there are likely to be few, if any, material price variances or material usage variances due to poor quality.

ii) The cost of labour will effectively become a fixed cost, the actual unit cost of labour simply depending on the volume produced. Labour efficiency variances could therefore be calculated but they will not reflect costs saved or excess wages paid. Labour rate variances are likely to be minimal if there is a guaranteed weekly wage.

iii) Predetermined standards conflict with the TQM philosophy of continual improvement.

iv) Continual improvements should alter prices, quantities of inputs and so on, whereas standard costing systems are best used in stable, standardised, repetitive environments.

v) Standard costing systems often incorporate a planned level of scrap in material standards. This is at odds with the TQM aim of 'zero defects'.

Results of these implications

i) There is less need for a standard costing system: variances are likely to be small or non-existent and, if incurred, non-controllable; the use of standards is inappropriate in a TQM environment.

ii) With the flexible work practices, capture of actual labour costs by individual jobs would be very difficult. Only material costs could be collected in the normal way. It is therefore unlikely that the full marginal cost of individual jobs could be collected.

d) A cost saving not recorded in the existing costing system

With the introduction of a system of just-in-time, the cost of having money tied up in high levels of stocks will be saved. This cost would not normally be captured by Barnet Ltd's existing costing system.

Note. A fuller answer has been given here than was required for assessment purposes.

12 a) **Background paper for meeting**

To: Jane Greenwood, Management Accountant
From: Assistant Management Accountant
Subject: Total quality management and the cost of quality
Date: xx/xx/xx

i) **The meaning of Total Quality Management**

Total Quality Management (TQM) is a philosophy that guides every activity within a business. It is concerned with developing and sustaining a culture of continuous improvement which focuses on meeting customers' expectations.

One of the basic principles of TQM is therefore a dissatisfaction with the status quo: the belief that it is always possible to improve and so the aim should be to 'get it more right next time'. This involves the development of a commitment to quality by all staff and a programme of continuous learning throughout the entire organisation, possibly by empowering employees and making them responsible for the quality of production or by introducing quality circles.

The customer-centred approach of TQM hinges upon identifying the 'customers', focusing attention on them and then meeting their needs in terms of price, quality and timing. Organisations must therefore be customer-oriented rather than, as is traditionally the case, production-oriented.

One of the goals of TQM is to get it right first time. By continuously improving towards zero defects, the quality of the product delivered to the customer is improved. The quality of output depends on the quality of materials input, however, and so either extensive quality control procedures are needed at the point where goods are accepted and inspected or quality assurance schemes, whereby the supplier guarantees the quality of the goods supplied, must be in place.

A small proportion of mistakes are inevitable in any organisation but more often than not those mistakes have been 'designed' into the production process. Because TQM aims to get it right first time, however, quality and not faults must be designed into an organisation's products and operations from the outset. Quality control must therefore happen at the production design and production engineering stages of a product's life, as well as actually during production.

In summary, TQM involves getting it right first time and improving continuously.

ii) **Failure of the current accounting system to highlight the cost of quality**

Traditionally, the costs of scrapped units, wasted materials and reworking have been subsumed within the costs of production by assigning the costs of an expected level of loss (a normal loss) to the costs of good production, while accounting for other costs of poor quality within production or marketing overheads. Such costs are therefore not only considered as inevitable but are not highlighted for management attention. Moreover, traditional accounting reports tend to ignore the hidden but real costs of excessive stock levels (held to enable faulty material to be replaced without hindering production) and the facilities necessary for storing that stock.

iii)/iv) **Explicit costs of quality**

There are four recognised categories of cost identifiable within an accounting system which make up the cost of quality.

1) Prevention costs are the costs of any action taken to investigate, prevent or reduce the production of faulty output. Included within this category are the costs of training in quality control and the cost of the design/development and maintenance of quality control and inspection equipment.

2) Appraisal costs are the costs of assessing the actual quality achieved. Examples include the cost of the inspection of goods delivered and the cost of inspecting production during the manufacturing process.

3) Internal failure costs are the costs incurred by the organisation when production fails to meet the level of quality required. Such costs include losses due to lower selling prices for sub-quality goods, the costs of reviewing product specifications after failures and losses arising from the failure of purchased items.

4) External failure costs are the costs which arise outside the organisation (after the customer has received the product) due to failure to achieve the required level of quality. Included within this category are the costs of repairing products returned from customers, the cost of providing replacement items due to sub-standard products or marketing errors and the costs of a customer service department.

v) **Quality costs not identified by the accounting system**

Quality costs which are not identified by the accounting system tend to be of two forms.

1) Opportunity costs such as the loss of future sales to a customer dissatisfied with faulty goods.

2) Costs which tend to be subsumed within other account headings such as those costs which result from the disruption caused by stockouts due to faulty purchases.

b) i) **Explicit cost of quality**

	£
Reworking (labour cost)	13,500
Customer support (contractors)	24,300
Store inspection costs	10,000
Cost of returns	4,500
	52,300

ii) **Cost of quality not reported in the accounting records**

Opportunity cost (lost contribution from 100 X4s due to faulty circuit board) = £795 (W1) x 100 = £79,500.

Workings

		£
1)	Labour (W2)	200
	Printed circuit board (£120,000 ÷ 1,000)	120
	Other material (£121,500 ÷ 900)	135
	Marginal cost	455
	Selling price	(1,250)
	Contribution	795

		£
2)	Total labour cost	193,500
	Less cost of reworking	(13,500)
		180,000

Unit cost per good unit = £180,000 ÷ 900 = £200

answers to chapter 8: BUDGETARY CONTROL SYSTEMS

1 a) A budget is a formalised, numerical plan of action for all areas of a business for the forthcoming period, normally set for the next twelve-month period.

b) A budgetary control system can help management to perform their duties and carry out their responsibilities in two main areas.

One of the roles of management is in terms of planning for the business – both long term strategic plans and shorter term operational plans. Budgets are formal, numerical plans which can help to ensure that all areas of the business are aiming at the same goals. For example, if the sales demand for the product is the key budget factor, by setting manufacturing budgets management can ensure that these are in line with the sales budget. It would be bad management to produce 100,000 units of a product if only 60,000 units of the product are likely to be sold in the forthcoming period.

A further example would be that, once the sales and manufacturing budgets are set, management can then ensure that the budgets for other areas of the business such as the canteen and the sales department are in line with these budgets. So, for example, if it is budgeted that there will be 200 factory workers each day then the canteen should not be budgeting to buy food for 400. Or if sales are expected to be 60,000 units in the period it is important that the sales department budgets in order to be able to deal with this level.

A further important role of management is that of control of operations and of costs in particular. A budgetary system can assist in this area as the eventual actual results can be compared to the budgeted figures and any variances can be calculated and investigated. Where necessary management can then take corrective action to deal with these variances from planned costs.

2 a) The strategic plans of a business are the long-term plans of the business. These plans will be based upon the strategic objectives of the management of the business which may concern maximisation of profitability, increase of market share, growth by acquisition of other businesses or expansion of the product range. Once the strategic objectives have been determined then the strategic plans are the long term plans of how the business is to meet these objectives.

Once the strategic plan is in place then the management can look at shorter term plans necessary in order to meet the strategic objectives of the business. These are the operational plans and will take a variety of forms such as plans for the purchase of fixed assets, plans for the amount of production and plans for the financing of the business. All of these plans take the form of budgets.

b) When a business is started then the management must determine a long-term plan of how the business is to be operated and where its future lies. This will mean that the senior management of the business must determine the strategic objectives of the business. The strategic plan will remain in place for the life of the business but may be altered from time to time as circumstances change or opportunities become available.

The strategic plan shows where the business is going but the next stage of the planning process is to determine how the business is going to get there. This will involve a detailed review of the business both from an internal and external perspective in order to decide what possible strategies there are in order to move the business closer to the strategic objective.

Information will need to be gathered about all of the resources of the business, the state of its products or services and the amount of finance that is available. External information about the market, competitors and the general economic environment will also be required. This detailed review of the position of the business is often called a SWOT analysis, a review of the strengths, weaknesses, opportunities and threats to the business.

Once this analysis has been carried out, management will be in a position to identify the various strategies that are available to the organisation, such as marketing a new product or concentrating on the production of its current products.

Once the various available strategies have been identified then the management will be in a position to choose which strategy is the most suitable and has the greatest potential for achieving the overall strategic objective. When the strategies for the future have been chosen then they can be co-ordinated into the strategic plan for the business.

Once the strategic plan is in place then the management can look at shorter term plans necessary in order to meet the strategies chosen for the business, the operational plans.

3 A capital budget details the timing and value of the purchases of fixed assets. This is important for a number of reasons.

- The purchase of fixed assets will normally be the most significant outgoing of a business and therefore it is important that such major purchases are properly planned.
- The purchase of fixed assets will normally be costly and it is therefore important that appropriate finance is available at the precise time that it is required.
- Fixed assets are frequently fundamental to the production and processes of an organisation therefore it is vital that fixed assets are fully functioning and are replaced or updated at the appropriate time.

4 Resource budgets are those that deal with all aspects of the short term operations of the business. The resource budgets will include:

Production budget – this is a budget for the number of units that it is planned to produce during the forthcoming period – this will be based upon the key budget factor which is frequently the sales demand which will be forecast in the sales budget.

Materials usage budget – this is based upon the production budget and is a budget for the estimated quantity of materials that is to be used in the forthcoming period.

Materials purchases budget – this is the amount of raw materials that must be purchased each period to satisfy the production and stock demands and will be expressed in both units and monetary amounts. These figures will be based upon the materials usage budget.

Labour usage budget – this is based upon the production budget and is an estimate of the labour hours required during the period to meet the production figures. The production budget will be the starting point for determining the labour usage budget.

Labour cost budget – this is based upon the labour usage budget and is the monetary cost of the labour hours required for the period including any overtime.

Machine hours budget – this is based upon the production plans and shows the number of hours that the machinery must be working in order to produce the required level of production. The figures can be calculated using the quantity of production from the production budget.

Variable overheads budget – this will be based upon the production budget as the variable overheads will vary with the amount of production. Therefore the production budget will provide the quantities of production which can then be used to determine the variable overheads expected to be incurred.

Fixed overheads budget – this is independent of the level of production as this should not affect the amount of fixed overheads. Therefore the budget for fixed overheads will be based upon estimates of fixed overhead costs and previous experience.

There may also be sundry other resource budgets such as the selling and distribution costs budget, advertising budget and the administration budget which will again all be set within the context of the sales budget.

5 a) The key budget factor is the element or resource of the business that is likely to be the one that places limitations on the activities of the business. It is unlikely in a business that it will be able to produce and sell an unlimited number of its products. There will normally be one factor at least that will limit the quantity of sales and/or production. The importance of the key budget factor is that as it places a limit on all of the other operations of the business then the forecast for the key factor must be made first and all other budgets will be based upon this one.

The most common key budget factor is that of sales demand. Therefore the sales forecast must be made first and the production budget will then be based upon the forecast sales levels.

b) Any three of the following:

- limitations on the amount of raw materials that can be purchased
- manpower limitations – a limit to the number of hours that can be worked in the period by the labour force
- capacity limitations – a limit to the number of machine hours available
- a limit to the quantity that can be produced by a production line in the period

6 i) There would appear to be no limits regarding demand for beds or the labour force. The key budget factor would seem to be the number of beds available.

ii) In a busy shopping centre demand for the ice cream is probably not the key factor therefore it is likely to be the quantity of ice cream that can be stored each day.

iii) Sales demand is not a limiting factor however as this is highly skilled work the available hours of the three partners wil be the key budget factor.

iv) As the products are similar to those of other manufacturers and therefore can be replaced by similar products by the retail stores then it is highly likely that the demand from the retail stores will be the key budget factor.

7 i) The budget manual is a set of detailed instructions as to how the budget is to be prepared. The budget manual might typically include the following:

- the names of the budget holders – those responsible for producing each budget
- to whom each budget holder reports
- an organisation chart
- the timescale for the production of each budget
- the procedures for preparing each budget
- the format of the budgets
- how and when actual performance is compared to budget

ii) The budget committee is responsible for co-ordinating and administering all of the individual budgets and will review and authorise each individual budget. The budget committee will normally be made up of senior executives and each function of the business should be represented on the budget committee in order to ensure that there is full communication between all areas of the business. The budget committee will normally be assisted by an accountant known as the budget officer.

iii) Budget holders are the managers within a business that are responsible for preparing each resource budget. In most cases the budget holder should be the manager who will also be responsible for ensuring that the activities meet the budget.

iv) The master budget is the final overall budget for all areas of the business. It is normally set out in the form of a budgeted profit and loss account, budgeted balance sheet and cash flow budget.

8 The budgeting process starts with the setting of the budget (forecast) for the key budget factor. This will frequently be the sales budget although if manufacturing resources are the key budget factor this may be the labour budget or machine hours budget. Once the key budget factor budget has been set then the production budget will be set by the production manager and the various other resource budgets set by the relevant budget holders.

Once the budget holder has drafted his budget then he will submit this to the budget committee. The budget officer will ensure that the budget is consistent with the other resource budgets checking, for example, that it has been prepared in line with the production budget.

There will then frequently be negotiations between the budget committee and the budget holder regarding the detailed content of the budget. The manager might for example have built in an increase in costs over previous years which the budget committee does not agree with. The budget holder may well have to change his draft budget and re-submit it to the budget committee a number of times before the budget committee is satisfied with it.

Once the budget committee have agreed all of the resource budgets with the budget holders then they will be formed into the master budget.

9 A rolling budget is one which is constantly being updated and added to. It will be set in detail for the next short accounting period and in outline for the remainder of the 12-month period. As each accounting period passes the details of the next period's budget are produced and the budget extended to maintain a 12-month coverage.

For example if budgets are set for each of 13 four-week periods in a year initially the detailed budget will be set for period 1 and the remaining 12 periods' budgets will be in outline. Towards the end of period 1 the detail for period 2's budget will be set and the outline budget for period 1 of the following year added.

The benefits of a rolling budget are that the detailed budgeting only has to be performed for the next accounting period rather than for periods a long time in advance therefore the budget is potentially more accurate. It also means that when setting the detail of each period's budget the budget holder can react to changes in circumstances that are revealed by comparison of the actual figures for each period to the budgeted figures.

10 i) Incremental budgeting is one of the most common methods in practice of setting budgets. Under this method the budget for the forthcoming period is set by taking the previous period's budget and adding a percentage to reflect any increases in prices since the last budget was set or any increase in activity level.

ii) Zero-based budgeting is a method of budgeting that looks at the costs of each cost centre from scratch for each period. Each cost is then considered in the context of the production budget and the amount of each cost must then be specifically justified and not just included in the budget because it was in last year's budget.

For each item of activity which causes a cost the following types of questions must be asked:

- is the activity necessary?
- are there alternatives to this activity?
- what are the costs of the alternative?
- what would happen if the activity were not carried out?
- is the expense of the activity worth the benefit?

By asking such questions the activity and its related costs can either be justified for inclusion in the budget or a cheaper alternative found.

iii) Activity-based budgeting is a system of setting budgets based upon Activity-based costing principles. Under this method of budgeting the costs that are incurred by each activity are budgeted for rather than the costs of individual cost centres. For example, a budget might be set for the production set-up process or the quality control procedures rather than the factory cost centre as a whole.

11 Spreadsheet design to produce the labour requirements budget for August

The labour requirements budget for August would be determined by the production budget, which is in turn dependent on the requirement for sales and stock. Consequently, there would be a 'cascade' approach.

Once the production requirement has been determined there would need to be an adjustment for the 10% defect rate. This would provide a figure for actual production required. This adjustment is complicated by the fact that whole units are required, and so a correction to bring the output up to the next complete unit may be necessary. This correction could be dispensed with in the interests of simplicity, however.

The next step would be to convert the actual production into labour hours by multiplying output by hours per unit. The hours per unit may well be contained in a data table to permit easy adjustment of the budget if production levels change.

The final step would be to convert the labour hours into money by reference to an hourly rate of pay. The hourly rate also could be located in the data table to permit easy amendment of the budget.

A cell layout diagram is set out below.

	A	B	C	D	E	F	G	H
1	**Labour budget**							
2	**Data table**							
3	Closing stock as a proportion of following month's sales						0.5	
4	Defect rate						0.1	
5	Labour hours per unit						10	
6	Labour wage rate per hour						£8	
7								
8	Month					*August*	*September*	
9	Budgeted sales units					300	600	
10	Opening stock					= F9 * G3		
11	Closing stock					= G9 * G3		
12	Good production required					= F9 – F10 + F11		
13	Actual production in units after adjustment for defect rate					= F12 /(1–G4)		
14	Labour hours budget					= F13 * G5		
15	Wages budget					= F14 * G6		

answers to chapter 9: FORECASTING INCOME

1 The general limitations of forecasting are:

- the less historical data that is used the more unreliable the results of the forecast will be
- the further into the future that the forecast considers the more unreliable it will become
- forecast figures will often be based upon the assumption that current conditions will continue in the future. A trend of results may be based upon historical data, but you cannot always assume that the trend will continue in the future
- if the forecast is based upon a trend there are always random elements or variations which cause the trend to change
- the forecast produced from the historical data may be quite accurate but the actual future results may be very different from the forecast figures due to changes in the political, economic or technological environment within which the business operates

2

	Trend	*Seasonal variation*		*Forecast*
Quarter 2 ((122,000 – 6,000) x 1.035)	120,060	–8,000	=	112,060
Quarter 3 (120,060 x 1.035)	124,262	+12,000	=	136,262
Quarter 4 (124,262 x 1.035)	128,611	–10,000	=	118,611

3

	Trend		*Seasonal variation*		*Forecast*
Quarter 1	340,000	x	0.82	=	278,800
Quarter 2	345,000	x	1.21	=	417,450
Quarter 3	350,000	x	1.07	=	374,500
Quarter 4	355,000	x	0.90	=	319,500

4

	Trend		Seasonal variation		Forecast
Quarter 1 (90,000/1.11) x 1.02)	82,703	x	0.69	=	57,065
Quarter 2 (82,703 x 1.02)	84,357	x	0.97	=	81,826
Quarter 3 (84,357 x 1.02)	86,044	x	1.23	=	105,834
Quarter 4 (86,044 x 1.02)	87,765	x	1.11	=	97,419

5

	Trend		Seasonal variation		Forecast
Quarter 1 (+ 4,500)	178,000	x	1.07	=	190,460
Quarter 2 (+ 4,500)	182,500	x	1.09	=	198,925
Quarter 3 (+ 4,500)	187,000	x	0.97	=	181,390
Quarter 4 (+ 4,500)	191,500	x	0.87	=	166,605

6 i)

	Actual	*Four-quarter moving average*	*Centred four-quarter moving average*	*Seasonal variation TREND*
2006				
Quarter 3	1,900			
Quarter 4	2,300			
2007		2,500		
Quarter 1	2,800		2,563	+237
		2,625		
Quarter 2	3,000		2,650	+350
		2,675		
Quarter 3	2,400		2,725	–325
		2,775		
Quarter 4	2,500		2,825	–325
2008		2,875		
Quarter 1	3,200		2,888	+312
		2,900		
Quarter 2	3,400		2,925	+475
		2,950		
Quarter 3	2,500		2,988	–488
		3,025		
Quarter 4	2,700		3,063	–363
		3,100		
2009				
Quarter 1	3,500			
Quarter 2	3,700			

ii)

Seasonal variation	*Quarter 1*	*Quarter 2*	*Quarter 3*	*Quarter 4*
2007	+237	+350	–325	–325
2008	+312	+475	–488	–363
	+549	+825	–813	–688
Average	+275	+412	–406	–344
Adjustment (63/4)	+15	+16	+16	+16
	+290	+428	–390	–328

iii) We can forecast the quarter 3 sales for 2009 by estimating the trend figure for that quarter and then applying the seasonal adjustment. The trend is increasing, however the rate of increase seems to have slowed in recent quarters. As an estimate therefore assume trend increase of say 65 units each quarter.

Trend 3,063 + 65 + 65 +65	3,258
Seasonal variation for quarter 3	–390
Forecast sales	2,868

iv) The forecast results may be different from the actual results if the trend changes in quarter 1 or 2 of 2009 and if the seasonal variation for quarter 3 is different from that predicted. The actual results could also be different to the forecast results due to any random factors that affect the sales for the quarter.

7 The main limitations of using time series analysis for forecasting are:

- unless the data used covers many years it is impossible to isolate the cyclical changes due to general changes in the economy
- the seasonal variations are an average of the seasonal variation for each period and again unless this is based on a large amount of historical data the figure could be misleading
- any random variations are ignored
- the trend and the seasonal variations are assumed to continue in the future in the same manner as in the past
- if the time series analysis is based upon historic value the figures will include past inflation which may not be an indication of the future amounts

8 a) The product life cycle is generally thought to split naturally into five separate stages:

- development
- launch
- growth
- maturity
- decline

During the development and launch stage of the product's life there are large outgoings in terms of development expenditure, fixed assets necessary for production, the building up of stock levels and advertising and promotion expenses. It is likely that even after the launch sales will be quite low and the product will be making a loss at this stage.

If the launch of the product is successful then during the growth stage there will be fairly rapid increases in sales and a move to profitability as the costs of the earlier stages are covered. However, these sales increases are not likely to continue indefinitely.

In the maturity stage of the product demand for the product will probably start to slow down and become more constant. In many cases this is the stage where the product is modified or improved in order to sustain demand and this may then see a small surge in sales.

At some point in a product's life, unless it is a consumable item such as chocolate bars, the product will reach the end of its sale life, this is known as the decline stage. The market will have bought enough of the product and sales will decline. This is the point where the business should consider no longer producing the product.

b) If the future demand for a product is to be forecast using time series analysis it is obviously important that the stage in the product life cycle that has been reached is taken into account. For example, if the trend is based upon the growth stage whereas in fact the product is moving into the maturity stage then the trend would show an overly optimistic forecast for sales.

9 Maturity stage.

10 i)

	A	B	C	D	E
1	Unit sales price – £	150			
2	Annual sales volume – units	180,000			
3	Seasonal variation	–14%	–28%	+20%	+22%
4		Quarter 1	Quarter 2	Quarter 3	Quarter 4
5	Seasonal variation – units	=(B2/4)*B3/100	=(B2/4)*C3/100	=(B2/4)*D3/100	=(B2/4)*E3/100
6	Quarterly volume – units	=(B2/4)+B5	=(B2/4)+C5	=(B2/4)+D5	=(B2/4)+E5
7	Quarterly sales – £	=B6*B1	=C6*B1	=D6*B1	=E6*B1

ii)

	A	B	C	D	E
1	Unit sales price – £	150			
2	Annual sales volume – units	180,000			
3	Seasonal variation – %	–14	–28	+20	+22
4		Quarter 1	Quarter 2	Quarter 3	Quarter 4
5	Seasonal variation – units	–6,300	–12,600	+9,000	+9,900
6	Quarterly volume – units	38,700	32,400	54,000	54,900
7	Quarterly sales – £	5,805,000	4,860,000	8,100,000	8,235,000

11 a) **Calculation of trend sales values from the regression line**

Quarter				
17		£(2,000,000 + (40,000 × 17))	=	£2,680,000
18		£(2,000,000 + (40,000 × 18))	=	£2,720,000
	or	£(2,680,000 + 40,000)	=	£2,720,000
19		£(2,720,000 + 40,000)	=	£2,760,000
20		£(2,760,000 + 40,000)	=	£2,800,000

Calculation of seasonally-adjusted sales

Quarter	*Trend value*	*Seasonal variation*	*Absolute variation*	*(i) Forecast*	*Percentage variation*	*(ii) Forecast*
	£		£	£	%	£
17	2,680,000	A	+350,000	3,030,000	+15	3,082,000*
18	2,720,000	B	+250,000	2,970,000	+10	2,992,000
19	2,760,000	C	–400,000	2,360,000	–15	2,346,000**
20	2,800,000	D	–200,000	2,600,000	–10	2,520,000

* £2,680,000 x 115%

** £2,760,000 x 85%

b) i)

Quarter	Actual	Absolute forecast	Residual error	Percentage forecast	Residual error
17	£	£	£	£	£
18	3,079,500	3,030,000	+49,500	3,082,000	–2,500
19	3,002,400	2,970,000	+32,400	2,992,000	+10,400
20	2,346,500	2,360,000	–13,500	2,346,000	+500
20	2,490,200	2,600,000	–109,800	2,520,000	–29,800

In each of the four quarters, the residual error associated with percentage seasonal variations is lower than that associated with absolute seasonal variations. On the basis of the sample of four quarters, the **percentage seasonal variations method appears to be the more accurate forecasting method**.

ii)

Quarter	Season	Trend	Seasonal variation	Forecast
		£	%	£
21	A	2,840,000*	+15	3,266,000
22	B	2,880,000	+10	3,168,000
23	C	2,920,000	–15	2,482,000
24	D	2,960,000	–10	2,664,000

*Trend for Q20 + £40,000

c) **MEMORANDUM**

To: Managing Director
From: Assistant Management Accountant
Date: xx.xx.xx
Subject: **Forecasting, seasonal variations and seasonally-adjusted data**

I have recently tested a statistical software package which can be used for estimating demand for fuel oil. I set out below some information which you may find useful.

i) **Seasonal variations** are regular, predictable and consistent changes in recorded values due to different circumstances which affect results at different times of the year, on different days of the week, at different times of day or whatever. For oil distribution, it is likely that demand will be higher in winter than in summer and this is reflected in the seasonal variations for our organisation produced by the software package. The sales revenue in Quarter A, which includes the winter months, is 15% above the average quarterly sales revenue whereas the sales revenue in Quarter C, which includes the summer months, is 85% of the average quarterly sales revenue.

Seasonally-adjusted data is actual data from which seasonal variations (derived from historic data) have been removed, to leave a figure which might be taken to indicate the trend (if we assume that any random variations are negligible). For example, the estimated seasonal variations within the actual sales revenue for Quarter 17 = 15/115 x £3,079,500 = £401,674, say £402,000. Deducting this from the actual sales revenue leaves an underlying figure of £(3,079,500 – 402,000) = £2,677,500.

ii) The percentage seasonal variations method of seasonal adjustment might be more accurate than the absolute seasonal variations method because the trend in sales turnover is increasing over time. When a trend is increasing, it is likely that absolute seasonal variations are also increasing. The absolute seasonal variations method simply adds absolute and unchanging seasonal variations to the trend figures whereas the percentage seasonal variations method, by multiplying the increasing trend values by a constant factor, produces seasonal variations which increase in time with the trend in sales.

iii) There are a number of ways in which an understanding of seasonal variations and seasonally-adjusted data can help us to be more efficient. For example, it helps in stock control. If we are able to forecast demand we will not have to hold excessive stock. This helps cash flow in two ways.

1) It reduces cash tied up in stocks.
2) It minimises the interest charges on amounts owing to Star Fuels.

Accurate forecasts of demand will also enable us to forecast future profit levels more accurately.

iv) There are, however, a number of limitations to this forecasting technique.

1) The use of the least squares regression equation assumes that there is a linear relationship between sales turnover and time.

2) The use of the equation also assumes that sales turnover is dependent only upon time. In reality it might depend on several other variables such as the actions of competitors or the state of the economy.

3) It assumes that what has happened in the past will provide a reliable guide for what will happen in the future. If, for example, a new competitor has entered the market, this will not be the case.

4) The data used was measured in monetary terms but part of any increase in sales turnover may be due to rising prices rather than increased demand. It might therefore be better to measure sales in litres rather than value.

5) The choice of a quarterly seasonal variation may be inappropriate. Forecasting on a weekly basis may be more suitable.

answers to chapter 10: FORECASTING EXPENDITURE

1 Total production $= \dfrac{129{,}000\,\text{kgs}}{5\,\text{kgs}}$

$= 25{,}800$ units

Monthly production $= \dfrac{25{,}800\,\text{kgs}}{12}$

$= 2{,}150$ units

2 a) Maximum shortage

	July	*Aug*	*Sept*	*Oct*	*Nov*	*Dec*
Requirement	4,800	4,300	4,100	4,900	4,200	5,000
Purchase	4,500	4,300	4,100	4,500	4,200	4,500
Shortfall	300	–	–	400	–	500

Total shortfall = 300 + 400 + 500

= 1,200 units

b) Purchasing plan

	July	*Aug*	*Sept*	*Oct*	*Nov*	*Dec*
Requirement	4,800	4,300	4,100	4,900	4,200	5,000
Purchase	4,500	4,500	4,500	4,500	4,500	4,500
Excess/(Shortfall)	(300)	200	400	(400)	300	(500)
Stock		200	600	200	500	–
Production	4,500	4,300	4,100	4,900	4,200	5,000

By purchasing the maximum available in August, September and November, even though it is not required, the shortages in October and December can be covered from materials held in stock. This leaves only the 300 kg shortage in July.

3 a) If the shortage is only temporary then there are a number of short-term solutions which could alleviate the problem.

- Using stocks of materials – the stocks of raw materials could be run down in order to maintain production and sales.
- Using stocks of finished goods – in order to maintain sales in the short-term finished goods stocks can be run down even though production levels are not as high as would be liked.
- Rescheduling purchases – if the amount of the raw material required is available in some periods but not in others then the raw materials purchases could be rescheduled to ensure that the maximum use is made of the available materials.

b) If the shortage is a long-term problem then the following are possible options for the business.

- Seeking an alternative supplier – this is an obvious solution but it may not always be possible to find another supplier who can supply the correct quality at an acceptable price.
- Finding an alternative material – in some instances a product can only be made from one particular material but it may be possible to adapt the design of the product and the manufacturing process in order to use a substitute material that is widely available.
- Manufacturing an alternative product – it may be possible to switch the production process to manufacture of an alternative product which uses a different material which is not in short supply.
- Buying in finished goods for resale – instead of producing the product it could be purchased in finished form from another producer who is not having the same problems with supply of the materials required. However this probably would lead to an under-utilisation of production resources and a major change in the organisation's strategy.

4 a)

	May	*June*	*July*	*Aug*	*Sept*	*Oct*
Material requirement	9,500	10,200	10,200	9,300	10,200	10,300
Potential shortage	–	200	200	–	200	300

Do not buy 10,000 kgs each month as this will lead to stocks that are not required. However buy enough in May and August to cover the potential shortages.

	May	*June*	*July*	*Aug*	*Sept*	*Oct*
Material requirement	9,500	10,200	10,200	9,300	10,200	10,300
Purchases	9,900	10,000	10,000	9,800	10,000	10,000
Stock	400	200	–	500	300	–
Production	9,500	10,200	10,200	9,300	10,200	10,300

b) No shortage

5 a) Total hours available (including overtime) = 12 x (38 + 8)
= 552 hours per week

Maximum production = 552/3
= 184 units

b) Possible solutions to this problem could be:

- increase the overtime worked – it may be possible to agree additional overtime with the employees in order to maintain production; however at 46 hours per week already this may not be an option here
- use sub-contractors – in some types of business it may be possible to use agency workers or to sub-contract the work in order to maintain production levels. This option is likely to be fairly costly
- use up finished goods stock – if production levels are lower than required to meet sales demand then for the short term sales can still be maintained by running down the finished goods stock. This is not, however, a long-term solution
- buying in finished goods stock – this could be an expensive option leaving factory capacity under-utilised and may have quality implications as well
- improving labour efficiency – this is not something that can be done quickly but with training over a period of time it may be possible to increase the number of employees with the skills required

6 Labour hours required = 1,860 units x 4 hours
= 7,440 hours

Labour hours available = 160 employees x 35 hours
= 5,600 hours

Overtime hours required = 7,440 – 5,600
= 1,840 hours

7 a) Hours of production line time = 2 shifts x 7 hours x 5 days x 2 production lines
= 140 hours

Maximum production = 140 hours x 30 units
= 4,200 units

b) If sales demand exceeds this maximum production level there are a number of options that could be considered.

- Introduce a third shift so that the production lines are in fact running for 21 hours a day.
- Lengthen the shift to, say, a 9 hour shift.
- Operate the factory for 6 or even 7 days a week.
- Speed up the production line so that more units are produced an hour.

8

	May	June	July	Aug	Sept	Oct
	£	£	£	£	£	£
Production costs (production units x £10.50)	37,800	30,450	33,600	32,550	35,700	42,000
Selling costs (sales units x £3.80)	13,300	11,400	11,400	12,160	13,300	14,440

9

Quarter 1	£657,000 x 128.4/126.4	=	£667,396
Quarter 2	£692,500 x 131.9/126.4	=	£722,633

10 Variable production costs

		£
January	4,200 x £25 x 137.3/135.2	106,631
February	4,400 x £25 x 139.0/135.2	113,092
March	4,500 x £25 x 139.6/135.2	116,161
April	5,100 x £25 x 140.3/135.2	132,310
May	5,300 x £25 x 141.2/135.2	138,380
June	4,800 x £25 x 143.0/135.2	126,923

Variable selling costs

January	4,100 x £8 x 141.5/140.5	33,033
February	4,300 x £8 x 143.0/140.5	35,012
March	4,650 x £8 x 143.7/140.5	38,047
April	4,700 x £8 x 144.4/140.5	38,644
May	5,000 x £8 x 145.1/140.5	41,310
June	5,100 x £8 x 146.0/140.5	42,397

11

		£
Rent	£65,000 x 1.055	68,575
Insurance	£15,700 x 1.10	17,270
Power	£84,000 x 171.2/166.3	86,475
		172,320

12 i)

	Machine hours	Cost £
June (lowest)	14,200	285,000
August (highest)	15,200	300,000
Increase	1,000	15,000

Variable cost = £15,000/1,000 hours
= £15 per hour

ii)

	£
June	
Variable element £15 x 14,200 hours	213,000
Fixed element (bal fig)	72,000
Total cost	285,000

13 a)

	Activity level	Cost £
July (lowest)	63,000	608,000
September (highest)	76,000	699,000
Increase	13,000	91,000

Variable element = £91,000/13,000
= £7 per unit

	£
July	
Variable element £7 x 63,000 units	441,000
Fixed element (bal fig)	167,000
Total cost	608,000

b) i) Production level of 74,000 units:

	£
Variable cost £7 x 74,000	518,000
Fixed cost	167,000
Total cost	685,000

ii) Production level of 90,000 units:

	£
Variable cost £7 x 90,000	630,000
Fixed cost	167,000
Total cost	797,000

c) The estimate for the 74,000 units of production is likely to be more accurate than the estimate for 90,000 units. Estimating the costs at 74,000 units is an example of interpolation, in that the estimate is being made for a production level that is within the range of production levels used to estimate the variable and fixed costs. 90,000 units of production is significantly higher than the levels of production used in estimating fixed and variable costs and therefore it is possible that the costs would behave differently at this level of production. This is an example of extrapolation.

14 a) y = a + bx

b) a is the point where the line intersects the vertical axis
b is the gradient of the line

c) a = the fixed element of the cost
b = the variable amount per unit/hour

15 Production costs = 138,000 + 6.4 x 105,000

= £810 000

16 Power costs:

		£
April	80,000 + 380,000 x 0.5	270,000
May	80,000 + 400,000 x 0.5	280,000
June	80,000 + 395,000 x 0.5	277,500
July	80,000 + 405,000 x 0.5	282,500
Aug	80,000 + 410,000 x 0.5	285,000
Sept	80,000 + 420,000 x 0.5	290,000

17 Month 1: sales trend = 3.1 + 0.9 x 25 (month 25)
= 25 600 units

Month 2: sales trend = 3.1 + 0.9 x 26
= 26 500 units

Month 3: sales trend = 3.1 + 0.9 x 27
= 27 400 units

18

	Trend		*Seasonal variation*		*Estimate of actual*
Quarter 1	400 + 105 x 13	=	1,765 – 175	=	1,590
Quarter 2	400 + 105 x 14	=	1,870 + 225	=	2,095
Quarter 3	400 + 105 x 15	=	1,975 + 150	=	2,125
Quarter 4	400 + 105 x 16	=	2,080 – 200	=	1,880

answers to chapter 11: PREPARING BUDGETS

1

	Units
Sales	13,800
Less: opening stock	(2,100)
Add: closing stock	1,500
Production	13,200

2

	Units
Sales	200,000
Less: opening stock	(35,000)
Add: closing stock (70% x 35,000)	24,500
Production	189,500

3 Production required = 16,200 x 100/97
= 16,702 units

4 a) **Production budget**

	Period 4 Units	*Period 5* Units	*Period 6* Units
Sales	10,800	11,500	11,000
Less: opening stock	(2,700)	(2,875)	(2,750)
Add: closing stock			
11,500 x 5/20	2,875		
11,000 x 5/20		2,750	
11,200 x 5/20			2,800
Good units required	10,975	11,375	11,050
Defective units			
10,975 x 4/96	457		
11,375 x 4/96		474	
11,050 x 4/96			460
Production	11,432	11,849	11,510

b)

	A	B	C	D	E
1		Period 4	Period 5	Period 6	Period 7
2	Sales – units	10,800	11,500	11,000	11,200
3	Opening stock	2,700	=B4	=C4	
4	Closing stock	=C2*0.25	=D2*0.25	=E2*0.25	
5	Good production	=B2-B3+B4	=C2-C3+C4	=D2-D3+D4	
6	Total production	=B5+(B5*4/96)	=C5+(C5*4/96)	=D5+(D5*4/96)	

5 Materials usage:

	Kg
25,400 x 5 kgs	127,000
Add: wastage 127,000 x 10/90	14,112
Raw material required	141,112

6 a) Materials usage budget

40,000 units x 5 kgs = 200,000 kgs

b) Materials purchases budget

	Kg
Raw materials required	200,000
Less: opening stock	(30,000)
Add: closing stock (30,000 x 80%)	24,000
	194,000

7 a) Materials usage budget

		Period 1	*Period 2*	*Period 3*
		Kg	Kg	Kg
Production x 8 kgs		256,000	280,000	320,000
Normal loss	256,000 x 20/80	64,000		
	280,000 x 20/80		70,000	
	320,000 x 20/80			80,000
Materials usage		320,000	350,000	400,000

Materials purchasing budget – units

	Period 1	*Period 2*	*Period 3*
	Kg	Kg	Kg
Materials usage	320,000	350,000	400,000
Less: opening stock	(64,000)	(87,500)	(100,000)
Add: closing stock			
350,000 x 5/20	87,500		
400,000 x 5/20		100,000	
480,000 x 5/20			120,000
	343,500	362,500	420,000

Materials purchasing budget – value

	Period 1	*Period 2*	*Period 3*
	Kg	Kg	Kg
343,500 kg x £2.50	858,750		
362,500 kg x £2.50		906,250	
420,000 kg x (£2.50 x 1.04)			1,092,000

b)

	A	B	C	D	E
1		Period 1	Period 2	Period 3	Period 4
2	Production – units	32,000	35,000	40,000	48,000
3	Usage before loss	=B2*8	=C2*8	=D2*8	=E2*8
4	Total usage	=B3*100/80	=C3*100/80	=D3*100/80	=E3*100/80
5	Opening stock	64,000	=B6	=C6	
6	Closing stock	=C4*5/20	=D4*5/20	=E4*5/20	
7	Purchases – units	=B4–B5+B6	=C4–C5+C6	=D4–D5+D6	
8	Purchases – £	=B7*2.5	=C7*2.5	=D7*2.5*1.04	

8 One unit requires 18 x 100/90 = 20 hours
20 units require 20 x 20 = 400 hours

9 Standard hours 120,000 x 4 = 480,000 hours
Actual hours 480,000 x 100/120 = 400,000 hours

10 Production budget

	Units
Sales	102,000
Less: opening stock	(17,000)
Add: closing stock (115,000 x 10/60)	19,167
Production	104,167

Labour usage budget

	Hours
Standard hours 104,167 x 5.5	572,919
Actual hours 572,919 x 100/95	603,073

11

	Period 1	*Period 2*	*Period 3*	*Period 4*
	£	£	£	£
Sales budget	120,000	136,000	156,000	148,400

Production budget

	Units	Units	Units	Units
Sales	3,000	3,400	3,900	3,500
Less: opening stock	(600)	(680)	(780)	(700)
Add: closing stock				
3,400 x 4/20	680			
3,900 x 4/20		780		
3,500 x 4/20			700	
4,000 x 4/20				800
	3,080	3,500	3,820	3,600
Defective units				
3,080 x 3/97	96			
3,500 x 3/97		109		
3,820 x 3/97			119	
3,600 x 3/97				112
	3,176	3,609	3,939	3,712

Materials usage budget

	Kg	Kg	Kg	Kg
Production x 4kg	12,704	14,436	15,756	14,848
Normal loss (x 10/90)	1,412	1,604	1,751	1,650
Materials usage	14,116	16,040	17,507	16,498

Materials purchasing budget

	Kg	Kg	Kg	Kg
Materials usage	14,116	16,040	17,507	16,498
Less opening stock	(4,200)	(5,614)	(6,127)	(5,774)
Add closing stock				
16,040 x 7/20	5,614			
17,507 x 7/20		6,127		
16,498 x 7/20			5,774	
16,200 x 7/20				5,670
Purchases	15,530	16,553	17,154	16,394

Labour budget – hours

	Hours	Hours	Hours	Hours
Standard hours				
Production x 2	6,352	7,218	7,878	7,424
Idle time (hours x 20/80)	1,588	1,805	1,970	1,856
Total hours	7,940	9,023	9,848	9,280

Labour budget – £

	£	£	£	£
7,940 x £8	63,520			
8,000 x £8		64,000	64,000	64,000
1,023 x £12		12,276		
1,848 x £12			22,176	
1,280 x £12				15,360
	63,520	76,276	86,176	79,360

12 a) i) Production days = 12 x 5 = 60 days

ii) Closing stock of finished goods:

Aye = 1,500 x 5/60 = 125 units
Bee = 2,400 x 5/60 = 200 units

iii) Labour hours available before overtime

= 12 weeks x 35 hours x 70 employees
= 29,400 hours

b) i) Production budget

	Aye Units	*Bee* Units
Sales	1,500	2,400
Less opening stock	(160)	(300)
Add closing stock	125	200
	1,465	2,300
Faulty production		
1,465 x 2/98	30	
2,300 x 2.5/97.5		59
	1,495	2,359

ii) Materials purchases

	Kg
1,495 x 4kg	5,980
2,359 x 7kg	16,513
	22,493
Less opening stock	(2,800)
Add closing stock (22,493 x 6/60)	2,250
	21,943

Materials budget – value £219,430

iii) Labour budget – hours

	Hours
Standard hours	
Aye 1,495 x 10 hours	14,950
Bee 2,359 x 7 hours	16,513
	31,463

Labour budget – value

	£
29,400 hours x £8	235,200
2,063 hours x £12	24,756
	259,956

c) Cost savings

	Opening stock	*Closing stock*	*Reduction*	*Saving* £
Aye	160	125	35 x £6 =	210
Bee	300	200	100 x £7 =	700
Raw materials	2,800	2,250	550 x £2 =	1,100
				2,010

13 a) i) 1) Number of production days in quarter 1 = 12 weeks × 5 days = 60 days

2) Quarter 1 closing finished goods stock:
Exe = 8 days × (930 ÷ 60 per day) = 124 units
Wye = 9 days × (1,320 ÷ 60 per day) = 198 units

3) Quarter 1 labour hours available before overtime

= 12 weeks × 35 hours × 46 employees = 19,320 hours

ii) 1) **Production budget for quarter 1, twelve weeks ending 24 March 2009**

		Exe Units		*Wye* Units
Budgeted sales		930		1,320
Required closing stock (from a))	124		198	
Opening stock	172		257	
Decrease in stock		(48)		(59)
Good production required		882		1,261
Failed product allowance (W) (× 2/98)		18	(× 3/97)	39
Total production required		900		1,300

Working

Good production represents (100 – 2)% of total Exe production.
882 units = 98% of total production
Total production = 882/98 × 100%
Alternatively, allowance = 2/98 of 882 = 2/98 × 882

2) **Material purchases budget for quarter 1, twelve weeks ending 24 March 2009**

		Litres
Material required for production:		
Exe (900 units × 6 litres)		5,400
Wye (1,300 units × 9 litres)		11,700
		17,100
Required closing stock (5 days × (17,100/60) litres per day)	1,425	
Opening stock	(1,878)	
Decrease in stock		(453)
Material purchases required		16,647
Value of material purchases required (× £15)		£249,705

3) **Production labour budget for quarter 1, twelve weeks ending 24 March 2009**

	Hours
Labour hours required for production:	
Exe (900 units × 12 hours)	10,800
Wye (1,300 units × 7 hours)	9,100
Total hours required	19,900
Labour hours available before overtime (from a)i)3))	19,320
Overtime hours required	580

Cost of budgeted labour hours

	£
Basic pay (19,900 hours × £6)	119,400
Overtime premium (580 hours × £1.80)	1,044
Total budgeted labour cost	120,444

iii)

	Opening stock	*Closing stock*	*Stock reduction*	*Storage cost per quarter* £ per unit	*Saving* £
Product Exe	172 units	124 units	48 units	4	192
Product Wye	257 units	198 units	59 units	5	295
Raw material	1,878 litres	1,425 litres	453 litres	1	453
Savings arising from changes in required stock levels					940

b) i)

	Q1 Units	*Q2* Units	*Q3* Units	*Q4* Units
Quarterly sales before seasonal variations (20,000 × 4)	5,000	5,000	5,000	5,000
Seasonal variations	(+20%)1,000	(+30%)1,500	(–10%)(500)	(–40%)(2,000)
Budgeted sales volume of Zed	6,000	6,500	4,500	3,000

ii)

A	B	C	D	E	F
1	Unit selling price	£90			
2	Annual volume	20,000			
3	Seasonal variations	20%	30%	– 10%	– 40%
4		Quarter 1	Quarter 2	Quarter 3	Quarter 4
5	Seasonal variations (units)	= (C2/4) * C3	= (C2/4) * D3	= (C2/4) * E3	=(C2/4) * F3
6	Quarterly volume	= (C2/4)+C5	= (C2/4)+D5	= (C2/4)+E5	= (C2/4)+F5
7	Quarterly turnover	= C6 * C1	= D6 * C1	= E6 * C1	= F6 * C1

c) ***Step 1.* Confirm that material is a limiting factor**

	Litres
Material requirements	
Exe (1,120 × 6)	6,720
Wye (1,480 × 9)	13,320
	20,040
Available supplies	18,870
Shortfall	1,170

***Step 2.* Identify the contribution earned per unit of limiting factor.**

The limiting factor is material and so we need to calculate, for each of the products, the contribution earned per unit for each litre of material used in the product.

	Exe	*Wye*
	£	£
Selling price	360	420
Variable cost	240	258
Unit contribution	120	162
Litres required per unit	6	9
Contribution per litre of material	£20	£18
Priority for production	1	2

Although Wyes have a higher unit contribution than Exes, Wyes require 50% more material that Exes. Because material is in short supply, it is more profitable to make Exes than Wyes.

***Step 3.* Work out the profit-maximising sales and production mix**

Sufficient Exes will be made to meet the full sales demand, and the remaining litres available will then be used to make Wyes.

Product	*Demand* Units	*Litres required*	*Litres available*	*Units produced*
Exe	1,120	6,720 (W1)	6,720	1,120
Wye	1,480	13,320 (W2)	12,150 (W3)	1,350 (W4)
		20,040	18,870	

Workings

1 Demand x 6
2 Demand x 9
3 18,870 – 6,720
4 12,150 litres/ 9 litres per unit

Given the limited availability of material, production in quarter 4 should be 1,120 units of Exe and 1,350 units of Wye.

14 a) i) **Gross production budget**

	Period 1		*Period 2*		*Period 3*		*Period 4*	
	Units		Units		Units		Units	
Sales		19,400		21,340		23,280		22,310
Closing stock (W1)	4,268		4,656		4,462		4,462	
Opening stock	3,880		4,268		4,656		4,462	
Increase/(decrease) in stock		388		388		(194)		–
Good production		19,788		21,728		23,086		22,310
Faulty production (W2)		612		672		714		690
Gross production		20,400		22,400		23,800		23,000

Workings

1 There are 4 x 5 days in each period.

Closing stock = 4 days' sales in the next period = 4/20 of next period's sales
Closing stock in period 1 = 4/20 x 21,340 = 4,268
Closing stock in period 2 = 4/20 x 23,280= 4,656
Closing stock in period 3 = 4/20 x 22,310 = 4,462
Closing stock in period 4 = 4/20 x 22,310 = 4,462

2 3% of gross production is scrapped. Good production therefore represents 97% (or 97/100) of gross production. Faulty production is 3% (or 3/100) of gross production and hence 3/97 of good production.

Faulty production is 3/97 x good production.

ii) **Material purchases budget**

	Period 1		Period 2		Period 3	
	Litres		Litres		Litres	
Material used in production (W1)		61,200		67,200		71,400
Closing stock (W2)	16,800		17,850		17,250	
Opening stock	16,500		16,800		17,850	
Increase/(decrease) in stock		300		1,050		(600)
Purchases		61,500		68,250		70,800

Workings

1 Each Gamma requires three litres of material.

Material used in production = 3 × gross production (from a)i))
Material used in production, period 1 = 3 × 20,400 = 61,200
Material used in production, period 2 = 3 × 22,400 = 67,200
Material used in production, period 3 = 3 × 23,800 = 71,400

2
- As we have already worked out, there are 20 days in each period.
- Closing stock must equal five days' gross production in the next period.
- Each Gamma requires three litres of material.
- Closing stock in period 1 = 5/20 × 22,400 (from a)i)) × 3 = 16,800
  Closing stock in period 2 = 5/20 × 23,800 × 3 = 17,850
  Closing stock in period 3 = 5/20 × 23,000 × 3 = 17,250

iii) **Cost of material purchases**

	Period 1	Period 2	Period 3
Material to be purchased (from a)ii))	61,500 litres	68 250 litres	70,800 litres
Cost per litre	× £8	× £8	× £8
Cost of material purchases	£492,000	£546 000	£566,400

iv) **Labour budget**

	Period 1	Period 2	Period 3
Gross production (units) (from a)i))	20,400	22 400	23,800
Labour hrs required per unit	× 0.5	× 0.5	× 0.5
Labour hrs required	10,200	11,200	11,900
Basic labour hrs available *	11,200	11,200	11,200
Surplus hrs/(overtime hrs)	1,000	–	(700)

* 70 workers × 40 hrs per wk × 4 wks = 11,200

v) **Cost of labour budget**

	Period 1	*Period 2*	*Period 3*
	£	£	£
Labour cost per period (guaranteed) *	67,200	67,200	67,200
Cost of overtime (700 × £9)	–	–	6,300
Cost of labour	67,200	67,200	73,500

* 70 workers x £240 x 4 wks

b) **MEMO**

To: Production director
From: Management accountant
Date: xx.xx.xx
Subject: **Budget 2009 – overtime and faulty production**

I have investigated the points you raised about the budget for 2009 and have set out my findings below.

i) **The value of possible overtime savings**

In period 3, 700 hours of overtime are needed to produce the required number of units. There are 1,000 surplus labour hours available in period 1, however. If an extra 1,400 units (700 hrs ÷ 0.5 hrs) were produced in period 1, using 700 of the surplus hours available, the need for overtime in period 3 would be removed and £6,300 (£9 overtime rate x 700 hrs) saved.

ii) **Extra costs to achieve overtime savings**

The extra 1,400 units produced in period 1 are not needed until period 3 and so would need to be stored until then. This would incur additional storage costs.

The cost of the raw materials for the extra units produced in period 1 will not be covered by the sales revenue from the units until period 3 at the earliest. Additional financing may therefore be required to purchase this raw material, with the result that the company incurs financing costs.

iii) **Advantages of using sampling to determine reasons for faulty production**

Instead of checking every Gamma produced to see whether or not it is faulty, a sample of Gammas can be inspected. This has a number of advantages.

1) It is likely to be cheaper to inspect a sample of Gammas rather than all those produced.

2) Inspection of all production would be extremely time-consuming and would slow down the time between the start of production and the transfer to finished goods.

3) Inspection may sometimes require destruction of the item in question. For example, testing fireworks involves setting them off.

Note. You are required to provide only two advantages.

iv) **Differences between various methods of sampling**

1) **Random sampling** involves selecting a sample (of Gammas in this instance) in such a way that every item in the population (ie all Gammas produced) has an equal chance of being included. Random samples are drawn up by listing all items in the population (sampling frame), numbering them and then selecting items using random number tables or random numbers generated by computer.

2) **Systematic sampling** can provide a good approximation to random sampling. It works by selecting every nth item after a random start. For example, if it was decided to select a sample of 20 from a population of 800, then every 40th (800 ÷ 20) item after a random start in the first 40 should be selected. If (say) 23 was chosen, the sample would include the 23rd, 63rd, 103rd, 143rd, ..., 783rd items.

3) **Stratified sampling** can often be the best method of choosing a sample (although it must be possible to divide the population into strata or categories for stratified sampling to be applied).

   Suppose we wanted to know whether the area of a particular country in which students live has any bearing on their success in the AAT exams. If we took a random sample of all AAT students in the country, it is conceivable that the entire sample might consist of AAT students living in one particular region. Stratified sampling removes this possibility.

   If the country's population of AAT students is divided into categories depending on where they live, random samples of students can be taken from each area of the country, the number in each sample being proportional to the total number of students in each category. So if there are 50,000 AAT students in the country in total, and 5,000 live in the north-west area, 10% of the sample should be chosen (randomly) from those living in the north-west.

v) **The form of sampling appropriate for our company**

Given that the faulty Gammas are thought to be caused by poor work practices of some of the production workers, those production workers need to be identified. It is therefore important to sample the work of every employee. By dividing the population of Gammas into categories based on the production worker who manufactured them, and applying **stratified sampling**, work of every employee would be inspected.

15 a) i) Production = sales + closing stock – opening stock.

Production budget for Antelopes for the four weeks ending 26 July 2008

		Units
Sales		141,120
Closing stock (W1)	42,336	
Opening stock	(30,576)	
Increase in stock		11,760
Good production required		152,880
Faulty production (W2)		3,120
Gross production		156,000

Workings

1 Demand in period 9 = 141,120 × 150% = 211,680
Number of days in period 9 = 4 × 5 = 20
Closing stock in period 8 = 4 days' sales in period 9
= 4/20 × 211,680 = 42,336

2 Faulty production = 2% (or 2/100) of gross production
100/2 × faulty production = gross production (1)

98% of gross production is good
good production = 98% (or 98/100) of gross production
100/98 × good production = gross production (2)

Equating (1) and (2):

100/2 × faulty production = 100/98 × good production
Faulty production = 2/98 × good production
= 2/98 × 152,880 = 3,120

Production budget for Bears for the four weeks ending 26 July 2008

		Units
Sales		95,000
Closing stock (W1)	30,875	
Opening stock	((25,175)	
Increase in stock		5,700
Good production required		100,700
Faulty production (W2)		5,300
Gross production		106,000

Workings

1) Demand in period 9 = 95,000 × 130% = 123,500
Closing stock in period 8 = 5 days' sales in period 9
= 5/20 × 123,500 = 30,875

2) Faulty production = 5/95 × good production
= 5/95 × 100,700 = 5,300

ii) Material purchases = materials used in production + closing stock – opening stock

Material purchases budget for the four weeks ending 26 July 2008

		Kgs
Materials used in production		
Antelopes: 156,000 (from a)i)) × 0.75 kgs		117,000
Bears: 106,000 (from a)i)) × 0.50 kgs		53,000
		170,000
Closing stock	40,000	
Opening stock	30,000	
Increase in stock		10,000
Material purchases		180,000

iii) **Cost of material purchases budget for the four weeks ending 26 July 2008**

= 180,000 kgs × £8
= £1,440,000

iv) **Labour budget in hours for the four weeks ending 25 July 2008**

	Hrs
Hours for Antelope production: 156,000 × 0.1 hrs	15,600
Hours for Bear production: 106,000 × 0.05 hrs	5,300
	20,900

v) **Cost of labour budget for the four weeks ending 26 July 2008**

= 140 employees × 4 weeks × guaranteed weekly wage of £228 = £127,680

b) i) **Labour**

Number of available labour hours in period 8 = 140 employees × 4 weeks × 38 hours = 21,280

Budgeted labour hours required in period 8 (from task a)iv)) = 20,900

Spare labour hours in period 8 = 21,280 – 20,900 = 380

In 380 hours, an extra 380/0.1 = 3,800 Antelopes could be produced.

Powdered rock

3,000 extra kgs of powdered rock could be purchased in period 8.

3,000/0.75 = 4,000 Antelopes could be made from this extra material.

Limiting factor

Extra production is therefore limited by the availability of labour to 3,800 Antelopes.

2% of production is faulty, however.

3,800 × 98% = 3,724 fault-free Antelopes could be produced.

ii) **Revised material purchases budget for the four weeks ending 26 July 2008**

	Kgs
Original budgeted material purchases (from task a)iii))	180,000
Additional materia purchases required for 3,800 Antelopes (3,800 × 0.75 kgs)	2,850
	182,850

16 a) i) **Production budget**

	Quarter 1		*Quarter 2*		*Quarter 3*		*Quarter 4*	
		Tins		Tins		Tins		Tins
Sales volume		2,910		3,395		3,880		4,365
Closing stocks (W1)	679		776		873		87	
Opening stocks (W2)	(582)		(679)		(776)		(87	
Increase in stock		97		97		97		–
Good production		3,007		3,492		3,977		4,365
Faulty production (W3)		93		108		123		135
Gross production		3,100		3,600		4,100		4,500

Workings

1 Closing stocks in each quarter must equal 12 days' sales volume of the nex quarter. There are 5 x 12 = 60 working days in each quarter. So closing stocks = 12/60 × next quarter's sales volume. With sales volume being the same as quarte 4 in quarter 5, closing stocks in quarter 4 will be the same as closing stocks ir quarter 3.

Sample work ng: closing stocks in quarter 1 = 12/60 x 3,395 = 679

2 Opening stocks of one quarter are the same as closing stocks of the previou quarter.

3 3% of finished production is faulty. Good production therefore represents 97% (o 97/100) of gross production. Faulty production is 3% (or 3/100) of gross productio and hence 3/97 of good production.

Therefore faulty production is 3/97 x good production.

Sample work ng: faulty production in quarter 1 = 3/97 x 3,007 = 93

ii) **Material purchases budget**

	Quarter 1		Quarter 2		Quarter 3		Quarter 4	
Gross production	3,100 tins		3,600 tins		4,100 tins		4,500 tins	
		Kg		Kg		Kg		Kg
Material used in production (W1)		21,700		25,200		28,700		31,500
Closing stock (W2)	2,520		2,870		3,150		3,150	
Opening stocks (W3)	(2,170)		(2,520)		(2,870)		(3,150)	
Increase in stocks		350		350		280		0
Purchases (kilograms)		22,050		25,550		28,980		31,500

Workings

1 Each tin requires 7 kgs of material and so material used in production = 7 x gross production (from (i))

2 Closing stocks in each quarter must equal six days' gross production and we already know there are 60 working days in each quarter. Therefore closing stocks = 6/60 × next quarter's material requirements.

Sample calculation: closing stocks in period 1 = 6/60 x material requirements in period 2 = 6/60 x 25,200 = 2,520

3 Opening stocks of one quarter are the same as closing stocks of the previous quarter.

iii) **Cost of material purchases budget**

	Quarter 1	Quarter 2	Quarter 3	Quarter 4
Material to be purchased (from ii))	22,050 kgs	25,550 kgs	28,980 kgs	31,500 kgs
Cost per kg	× £12	× £12	× £12	× £12
Cost of material purchases	£264,600	£306,600	£347,760	£378,000

iv) **Labour budget**

	Quarter 1	Quarter 2	Quarter 3	Quarter 4
Gross production units (from i))	3,100	3,600	4,100	4,500
Labour hours required per unit	× 3	× 3	× 3	× 3
Labour hours required	9,300	10,800	12,300	13,500
Guaranteed hours (W)	12,180	12,180	12,180	12,180
Surplus hours/ (overtime hours)	2,880	1,380	(120)	(1,320)

Working

Guaranteed hours = 35 hours × 12 weeks × 29 workers

v) **Cost of labour budget**

	Quarter 1	*Quarter 2*	*Quarter 3*	*Quarter 4*
	£	£	£	£
Guaranteed wages per period (W1)	97,440	97,440	97,440	97,440
Overtime (W2)			1,320	14,520
	97,440	97,440	98,760	111,960

Workings

1 Guaranteed wages = £280 x 12 weeks x 29 workers = £97,440
2 Overtime = overtime hours x £11.00 per overtime hour.

b) **MEMO**

To: Jemma Hughes
From: Accounting technician
Date: xx.xx.xx
Subject: **Cost savings and forecasting**

Following our discussions, I have looked into the points you raised and set out my findings below.

i) **Revised budget of labour hours to reduce overtime**

By rescheduling overtime as shown in the budget below, the total overtime hours can be reduced, with production being carried out within guaranteed hours in quarters 1 and 2, when there are surplus hours.

	Quarter 1	*Quarter 2*	*Quarter 3*	*Quarter 4*
Surplus hours/ (overtime hours)	2,880	1,380	(120)	(1,320)
Original hours worked (from a) iv))	9,300	10,800	12,300	13,500
Reschedule quarter 3's overtime		120	(120)	
Reschedule quarter 4's overtime	60	1,260		(1,320)
Revised labour hours	9,360	12,180	12,180	12,180

ii) **Revised production budget**

A revised production budget which takes account of the rescheduling in a) is shown below.

	Quarter 1	*Quarter 2*	*Quarter 3*	*Quarter 4*
Revised labour hours (from i))	9,360	12,180	12,180	12,180
Revised production budget (tins) (W)	3,120	4,060	4,060	4,060

Working

Each tin requires three labour hours and so the revised production budget = revised labour hours ÷ three labour hours per tin.

iii) **Forecast trend**

Using the regression line y = 1,000 + 100x established by the sales director, the trend for quarters 1 to 4 can be established (with x in quarter 1 = 25).

Quarter 1: $1{,}000 + (100 \times 25) = 3{,}500$ tins
Quarter 2: $1{,}000 + (100 \times 26) = 3{,}600$ tins
Quarter 3: $1{,}000 + (100 \times 27) = 3{,}700$ tins
Quarter 4: $1{,}000 + (100 \times 28) = 3{,}800$ tins

iv) **Forecast sales volume**

The forecast sales volume is established by adjusting the trend values set out in (iii) above by the seasonal variations calculated by the sales director.

Quarter 1: $3{,}500 - 500 = 3{,}000$ tins
Quarter 2: $3{,}600 - 300 = 3{,}300$ tins
Quarter 3: $3{,}700 + 300 = 4{,}000$ tins
Quarter 4: $3{,}800 + 500 = 4{,}300$ tins

v) **Reasons why linear regression might give inaccurate estimates of demand**

There are several reasons why linear regression might give inaccurate estimates of the demand for tins of A120. (You were required to provide only three reasons.)

- The level of demand for A120 may not be dependent on time but instead might be influenced by one or more other factors (such as economic factors and changes in taste and fashion).
- The relationship between sales of A120 and time might not be linear but instead might follow a curvilinear pattern
- There is no guarantee that what has happened in the past will provide a reliable guide to the future. For example, a new competitor entering the market could have a significant impact on levels of demand for Dobra's products.
- The amount of data used to determine the regression equation (24 observations) may be too small to provide accurate enough estimates.

answers to chapter 12: RECONCILING BUDGETS AND ACTUAL FIGURES

1 A fixed budget is a budget that is set in advance of a period and its purpose is to provide a single achievable target for the entire organisation to work to. This target level of activity means that all areas of the business will be coordinated towards achieving this goal. The purpose of the fixed budget is to aid in the planning processes of the business. The budget will set out the resources that are required in order to achieve that target.

A flexed budget is a budget that is prepared once the actual results are known. The flexed budget is prepared at the actual activity level that was achieved in the period in order to show what the standard costs should have been at that activity level. When these costs are then compared to the actual costs meaningful variances can be calculated. The comparison of the flexed budget to the actual figures is therefore part of the control process.

2 £15,000 is the cost of 3 supervisors therefore each one costs £5,000 per period.

At a production level of 330,000 units four production supervisors will be required costing £20,000 for the period.

3

	112,000 units
	£
Materials (112,000 x £2.40) (W)	268,800
Labour (112,000 x £1 + 24,000) (W)	136,000
Production overhead (fixed)	38,000

Working

Materials	100,000 units	£2.40 per unit
	120,000 units	£2.40 per unit

Therefore a variable cost – £2.40 per unit

Labour	100,000 units	£1.24 per unit
	120,000 units	£1.20 per unit

Therefore a semi-variable cost

Variable element = £20,000/20,000 units
= £1 per unit

	£
At 100,000 units:	
Variable cost	100,000
Fixed cost (bal fig)	24,000
Total cost	124,000

4 Production overhead (72,000 x £7 + £104,000) (W) = £608,000

Working

$$\text{Variable element of cost} = \frac{£664{,}000 - 524{,}000}{20{,}000\text{ units}}$$

$$= £7 \text{ per unit}$$

	£
At 60,000 units:	
Variable element 60,000 x £7	420,000
Fixed element (bal fig)	104,000
Total cost	524,000

5

	Quarter 4 budget
	£
Sales (15,000 units)	97,500
Material	(41,250)
Labour (8 x £3,500)	(28,000)
Production overhead	(18,000)
Gross profit	10,250
General expenses (6,400 + 15,000 x £0.28)	10,600
Operating loss	(350)

6 i)

	Budget *28,000 units*	*Actual* *31,500 units*	*Variances*
	£	£	£
Sales	406,000	441,000	35,000 (F)
Materials	165,200	180,400	15,200 (A)
Labour	100,800	115,600	14,800 (A)
Production overhead	37,500	39,000	1,500 (A)
Gross profit	102,500	106,000	3,500 (F)
General expenses	55,600	68,900	13,300 (A)
Operating profit	46,900	37,100	9,800 (A)

ii)

	Flexed Budget 31,500 units	Actual 31,500 units	Variances
	£	£	£
Sales	456,750	441,000	15,750 (A)
Materials	185,850	180,400	5,450 (F)
Labour	113,400	115,600	2,200 (A)
Production overhead	37,500	39,000	1,500 (A)
Gross profit	120,000	106,000	14,000 (A)
General expenses (W)	60,850	68,900	8,050 (A)
Operating profit	59,150	37,100	22,050 (A)

Working

General expenses:

At 28,000 units – Variable element = £55,600 – 13,600/28,000
= £1.50 per unit

At 31,500 units:	£
Variable element 31,500 x £1.50	47,250
Fixed element	13,600
Total cost	60,850

iii) The variances calculated when using the original fixed budget show favourable sales and gross profit variances and fairly large adverse cost variances culminating in an adverse net profit variance.

When the actual results are compared to the flexed budget the variances are different.

There is an adverse sales variance and an adverse gross profit variance. The materials now show a favourable variance and the other variances are not so large. The final net profit variance however is much larger than the variance when compared to the fixed budget.

7

	Flexed budget 230,000 units		Actual 230,000 units		Variances
	£	£	£	£	£
Sales		1,564,000		1,532,000	32,000 (A)
Materials	793,500		783,200		10,300 (F)
Labour	433,500		428,600		4,900 (F)
Production expenses	180,000		173,500		6,500 (F)
Production cost		1,407,000		1,385,300	
Gross profit		157,000		146,700	10,300 (A)
General expenses		72,000		74,700	2,700 (A)
Operating profit		85,000		72,000	13,000 (A)

Working

Labour – semi-variable cost

Variable element $= \dfrac{£449,000-387,000}{40,000}$

$= £1.55$

Fixed element = £387,000 – (200,000 x 1.55)

= £77,000

At 230,000 = £77,000 + (230,000 x 1.55)

= £433,500

Production expenses – semi-variable cost

Variable element $= \dfrac{£186,000-162,000}{40,000}$

= £0.60 per unit

Fixed element = £162,000 – (200,000 x 0.60)

= £42,000

At 230,000 = £42,000 + (230,000 x 0.60)

= £180,000

8 i) **Quarter 2 budget**

	£	£
Sales 50,000 units		400,000
Materials	165,400	
Labour	69,800	
Cost of production 56,000 units	235,200	
Less: closing stock	25,200	
Cost of sales		210,000
Gross profit		190,000
Production overhead		56,000
General expenses		52,000
Operating profit		82,000

ii)

	£
Profit per absorption costing budget	88,000
Less: production overhead included in closing stock (6,000 x £1)	(6,000)
Profit per marginal costing budget	82,000

9 Budgeted level of activity $= \dfrac{£3{,}034{,}000}{£16.40}$

$= 185{,}000$ units

10 Budgeted level of activity $= \dfrac{£331{,}200}{£1.20}$

$= 276{,}000$ units

11 Overhead absorption rate $= \dfrac{£84{,}000}{24{,}000 \text{ units}}$

$= £3.50$ per unit

Overhead absorbed $= £93{,}600 - £3{,}650$

$= £89{,}950$

Actual activity level $= \dfrac{£89{,}950}{£3.50}$

$= 25{,}700$ units

12 Overhead absorption rate $= \dfrac{£483{,}000}{70{,}000 \text{ units}}$

$= £6.90$ per unit

Overhead absorbed $= £490{,}000 + £15{,}080$

$= £505{,}080$

Actual activity level $= \dfrac{£505{,}080}{£6.90}$

$= 73{,}200$ units

13 i) A responsibility centre is an area of a business for which costs or revenues are gathered and compared to budgets for control purposes. Responsibility centres are known as such due to the fact that each of these areas of the business has a manager that is responsible for the activities of that area.

ii) Responsibility accounting is a method of budgeting and comparing actual costs to budgets for each of the responsibility centres with the manager of that responsibility centre being answerable for variances that are under his control.

iii) An expense centre is an area of the business for which costs can be ascertained. This may be the entire factory or a smaller area such as a single machine.

iv) A profit centre is an area of the business for which both revenues and costs can be ascertained and therefore a profit or loss for a period can be determined. Often profit centres are larger areas of the business such as an entire division or geographical sales area.

14 The importance of identifying controllable variances is in the area of motivation or de-motivation of management. If variances are reported as part of the responsibility of a manager over which he has no control then this will have a de-motivational effect. If a manager is constantly held responsible for an adverse variance in a cost, the level of which he cannot influence, then this will not have a positive effect on the performance of this manager.

Investigating the causes of variances and determining any interdependence between the variances is an important aspect of management control as in a system of responsibility accounting the managers responsible for various elements of the business will be held accountable for the relevant variances. However they should only be held accountable for variances that are within their control.

There may be variances caused by factors which are beyond the manager's control such as an increase in rent or business rates. There may also be variances in a manager's responsibility centre which have not been caused by his actions but by those of another responsibility centre manager.

An example is a favourable material price variance caused by purchasing a lower grade of material which leads directly to an adverse materials usage variance as the lower grade of material means that there is greater wastage. The initial reaction might be to give credit to the purchasing manager for the favourable variance and to lay blame for the adverse usage variance on the production manager. However the true picture is that, in the absence of any further reasons for the variance then the responsibility for both variances lies with the purchasing manager.

15 The process of continual comparison of actual results to budgeted results is known as feedback.

The budget period is normally for the forthcoming year; however, the feedback process should take place on a much more frequent basis .The calculation and reporting of variances should take place on a regular basis and will be daily, weekly or monthly depending upon the organisation. Any resulting action that must be taken in order to eliminate variances or improve efficiency should then be taken as soon as possible.

The information that is being received about the current performance of the business in terms of the current actual results can then also be used to influence the budget for future periods. This system of using information about the current performance for budgeting for the future is known as feedforward.

16 a) i) Budgeted unit selling price $= \dfrac{£660{,}000}{30{,}000}$

$= £22$ per unit

ii) Budgeted unit material cost $= \dfrac{£252{,}000}{30{,}000}$

$= £8.40$ per unit

iii) Marginal element of factory power $= £83{,}600 - £20{,}600$

$= £63{,}000$

Budgeted marginal cost per unit $= \dfrac{£63{,}000}{30{,}000}$

$= £2.10$ per unit

iv) Actual marginal cost $= £88{,}600 - £20{,}600$

$= £68{,}000$

Actual marginal cost per unit $= \dfrac{£68{,}000}{34{,}000}$

$= £2.00$ per unit

b)

	Flexed budget		*Actual*		*Variance*
Units	*34,000*		*34,000*		
	£	£	£	£	£
Sales (34,000 x £22)		748,000		697,000	51,000 (A)
Direct costs					
Materials (34,000 x £8.40)	285,600		299,200		13,600 (A)
Factory power					
(34,000 x £2.10)	71,400		68,000		3,400 (F)
		357,000		367,200	
Contribution		391,000		329,800	
Labour	180,000		192,600		12,600 (A)
Factory power	20,600		20,600		–
Fixed overheads	75,000		79,000		4,000 (A)
Fixed costs		275,600		292,200	
Operating profit		115,400		37,600	77,800 (A)

c) The original budget was a fixed budget based upon the budgeted sales and production of 30,000 units. The flexed budget is based upon sales of 34,000 units therefore the anticipated increases in sales revenue and variable costs is built into this budget.

The original fixed budget and actual results were based on absorption costing whereas the flexed budget is based upon marginal costing. Under absorption costing the fixed production overheads are included in the closing stock valuation and therefore carried forward to be charged in the next accounting period. Under marginal costing all of the fixed overheads are charged in the current period. As the stock levels are rising, under absorption costing more costs are being carried forward to the next period resulting in a higher budgeted profit figure than under marginal costing.

d) One reason for the flexed budget being a better measure of management performance is that when comparing the budget to the actual results it is comparing like with like. As the activity level has increased above the original budgeted level the flexed budget reflects the related expected increases in variable costs and revenues.

Furthermore, the flexed budget has been produced under marginal costing principles whereas the original budget was prepared under absorption costing principles; under the latter profits can be boosted by increasing stock levels, as we have here, as more costs can be deducted from this period's figures to be charged in the next period's figures.

17 a) i) **Calculation of fixed costs and variable unit costs**

	Original budget	*Revised budget*	*Difference*		*Variable cost per unit*
Production and sales units	24,000	20,000	4,000		
	£	£	£		£
Variable costs					
Material	216,000	180,000	36,000	(÷ 4,000)	9
Labour	288,000	240,000	8,000	(÷ 4,000)	12
Semi-variable costs					
Heat, light and power	31,000	27,000	4,000	(÷ 4,000)	1

The fixed element of heat, light and power costs can now be determined using figures from the original budget.

	£
Total costs	31,000
Variable cost (24,000 units x £1)	24,000
Therefore fixed costs of heat, light and power	7,000

ii) **Flexible budget comparison for the year ended 31 May 2008**

		Flexible budget		*Actual results*	*Variance*
Fasta production and sales units		22,000		22,000	
		£		£	£
Variable costs					
Material	22,000 × £9	198,000	(£206,800 + £7,520)	214,320	16,320 (A)
Labour	22,000 × £12	264,000		255,200	8,800 (F)
Semi-variable costs					
Heat, light and power:					
variable 22,000 × £1		22,000			
fixed		7,000			
		29,000	(£33,400 – £7,520)	25,880	3,120 (F)
Fixed costs					
Rents, rates and depreciation		40,000		38,000	2,000 (F)
		531,000		533,400	2,400 (A)

Note: (A) denotes an adverse variance. (F) denotes a favourable variance.

b) **MEMO**

To: Steven Jones, managing director
From: Management accountant
Date: xx.xx.xx
Subject: **Flexible budget statement for the year ended 31 May 2008**

This memorandum deals with your queries regarding the latest flexible budget statement.

i) **Why the flexible budgeting variances differ from those in the original statement**

The variances in the original statement were derived from a comparison of the budgeted costs for 20,000 units with the actual costs for 22,000 units. Since variable costs increase when output increases, the actual costs are almost certain to be higher than the budget costs, with consequent adverse variances.

The flexible budget statement compares like with like, by determining the budgeted costs for the actual volume of 22,000 units and comparing these with the actual results.

The resulting mixture of adverse and favourable variances is much more realistic. Your assertion that the large reduction in adverse variances is due to the introduction of participative budgeting is not necessarily true.

ii) **Two reasons why a favourable cost variance may have arisen**

1) **Managers may have included unrealistically high costs in the original budget.** This is a problem which can arise with participative budgeting; managers include extra cost allowances to ensure that they achieve their budgets. The submitted budgets therefore need careful checking, although this may be difficult because the managers themselves are the ones with the technical expertise.

2) **Costs may have been lower than the level expected when the original budget was determined**. For example, an expected rise in rent or rates costs may not have occurred. Such savings are not necessarily the result of management control action.

iii) **Two reasons why higher sales volume may not be the result of improved motivation**

1) The **market** for Fastas may have **expanded** and Rivermede could have reaped the benefit of a general increase in the demand for this product. This general market increase is not necessarily the result of improved motivation of sales staff.

2) The sales staff may have **submitted an unrealistically low sales target** for the budget, to ensure that they achieve the target. Thus the fact that the sales volume is higher than budget may be a result of participative budgeting, but it may be due to manipulation of the system rather than improved motivation.

18 a) i) 1) Budgeted selling price = £960,000 turnover ÷ 20,000 units = £48 per unit

2) Budgeted material cost = £240,000 material cost ÷ 20,000 units
= £12 per unit

3) Total budgeted marginal cost of light, heat and power

= £68,000 – fixed cost £20,000 = £48,000

Budgeted marginal cost of light, heat and power per unit

= £48,000 ÷ 20,000 = £2.40 per unit

4) Actual marginal cost of light, heat and power

= £74,500 production cost – fixed costs £12,000
= £62,500

Actual marginal cost of light, heat and power per unit

= £62,500 ÷ 25,000 units produced = £2.50 per unit

ii) **HFD Processes Ltd**
Flexible budget statement for year ended 30 November 2008

	Flexible budget		*Actual results*		*Variance*
Sales units	22,000 units		22,000 units		
	£	£	£	£	£
Turnover					
(22,000 × £48 (from a)i)1))		1,056,000		1,012,000	44,000 (A)
Variable costs					
Material (22,000 × £12)	264,000		261,800		2,200 (F)
Light, heat and power					
(22,000 × £2.40)	52,800		55,000*		2,200 (A)
		316,800		316,800	
Contribution		739,200		695,200	
Fixed costs					
Production labour	260,000		273,000		13,000 (A)
Light, heat and power	20,000		12,000		8,000 (F)
Fixed overheads	400,000		430,000		30,000 (A)
		680,000		715,000	
Operating profit/(loss)		59,200		(19,800)	79,000 (A)

Note: (A) denotes an adverse variance; (F) denotes a favourable variance.

*Variable cost of light, heat and power = £2.50 (from (a)) ÷ 22,000 = £55,000

b) **MEMO**

To: Chief executive of HFD plc
From: Management accountant
Date: xx.xx.xx
Subject: **Flexible budget statement for year ended 30 November 2008**

This memorandum addresses your concerns regarding the results shown in the flexible budget statement.

i) **Why the flexible budget operating statement shows different results from the original operating results**

1) The flexible budget is prepared on a marginal cost basis whereas the original budget and actual results were prepared on an absorption cost basis. Since production was higher than sales, some fixed overhead was carried forward in stock with absorption costing. With marginal costing, however, all of the fixed overheads are charged as period costs against the sales for the period, resulting in a lower reported profit figure.

2) The flexible budget is a realistic target for costs and revenues for the actual activity level of 22,000 units sold. The 2,000 units sold in excess of the original budgeted amount would be expected to increase both revenue and variable costs. The flexible budget makes allowances for these increases caused by the change in volume.

ii) **Why the flexible budget operating statement might be a better measure of management performance**

The flexible budget statement compares like with like. When the activity level changes, the expected revenue and variable costs also change. It is therefore logical to alter the budget to allow for these changes. The resulting variances will provide a better measure for management performance.

Furthermore the profit shown in the original statement, which was prepared on an absorption costing basis, can be distorted by increases or decreases in stock, as fixed overheads are carried forward in, or 'released from', stock. The use of marginal costing, however, avoids such profit distortions.

19 a) i) 1) **Budgeted selling price per Omega**

Turnover ÷ sales volume = selling price
£1,440,000 ÷ 36,000 = selling price
£40 = selling price

2) **Budgeted material cost per Omega**

Material is a variable cost and so total material cost ÷ sales volume * = material cost per unit

£432,000 ÷ 36,000 = material cost per unit
£12 = material cost per unit

* Production equals sales and so material cost of production is the same as material cost of sales.

3) **Budgeted labour cost per Omega**

Labour is a variable cost and so total material cost ÷ sales volume = labour cost per unit

£216,000 ÷ 36,000 = labour cost per unit
£6 = labour cost per unit

4) **Budgeted variable cost of light, heat and power per Omega**

	£
Total budgeted cost	92,000
Fixed element	20,000
Variable element	72,000

Variable cost per unit = £72,000/36,000 = £2

5) **% of cost of production carried forward in closing stock**

Cost of production = £1,318,000

Closing stock = £164,750

Closing stock as a % of the cost of production = (164,750/1,318,000) x 100% = 12.5%

6) Material cost of sales = 87.5% x £500,000
= 87.5/100 x £500,000
= £437,500

Labour cost of sales = 87.5% x £232,000
= 87.5/100 x £232,000
= £203,000

Variable production cost of light, heat and power = £(96,000 – 12,000)
= £84,000

Variable cost of sales of light, heat and power = 87.5% x £84,000
= 87.5/100 x £84,000
= £73,500

Actual variable cost of sales

	£'000
Material	437.5
Labour	203.0
Light, heat and power	73.5
	714.0

7) **Total actual fixed costs**

	£'000
Light, heat and power	12.0
Depreciation	70.0
Other fixed overheads	420.0
	502.0

ii) **Hall Ltd – Flexible budget statement for year ended 30 November 2008**

	Original budget	*Flexed budget*		*Actual results*		*Variances*	
Sales volume (units)	36,000	35,000		35,000		–	
	£	£		£		£	
Turnover	1,440,000	1,400,000	(W1)	1,365,000		35,000	(A)
Variable costs							
Material	432,000	420,000	(W2)	437,500	(from vi))	17,500	(A)
Labour	216,000	210,000	(W3)	203,000	(from vi))	7,000	(F)
Light, heat, power	72,000	70,000	(W4)	73,500	(from vi))	3,500	(A)
	720,000	700,000		714,000		14,000	(A)
Contribution	720,000	700,000		651,000		49,000	(A)
Fixed costs							
Light, heat, power	20,000	20,000		12,000		8,000	(F)
Depreciation	100,000	100,000		70,000		30,000	(F)
Other fixed o'ds	400,000	400,000		420,000		20,000	(A)
	520,000	520,000		502,000		18,000	(F)
Profit	200,000	180,000		149,000		31,000	(A)

Workings

1 35,000 × £40 = £1,400,000
2 35,000 × £12 = £420,000
3 35,000 × £6 = £210,000
4 35,000 × £2 = £70,000

b) **Memo**

To: Harry Easton, Chief executive
From: Assistant management accountant
Date: xx.xx.xx
Subject: **Hall Ltd – Flexible budget statement for year ended 30 November 2008**

This memorandum addresses your concerns regarding the results shown in the flexible budget.

i) 1) **Why there is a difference between the original budget and the flexible budget**

The original budget was for planning purposes and was based on sales and production volumes of 36,000 units. It provided a target at which management should have aimed. The flexible budget is based on sales and production volumes of 35,000 units. It is for control purposes and shows what costs and revenues should have been given actual sales and production volumes. The revenue and variable costs in the flexible budget will therefore be less than those in the original budget given the different volumes, although the fixed costs are the same.

2) **Why there is a difference between the original actual operating profit and the flexible budget actual operating profit**

The original actual results were prepared using absorption costing, which involves matching all costs (including fixed costs) against revenue. Units in closing stock are therefore valued at full cost so that all costs including fixed costs can be matched against the revenue from the units when they are eventually sold in a later period. So not all fixed costs are charged in the period. Marginal costing, on the other hand, which was used to prepare the flexible budget, requires that all fixed costs are written off in the period in which they are incurred.

ii) **Why the actual operating profit was greater than the budgeted operating profit, despite a lower sales volume**

1) Because the actual level of production was greater than the actual level of sales, the use of absorption costing means that some of the fixed overhead is carried forward in the closing stock valuation to be charged against next year's profit.

2) The actual contribution per unit was higher than the budgeted contribution per unit, and actual fixed costs were lower than budgeted fixed costs.

20 a) i) **Budgeted selling price per CD player** = turnover/sales volume (£3,200,000/80,000 or £4,000,000/100,000) £40.00

ii) **Budgeted bought-in material cost per CD player** = bought-in materials/production volume (£1,600,000/80,000 or £2,000,000/100,000) £20.00

iii) **Labour unit variable cost**

Using the incremental approach:

	Volume		*Cost*
	100,000		£760,000
	80,000		£640,000
Incremental volume of	20,000	has an incremental cost of	£120,000

Therefore variable cost per unit = £120,000/20,000 = £6 per unit

iv) **Budgeted total labour fixed cost**

	£
Total cost	760,000
Total variable cost (£6 × 100,000)	600,000
Fixed cost	160,000

An identical answer is possible by using the total cost for 80,000 CD players and deducting the total variable cost based on 80,000 CD players.

v) **Budgeted variable cost of light, heat and power**

Using the incremental approach:

	Volume		*Cost*
	100,000		£450,000
	80,000		£370,000
Incremental volume of	20,000	has an incremental cost of	£80,000

Therefore variable cost per unit = £80,000/20,000 = £4 per unit

vi) **Budgeted total light, heat and power fixed cost**

	£
Total cost	450,000
Total variable cost (£4 x 100,000)	400,000
Fixed cost	50,000

An identical answer is possible by using the total cost for 80,000 CD players and deducting the total variable cost based on 80,000 CD players.

b) **Flexible budget statement for the year ended 31 May 2008**

	Flexible budget	*Actual results*	*Variances*
Production and sales volume (CD players)	140,000	140,000	
	£'000	£'000	£'000
Conversion costs			
Labour (W1)	1,000	972	28 (F)
Light, heat and power (W2)	610	586	24 (F)
Rent, rates and insurance (W3)	200	200	–
Depreciation (W4)	150	132	18 (F)
Total conversion costs	1,960	1,890	70 (F)
Bought-in materials (W5)	2,800	3,220	420 (A)
Total expenses	4,760	5,110	350 (A)
Turnover (W6)	5,600	6,440	840 (F)
Operating profit	840	1,330	490 (F)

Workings

1 Variable cost of 140,000 CD players + labour fixed cost = (£6 × 140,000) + £160,000 = £1,000,000

2 Variable cost of 140,000 CD players + light, heat and power fixed cost = (£4 × 140,000) + £50,000 = £610,000

3 Fixed cost so the same at all levels of production

4 Fixed cost so the same at all levels of production

5 Cost of 140,000 CD players = £20 × 140,000 = £2,800,000

6 Turnover from 140 000 CD players = £40 × 140,000 = £5,600,000

c) **MEMO**

To: Mike Jones
From: Assistant management accountant
Date: xx.xx.xx
Subject: **Performance related pay**

i) **Possible reasons for improved profit**

The improved profitability may have occurred even without the introduction of performance related pay.

1) KBV Sound cannot control the volume of sales as the only customer is the parent company. It therefore depends entirely on the level of demand from KBV Motors. This year KBV Motors required 40,000 more CD players than budgeted and so, even without performance related pay, the sales volume target would have been exceeded. All other things being equal (ie no increase in fixed costs and variable costs per unit), this increase in demand would have increased profit.

2) Part of the improved profit arose from a change in accounting policy on deprecation. There were no fixed asset purchases or sales and hence the actual annual depreciation figure would have been known and should have been the same as the budgeted figure. The actual figure was less than the budgeted figure and so actual profit was greater than budgeted.

3) The selling price per CD player is set at twice the cost of the bought-in materials. This means the more managers pay for the bought-in materials, the higher the price they can charge KBV Motors and so the higher the profit KBV Sound can report. (Such a policy leads to inefficiencies, however, as managers are motivated to pay as much as possible for bought-in materials.)

4) Fixed costs are the same irrespective of the level of production and sales. Hence the contribution will increase, all other things being equal, if actual volumes are greater than budgeted volumes and, with fixed costs remaining constant, so will profitability.

Note: You were required to provide only three reasons.

ii) **General conditions for improved performance**

There are several conditions necessary if performance related pay is to lead to improved performance.

1) Managers need to know the objectives of the organisation.

2) Budgets must tie in with those objectives.

3) Managers must feel that the objectives are achievable (although they should provide a challenge).

4) Managers must want to achieve those objectives.

5) Managers must be able to influence the achievement of the objectives.

6) The level of rewards – both financial and non-financial – should motivate managers.

7) Managers must have the skills necessary to achieve the targets.

8) There should be a short period of time between effort and reward.

9) The actual results should not be capable of being manipulated.

Note: You were required to provide only three reasons.

UNIT 8

PRACTICE EXAM 1

HEETME LTD

ANSWERS

ANSWERS

SECTION 1

Task 1.1

a) i) Standard cost per litre of paint = Total budgeted cost / number of litres
£25,000 / 1,000 = £25 per litre

ii) Standard usage of glass per solar panel = Total budgeted usage / number of production units
10,000/2,000 = 5 kilograms per solar panel

iii) Actual labour rate per hour = Total budgeted labour cost / total budgeted hours
£28,000/4,000 = £7 per hour

iv) Standard labour hours for actual production = Standard labour hours for one unit of production x actual production
= 4,000/2,000 x 2,100 = 4,200 hours

v) Budgeted total cost per solar panel = Budgeted total cost / budgeted production
= £293,000 / 2,000 = £146.50 per solar panel

vi) Total standard cost of actual production = Standard cost per panel x actual production
= £146.50 x 2,100 = £307,650

b) i) Direct material (glass) price variance

	£
Actual direct materials cost	147,000
Standard cost for actual material used £120,000/10,000 x 10,500	126,000
	21,000 Adverse

ii) Direct material (glass) usage variance

	Kg
Actual glass usage	10,500
Standard usage for actual production (5kg x 2,100)	10,500 Kg
Variance	NIL

Note: If there had been a variance it would be valued at standard cost (£12).

iii) Direct labour rate variance

	£
Actual labour cost	28,000
Standard cost for actual hours (£28,000/4,000) x 4,000	28,000
Variance	NIL

iv) Direct labour efficiency variance

	Hours
Actual labour hours	4,000
Standard hours for actual production (2,100 x 2)	4,200
	200 Fav

@ standard cost per hour
200 hours @ £7 per hour = £1,400 Fav

v) Fixed overhead expenditure variance

	£
Actual fixed overhead expenditure	130,000
Budgeted fixed overhead expenditure	120,000
	10,000 Adverse

vi) Fixed overhead efficiency variance

Fixed overheads are absorbed on labour hours	
Direct labour efficiency variance	200 hours favourable
@ standard fixed overhead absorption rate per hour (£120,000 / 4,000 hours) = £30	£6,000 favourable

c) An adverse (sometimes called unfavourable) variance reduces profit. They either increase costs or decrease revenue. Favourable variances are the opposite and increase profit.

d)

From: An Other Student
To: Chief Accountant
Sent: 1 December 2008
Subject: Variance Report

i) **Direct material (glass) price variance**

The direct material price variance was adverse which means that more was spent per kg on glass. This ties in with the information from the Production Director that better quality glass was purchased. The glass cost an additional £2 per kg which for the actual amount purchased gave an adverse variance of £21,000. The improved quality of the glass may impact on other variances, for example, less may be used, giving a better usage variance,or a higher price may be charged.

ii) **Direct material (glass) usage variance**

The usage variance is zero. This indicates that the actual amount of glass used for each panel was as expected. Thus the better quality of the glass did not result in less being used per panel.

iii) **Direct labour rate variance**

The direct labour rate variance is zero too. This indicates that the actual amount paid per hour was exactly as expected.

iv) **Direct labour efficiency variance**

The direct labour efficiency variance was £1,400 favourable. This means that less labour was used for the actual level of production than was expected. This may be due to the increased quality of the glass as was suggested by the Production Director.

Task 1.2

a) **Total direct material (paint) variance**

	£
Actual expenditure on paint	29,900
Standard cost of actual production (£25,000/2,000) x 2,100	26,250
	3,650 Adverse

Total variance

The total direct material variance is the difference between the amount spent on paint and the amount budgeted to be spent for the actual amount of production. This is can be seen as comparing the actual cost compared to the flexed budget.

Thus the cost of painting a solar panel should be £12.50 and 2,100 were produced. The flexed budget cost was therefore £12.50 x 2,100 = £26,250. This flexed budget can be compared with the actual expenditure of £29,900.

The difference between the actual expenditure and the standard cost of actual production is the total direct material (paint) variance. The difference of £3,650 adverse indicates that more has been spent than budgeted.

This variance could be the result of two factors, the price per litre of paint and the amount of paint used per panel being different from the budget.

b) **Direct material (paint) price variance**

	£
Actual direct materials cost	29,900
Standard cost for actual material used (£25,000 / 1,000) x 1,150	28,750
	1,150 Adverse

Price variance

The price variance compares the actual cost of the paint and the standard cost of the paint for the actual materials used. Thus, 1,150 litres should cost £28,750 at the standard price of £25 per litre but actually cost £29,900. The adverse variance shows that £1,150 more than expected was paid.The price actually paid for the paint was £26 per litre (£29,900/1,150 litres). The price variance should not be considered in isolation and the quality of the paint should also be considered.

c) **Direct material (paint) usage variance**

	Litres
Actual paint usage	1,150
Standard usage for actual production (0.5 litres x 2,100)	1,050
Variance	100 Adverse
At standard cost (£25 per litre)	2,500 Adverse

Usage variance

The usage variance compares the actual amount of materials used for the actual level of production and the amount of paint which should have been used. An extra 100 litres were used. The effect of this alone, as we have already considered the price variance, is an extra cost of £2,500.

Task 1.3

Expected price of glass

In January:

a = 9
b = 0.1
X = 31

Therefore Y = 9 + (31 x 0.1) = £12.10 per kilogram

In February:

a = 9
b = 0.1
X = 32

Therefore Y = 9 + (32 x 0.1) = £12.20 per kilogram

SECTION 2

Task 2.1

a)

Note all monetary amounts in '000 for (i) and (ii)

		SP2000	SP3000
i)	Gross profit margin = Gross Profit/Turnover x 100	(1,014/1,800) x 100 = 56.33%	(905/1,500) x 100 = 60.33%
ii)	Operating profit margin = Operating Profit/Turnover x 100	(414/1,800) x 100 =23.00%	(305/1,500) x 100 =20.33%
iii)	Direct materials cost per unit = Direct materials cost/sales units	£540,000/9,000=£60.00	£300,000/5,000=£60.00
(iv)	Direct labour cost per unit = Direct labour cost/sales units	£126,000/9,000=£14.00	£175,000/5,000=£35.00
v)	Fixed production overheads cost per unit = Fixed prod'n o/hds cost/sales units	£120,000/9,000=£13.33	£120,000/5,000=£24.00
vi)	Return on net assets = Operating profit / Net assets x 100	£414,000/£2,014,000 x 100 = 20.56%	£305,000/£ 1,905,000 x 100 = 16.01%
vii)	Stock Turnover = (Stock of material/Direct materials) x 365	£60,000/£540,000 x 365 = 40.56 days	£60,000/£300,000 x 365 = 73.00 days

Tip: The Chief Assessor for this paper has indicated that 'candidates must be able to calculate a range of indicators including those in previous papers as well as this paper. Future exams may require candidates to calculate a range of indicators including those not assessed in recent exams.' Be prepared!

b)

From: An Other Student
To: Finance Director
Sent: 1 December 2008
Subject: Performance indicators

i) **Gross profit margin**

The gross margin for the SP3000 is higher than the SP2000 by 4%.

This difference can be explained by differences in the selling price per unit and the cost of production of each unit.

The selling price of the SP3000 is £300 per unit whereas the selling price of the SP2000 is £200 per unit. If the cost of production for both products was the same then the SP3000 would have a higher gross margin.

The cost of production of the two products should be compared:

- The direct material cost of glass is constant at £60 per unit and so does not affect the margin.
- The direct labour cost per unit is much higher for the SP3000. This will reduce the gross margin for the SP3000.
- The fixed costs per unit are also higher for the SP3000 because less volume is produced (£24 per unit as opposed to £13.33 per unit for SP2000). Again this will reduce the margin for the SP3000.

The higher unit selling price of the SP3000 more than outweighs the additional costs per unit and hence the SP3000 has a higher gross margin.

ii) **Return on net assets**

The SP2000 has a higher return on net assets (RONA) than the SP3000 because its' operating profits are larger relative to its net assets. Thus it generates an additional £109,000 but only uses an additional £109,000 of net assets.

Task 2.2

a) Revised production in units to make 9,000 units of good production

	Units
Good production required	9,000
Reject production (10% of total production)	1,000
Revised Production	10,000

Tip: Remember to continue even if you are unsure of your answer to this part of the question. If you did get the answer to this part wrong the own figure rule means that you will not suffer a large reduction in marks because of this error.

b) Additional units produced = 1,000 units

		£
Materials costs	£60 x 1,000 units	60,000
Labour costs	£14 x 1,000 units	14,000
Total additional cost		74,000

c)

	£
Original gross profit	1,014,000
less: Total additional cost of additional units produced	74,000
Revised gross profit	940,000
Original operating profit	414,000
Less: Total additional cost of additional units produced	74,000
Revised operating profit	340,000

d)

	£
Original net assets	2,014,000
Less: Total additional cost	74,000
Revised net assets	1,940,000

Task 2.3

a)

Year	*0*	*1*	*2*	*3*	*4*	*5*
	£'000	£'000	£'000	£'000	£'000	£'000
Purchase Price	300					
Running cost		30	30	30	30	30
Residual value						(50)
Net Cost	300	30	30	30	30	(20)
Discount factor	1.00	0.952	0.907	0.864	0.823	0.784
Present cost	300	28.560	27.210	25.920	24.690	(15.680)

Net Present Cost = £390,700

The discounted lifecycle cost of the machine is £390,700.

b)

Year	*0*	*1*	*2*	*3*	*4*	*5*
	£'000	£'000	£'000	£'000	£'000	£'000
Labour cost Saving (W1)	0	105	105	105	105	105
Discount factor	1.00	0.952	0.907	0.864	0.823	0.784
Present value		99.960	95.235	90.720	86.415	82.320

Net Present Labour Cost Saving = £454,650

The discounted labour savings are £454,650

Working

3 hours saving per unit x 5000 units x £7 = £105,000

c)

	£
The discounted lifecycle cost of the machine	(390,700)
The discounted labour savings	454,650
Investing in the new machine saves	63,950

Investment in the new machine will be financially beneficial.

Tip: lifecycle costing and simple discounting are fundamental management accounting knowledge which are assessed in every ECR paper.

UNIT 8

PRACTICE EXAM 2

GRIPPIT LTD

ANSWERS

ANSWERS

SECTION 1

a) i) standard labour rate per hour = budgeted labour cost / budgeted labour hours

= £4,800 / 600

= £8 per hour

ii) standard labour hours for actual production = standard labour hour per tonne x actual production

= 600hours/200 tonnes x 210 tonnes

= 630 hours

iii) budgeted cost per tonne of Crumb = total budgeted cost / budgeted output

= £94,800 / 200 tonnes

= £474

iv) budgeted overhead absorption rate per tonne = fixed overheads / budgeted output

= £90,000 / 200 tonnes

= £450

v) overheads absorbed into actual production = actual production x absorption rate

= 210 units x £450

= £94,500

vi) the total standard cost of actual production = standard cost per tonne x actual output

= (94,800/200 tonnes) x 210 tonnes

= £99,540

Tip: This topic is assessed in EVERY exam!

b) i) Direct labour rate variance

	£
Actual hours at standard rate (600 x £8)	4,800
Actual hours at actual rate	5,100
Labour rate variance	300 Adv

ii) Direct labour efficiency variance

	£
Standard hours for actual production at the standard rate	
3 x 210 x £8	5,040
Actual hours for actual production at the standard rate	
600 x £8	4,800
Labour efficiency variance	240 Fav

iii) Fixed overhead expenditure variance

	£
Budgeted fixed overhead	90,000
Actual fixed overhead	95,000
Fixed overhead expenditure variance	5,000 Adv

iv) Fixed overhead volume variance

	£
Actual production at absorption rate per unit (210 x £450	94,500
Budgeted production at absorption rate per unit	90,000
Fixed overhead volume variance	4,500 Fav

Note: There are numerous ways of laying out variance calculations. If correct they will be given credit.

c) *Reconciliation or operating statement – May 2008*

	Variances *Adverse*	*Favourable*	
	£	£	£
Total standard cost –			
Budgeted/Standard cost for actual production (210 x £474)			99,540
Direct labour rate	300		
Direct labour efficiency		240	
Fixed overhead expenditure	5,000		
Fixed overhead volume		4,500	
Total variance	5,300	4,740	560 Adv
Actual cost of actual production			100,100

Tip: Even if unsure of your answers from Task 1.1b) carry forward these figures.

d)

To:	Finance Director	**Subject:**	Explanation of variances
From:	AAT student	**Date:**	16 June 2008

i) **Direct labour rate variance**

The direct labour variance was £300 adverse / unfavourable. This was because of labour actually costing £8.50 an hour compared to the £8 budgeted cost - an increase of 50p an hour. Half of this variance can be explained by a pay rise of 25p an hour. The remaining variance should be investigated but may be a result of overtime, incorrect budgeting figures or a change in the type or mix of labour used.

ii) **Direct labour efficiency variance**

The direct labour efficiency variance was £240 favourable. This may in part be as a result of the software upgrade. The upgrade should increase labour efficiency by 10% to reduce the standard time to 2.7 hours per tonne; the actual labour time was 2.86 hours per tonne (actual hours of 600 divided by the actual output of 210). The underperformance of the new software should be examined.

iii) **Fixed overhead expenditure variance**

The fixed overhead expenditure variance was £5,000 adverse / unfavourable. The software upgrade cost £120,000 for a 2-year licence. The cost per month is , therefore, £120,000 divided by 24 which is £5,000 per month. The £5,000 adverse variance may be explained by the upgrade.

iv) **Fixed overhead volume variance**

This fixed overhead volume variance was £4,500 favourable. This was because actual output was higher than budgeted output (210 not 200). This could be due to the software upgrade improving labour efficiency which in turn produced more output per hour and hence increased the volume.

Tip: Check that you get the easy marks for the memo headings

Task 1.2

Standard cost card for production of 250 tonnes of rubberised asphalt

		Quantity	*Unit price*	*Total cost*
			£	£
Crumb	tonnes	50	474	23,700
Asphalt	tonnes	200	150	30,000
Direct labour	hours	800	10	8,000
Fixed production overheads	tonnes	250	600	150,000
Standard cost				211,700

Task 1.3

a) Y = a + bX

For June, X = 26, therefore Y = 125 + (2 x 26) = £177 per tonne
For July = X = 27, therefore Y = 125 + (2 x 27) = £179 per tonne

b) As May is the base, May = 100 when price was £175 per tonne

Therefore, June = 177/175 x 100 = 101.14
July = 179/175 x 100 = 102.29

Note: Answers are given to 2 decimal places

SECTION 2

Task 2.1

a)

		Scenario 1	Scenario 2
i)	Gross profit margin = Gross Profit / Turnover x 100	(4,500 / 12,500) x 100 = 36.00%	(4,000 / 14,000) x 100 = 28.57%
ii)	Net profit margin = Net Profit / Turnover x 100	(2,150 / 12,500) x 100 = 17.20%	(1,650 / 14,000) x 100 = 11.79%
iii)	Direct materials cost per unit = Direct materials cost / sales units	£3,000,000 / 10,000 = £300	£4,200,000 / 14,000 = £300
iv)	Direct labour cost per unit = Direct labour cost / sales units	£2,000,000 / 10,000 = £200	£2,800,000 / 14,000 = £200
v)	Fixed production cost per unit = Fixed production cost / sales units	£3,000,000 / 10,000 = £300	£3,000,000 / 14,000 = £214.29
vi)	Gearing = Debt / (debt + equity)	12,000 / (12,000 + 8,400)= (0.5882 or 58.82%)	11,300/(11,300+8,400)= 0.5736 or 57.36%
	Alternative answer for gearing: Gearing = Debt / equity	12,000/8,400 = (1.4286 or 142.86%)	11,300/8,400 = (1.3452 or 134.52%)
vii)	Interest cover = Operating profit / interest payable	2,750/600 = 4.58	2,250/600 = 3.75

b)

To:	Finance Director	**Subject:**	Gross profit margin, gearing and interest cover
From:	AAT Trainee	**Date:**	16 June 2008

i) **Gross profit margin**

The gross profit margin for scenario 1 is 36% and scenario 2 is 28.57%. Direct materials and labour are the same under both scenarios so that the higher gross profit margin for Scenario 1 must be as a result of differences in sales price per unit or fixed production overheads. In fact the fixed costs per unit are higher under scenario 1 because less volume is produced (£300 per unit as opposed to £214.29 per unit for scenario 2). Therefore the reason for the higher gross margin is the higher price per unit (£1,250 and £1,000 respectively).

ii) **Gearing and interest cover**

The level of gearing for both scenarios is at a similar level. Everything else being equal the higher the gearing ratio the higher the risk. This is because debt has interest payments that have to be made from operating profit. However, the gearing indicator cannot be considered in isolation.

The level of interest cover shows how many times Voltair can pay its interest payable out of operating profit. For scenario 1 the profit is 4.58 times greater than interest payable. This falls slightly to 3.75 times for scenario 2 due to the fall in profits, as the interest payable is constant under both scenarios.

Both scenarios have a relatively high interest cover and this does not appear to be a problem for the business.

Task 2.2

a) i) Full production cost per turbine based upon production of 10,000 turbines = £8,000,000

Therefore cost per turbine = £8,000,000 / 10,000 = £800.00

ii) Unavoidable fixed production cost = £3,000,000 - £1,950,000 = £1,050,000

Therefore unavoidable fixed production cost per turbine for 10,000 units = £1,050,000 / 10,000 = £105.00

iii) Avoidable production cost per turbine for 10,000 units = £800 - £105 = £695.00

b) i) Full production cost per turbine based upon production of 14,000 turbines = £10,000,000

Therefore cost per turbine = £10,000,000 / 14,000 = £714.29

ii) Unavoidable fixed production cost = £3,000,000 - £1,950,000 = £1,050,000

Therefore unavoidable fixed production cost per turbine for 14,000 units = £1,050,000 / 14,000 = £75.00

iii) Avoidable production cost per turbine for 14000 units = £714.29 - £75.00 = £639.29

c) **To:** Managing Director **Subject:** Outsourcing/contracting out
From: AAT Trainee **Date:** 16 June 2008

This report will make recommendations whether, at different demand levels, Voltair should contract out the manufacture of wind turbines. It will also outline other considerations that need to be taken into account when making the decision.

i) **Demand of 10,000 turbines**

If production was outsourced then Voltair would avoid incurring costs of £695 per turbine at demand of 10,000 units. This is the avoidable production cost per turbine (see above). This relevant saving should be compared to the cost of each turbine if outsourced which is £650. Using this information alone the decision should be to outsource.

ii) **Demand of 14,000 turbines**

If production was outsourced then Voltair would avoid incurring costs of £639.29 per turbine at demand of 14,000 units. This is the avoidable production cost per turbine (see above). This relevant saving should be compared to the cost of each turbine if outsourced which is £650 Using this information alone the decision should be NOT to outsource.

iii) **Other considerations**

The above analysis may be inadequate without other considerations that need to be taken into account:

- Accuracy of the data upon which the decision is made. It is an estimate of future demand.
- Is the outsourced product of similar quality? For instance, delivery reliability, physical quality, durability, availability of parts etc..
- Cash flow and finance considerations.

Note: other valid considerations would also be given credit. e.g. response of stakeholders to the decision such as shareholders, customers, other suppliers and so on.

Task 2.3

a) Lifecycle Costing means evaluating what a product or service will cost over its entire life cycle Acquisition costs are only one element, other costs will include operating, maintenance and decommissioning costs.

Target costing involves setting a target cost by subtracting a desired profit margin from a competitive market price. A target cost is the maximum amount of cost that can be incurred on a product and with it the firm can still earn the required profit margin from that product at a particular selling price.

b) Target cost = market price – desired profit margin

= £25 – (£25 x 30%)

= £25 – £7.50

= £17.50

UNIT 8

PRACTICE EXAM 3

TEESRUS LTD

ANSWERS

ANSWERS

SECTION 1

Task 1.1

a) **Production budget (units)**

i) **Budgeted production overheads**

Budgeted production × Fixed overhead absorption rate = 80,000 boxes × £1 per box
= £80,000

ii) **Actual number of tea bags used in production**

Transfer from bagging division – closing stock = 8,500,000 – 50,000
= 8.450,000 bags

iii) **Standard usage of tea bags for actual production**

100 tea bags × 84,000 boxes = 8,400,000 tea bags

b) i) **Direct materials (tea bags) usage variance**

	£
Standard cost of standard usage 8,400,000 (part a) x 0.033	277,200
Standard cost of actual usage 8,450,000 (part a) x 0.033	278,850
	1,650 (A)

ii) **Direct packing materials price variance**

	£
Standard cost of actual usage 4,200 × £2	8,400
Actual cost of actual usage	8,800
	400 (A)

iii) **Fixed overhead expenditure variance**

	£
Budgeted fixed overhead	80,000
Actual fixed overhead	85,000
	5,000 (A)

iv) **Fixed overhead capacity variance**

	£
Budgeted hours at standard cost 80,000 x 0.02 x £50	80,000
Actual hours at standard cost 1,800 x £50	90,000
	10,000 (F)

c) i) **Total standard cost of actual production**

£4.60 × 84,000 boxes = £386,400

ii) **Total actual cost of actual production**

	£
Materials – tea bags 8,450,000 x £0.033	278,850
Materials – packing	8,800
Labour (1,800 hours @ £9.50)	17,100
Fixed overheads	85,000
	389,750

d) **Operating statement**

	Variances *Favourable* £	*Adverse* £	£
Total standard cost of actual production			386,400
Materials (tea bags) price variance	–	–	
Materials (tea bags) usage variance		1,650	
Packing materials price variance		400	
Packing materials usage variance	–	–	
Direct labour rate variance	900		
Direct labour efficiency variance		1,200	
Fixed overhead expenditure variance		5,000	
Fixed overhead efficiency variance		6,000	
Fixed overhead capacity variance	10,000		
	10,900	14,250	3,350
Total actual cost of actual production			389,750

e) **REPORT**

To: Finance Director
From: Accounting Technician
Date: December 2007
Subject: Production cost variances

As requested I have calculated the production cost variances for November 2007 and produced an operating statement reconciling total standard cost of actual production to total actual cost of actual production.

There is a direct materials (tea bags) adverse usage variance of £1,650. This means that more tea bags are being used than the standard of 100 per box. This may be due to more being put in a box or due to other forms of wastage such as tearing of tea bags before packing. As we have both 3 machines nearing the end of their operational life as well as 2 new operators who are still being trained it is likely that the cause of this variance is due to either inefficiencies in the machinery or with the 2 new operatives.

The direct labour rate variance is £900 favourable and as a pay rise is still outstanding it is probably the case that the pay rise has already been built into the standard cost but is not yet being paid to the employees.

There is also a direct labour adverse efficiency variance of £1,200 which again may be due to the combination of the inexperienced operators and the older machinery.

Task 1.2

Standard cost card for 1,000 tea bags

	£
Direct materials – tea (3kg × £5)	15.00
Direct materials – bags (1,000 × £0.006)	6.00
Direct labour $\left(\frac{1{,}000}{5{,}000\,\text{hours}} \times £10\right)$	2.00
Fixed overhead $\left(\frac{0.2\,\text{hours} \times £200{,}000}{4{,}000\,\text{hours}}\right)$	10.00
	33.00

Task 1.3

a) $$\text{June} = \frac{£4.95}{£4.80} \times 100 = 103.13$$

$$\text{November} = \frac{£5.10}{£4.80} \times 100 = 106.25$$

b) $$\text{January 08 cost} = \frac{£4.80 \times 108.25}{100} = £5.20$$

c) $$\text{Percentage increase} = \frac{£5.20 - £4.80}{£4.80} \times 100$$

$$= 8.33\%$$

SECTION 2

Task 2.1

		Actual	*Budgeted*
a)	i) **Cost of tea pickers as a percentage of turnover**		
	$\frac{132,000}{787,500} \times 100$	16.76%	
	$\frac{150,000}{1,125,000} \times 100$		13.33%
	ii) **Cost of tea processor operators as a percentage of turnover**		
	$\frac{35,000}{787,500} \times 100$	4.44%	
	$\frac{50,000}{1,125,000} \times 100$		4.44%
	iii) **Cost of seeds and fertilisers as a percentage of turnover**		
	$\frac{75,000}{787,500} \times 100$	9.52%	
	$\frac{75,000}{1,125,000} \times 100$		6.67%
	iv) **Gross profit margin**		
	$\frac{485,500}{787,500} \times 100$	61.65%	
	$\frac{790,000}{1,125,000} \times 100$		70.22%
	v) **Operating profit margin**		
	$\frac{35,500}{787,500} \times 100$	4.51%	
	$\frac{290,000}{1,125,000} \times 100$		25.78%

	Actual	Budgeted
vi) **Return on net assets**		
$\frac{35{,}500}{935{,}500} \times 100$	3.79%	
$\frac{290{,}000}{1{,}190{,}000} \times 100$		24.37%
vii) **Net asset turnover**		
$\frac{787{,}500}{935{,}500}$	0.84	
$\frac{1{,}125{,}000}{1{,}190{,}000}$		0.95

b)

REPORT

To: Finance Director
From: Accounting Technician
Date: December 2007
Subject: Operating performance of tea plantation.

You have asked for this report to explain the changes in gross profit margin and operating profit margin from the budgeted figures for the year to the actual figures for the year.

Starting with the gross profit margin this has fallen from a budgeted figure of 70.22% to an actual of 61.65%. This is all set in the context of the a lower than expected tea crop due to bad weather leading to turnover being only 70% of the budgeted figure. This is exactly in line with the amount of tea harvested in kilograms which was also 70% of the budgeted figure.

The tea pickers and tea processor operators are employed as and when they are needed so we were able to reduce costs here by only employing enough to cover the lower harvest. Therefore only 440 tea pickers were employed rather than the budgeted figure of 500. This has meant that the cost of tea pickers as a percentage of turnover has increased from the budgeted figure but not excessively so. The reason for this increase has been that the tea pickers have been hampered by the poor tea crop and could not harvest as quickly and therefore still took the full 100 days budgeted to pick 70% of the budgeted crop. However the costs of the tea processors were held in check and these are the same as a percentage of turnover as was budgeted.

Two of the major reasons for the overall fall in gross profit margin are that the depreciation of the tea machines is a fixed cost and the cost of seeds and fertilisers are committed at the start of the season and do not respond to a change in turnover or harvest level. Therefore these two figures which are the same as the budgeted figures do of course mean that in percentage terms the gross profit has reduced.

The operating profit margin is only 4.51% compared to the budgeted figure of 25.78%. This is clearly partly caused by the lower than budgeted gross profit margin but also due to the fixed nature of the administration costs and to a degree the distribution costs. Although turnover and harvest are 70% of the budgeted figure the administration costs remain the same as budgeted and the distribution costs are still 86% of the budgeted figure. There should also be some concern about the way in which we are using our asset base as the net asset turnover is only 0.84 compared to the budgeted figure of 0.95. All of these factors have contributed to a significant decline in operating profit margin and also return on net assets.

I hope that this information has been of use to you.

Task 2.2

a) **Budgeted profit and loss accounts**

		Pickmaster	*Pickmaster2*
		£	£
Turnover		1,125,000	1,125,000
Cost of sales			
Tea pickers		50,000	150,000
Tea processor operators	(10 × £6 × 100 × 8)	48,000	
	(1 × £6 × 100 × 8)		4,800
Depreciation of tea machines	(8 × £2,000)	16,000	
	(8 × £9,000)		72,000
Seed and fertiliser costs		75,000	75,000
Total cost of sales		289,000	301,800
Gross profit		836,000	823,200
Administration costs		150,000	135,000
Distribution costs		350,000	350,000
Operating profit		336,000	338,200
Net assets at year end			
Budgeted net assets		935,500	935,500
Operating profit		336,000	338,200
Net assets		1,271,500	1,273,700

Tutorial note. The value of the new machines has not been included in the net asset figure as their purchase would have to be funded in some way ie bank loan, leasing, leading to an increase in liabilities which would cancel out the increase in asset values. This will not be an exact cancellation but we have no information about the method of funding.

		Pickmaster %	*Pickmaster2* %
b) i)	**Gross profit margin**		
	$\frac{836,000}{1,125,000} \times 100$	74.31	
	$\frac{823,200}{1,125,000} \times 100$		73.17
ii)	**Operating profit margin**		
	$\frac{336,000}{1,125,000} \times 100$	29.87	
	$\frac{338,200}{1,125,000} \times 100$		30.06
iii)	**Return on net assets**		
	$\frac{336,000}{1,271,500} \times 100$	26.43	
	$\frac{338,200}{1,273,700} \times 100$		26.55

c) **REPORT**

To: Managing Director
From: Accounting technician
Date: December 2007
Subject: Purchase of new machinery

I have been asked to write this report with regard to the decision as to whether to replace our current tea machines with eight new Pickmaster machines or Pickmaster 2 machines.

i) In terms of our profitability and return on net asset there is little to be chosen between the two options. The Pickmaster machines give a slightly higher gross profit margin due to the much smaller depreciation charge although costing more in terms of tea processor operators. However due to a reduction in administration costs if the Pickmaster2 machines are purchased then the gross profit and gross profit margins hardly differ under the two options. Equally the return on net assets under each of the two options is very similar.

ii) Firstly we need to consider the funding of the purchase of these machines. If the Pickmaster machines are purchased then they will cost £160,000 (8 x £20,000) but if the Pickmaster2 machines are purchased then these will cost £720,000 (8 x £90,000). These purchases will have to be funded in some way such as a bank loan or by purchasing them under lease finance. In either event if the Pickmaster2 machines are purchased then this will significantly increase the gearing of the organisation and incur high service costs in the form of interest payments on a loan or finance charges on a lease.

The second consideration is the relative benefits and costs of the two machines. The advantage of the Pickmaster2 is that only 1 operator per day is required rather than 10. However these operators are employed as and when needed on temporary contracts therefore if the harvest was low again as in 2007 less operatives could be employed. However the depreciation charges on the machines at £72,000 (8 x £9,000) for the Pickmaster2 machines compared to £16,000 (8 x £2,000) for the Pickmaster machines are fixed costs that will be incurred whatever the level of turnover and harvest. Therefore if there is a low harvest investment in the Pickmaster2 machines will depress profit.

(**Tutorial note.** A third consideration might be the expected residual value of each type of machine at the end of the 10-year period but only two further considerations were required for the task).

iii) As the choice of machines has little effect on profit at the budgeted level but the Pickmaster2 machines increase the risk of the operation, due to increased gearing and depreciation charges, then on balance purchase of the Pickmaster machines for £160,000 would be recommended.

Task 2.3

a) Life cycle costing is an accounting technique whereby the cost of an activity, project or piece of machinery is considered and calculated over the whole of its economic life, from purchase through to eventual disposal. Therefore the initial cost of investment is only part of the cost of the project and other costs will include operating costs and revenues, maintenance costs, decommissioning costs and final residual value.

b) In a life cycle costing analysis the cash flows relating to the project are considered over its entire life which may spread over many years. As with any project being considered where cash flows in the future are being assessed then the time value of money must be considered in order to calculate a net present value. Therefore to find the true cost of the cash flows associated with the project discounted cash flow techniques must be used to reflect the time value of money.

UNIT 8

PRACTICE EXAM 4

FOODDRINK LTD

ANSWERS

SECTION 1

Task 1.1

a) i) **Standard price of materials per kilogram**

$$\frac{£5,400}{450} = £12 \text{ per kg}$$

ii) **Standard usage of materials for actual production**

$$\text{Standard usage per unit of production} = \frac{450}{9,000}$$

$$\text{Standard usage for actual production} = 9,900 \times \left(\frac{450}{9,000}\right) = 495 \text{ kgs}$$

iii) **Standard labour rate per hour**

$$\frac{4,500}{300} = £15$$

iv) **Standard labour hours for actual production**

$$\text{Standard labour hours per unit} = \frac{300}{9,000}$$

$$\text{Standard labour hours for actual production} = 9,900 \times \left(\frac{300}{9,000}\right) = 330 \text{ hours}$$

v) **Budgeted overhead absorption rate per unit**

$$\frac{18,000}{9,000} = £2$$

vi) **Overheads absorbed into actual production**

9,900 × £2 = £19,800

b) i) **Direct material price variance**

Standard cost of 594 kgs = 594 × £12 = £7,128

Actual cost of 594 kgs = £6,534

Material price variance = £594 (F)

Alternatively

Actual price of materials = $\frac{£6,534}{594}$ = £11

Material price variance = 594 × £(12 – 11) = £594 (F)

ii) **Direct material usage variance**

Standard usage to produce 9,900 units at standard cost = 495 × £12 = £5,940

Actual usage to produce 9,900 units at standard cost = 594 × £12 = £7,128

Materials usage variance = £1,188 (A)

Alternatively

Materials usage variance = (495 – 594) × £12 = £1,188 (A)

iii) **Direct labour rate variance**

Standard cost of 325 hours of labour = 325 × £15 = £4,875

Actual cost of 325 hours of labour = £4,225

Labour rate variance =£650 (F)

Alternatively

Actual rate of labour = $\frac{£4,225}{325}$ = £13

Labour rate variance = 325 × £(15 – 13) = £650 (F)

iv) **Direct labour efficiency variance**

Standard hours to produce 9,900 units at standard rate = 330 × £15 = £4,950

Actual hours to produce 9,900 units at standard rate = 325 × £15 = £4,875

Labour efficiency variance = £75 (F)

Alternatively

Labour efficiency variance = (330 – 325) × £15 = £75 (F)

v) **Fixed overhead expenditure variance**

£18,000 – £19,000 = £1,000 (A)

vi) **Fixed overhead volume variance**

(9,000 – 9,900) × £2 = £1,800 (F)

c) Budgeted costs for actual production 9,900 units × £3.10 (W) = £30,690

	Favourable	Adverse	
	£	£	£
Variances			
Direct material price	594		
Direct material usage		1,188	
Direct labour rate	650		
Direct labour efficiency	75		
Fixed overhead expenditure		1,000	
Fixed overhead volume	1,800		
Total variance	3,119	2,188	(931)
Actual cost of actual production			29,759

WORKING

$$\text{Standard cost per unit} = \frac{£27,900}{9,000} = £3.10$$

d) Under standard absorption costing the fixed costs are absorbed into production. Therefore, the unit cost includes an amount of the fixed costs. As the volume of output changes, the fixed costs will be under or over absorbed. For example, if the actual production exceeds the budget, the fixed costs will be over-absorbed (ie, too much fixed cost is added to the cost of production). This results in a favourable volume variance. Also the stock valuation will include an element of fixed cost.

Under marginal costing the fixed costs are treated as a period cost. Therefore the unit cost does not include fixed costs. The only fixed overhead variance will be an expenditure variance equal to the difference between the budget and actual fixed cost. There will be no volume variance. Similarly stock valuation will not include fixed costs.

e) The fixed overhead volume variance can be split into the capacity and efficiency variance. To do this the fixed cost has to be absorbed per labour hour. The capacity variance then calculates the increase or decrease of hours worked due to the availability of direct labour - If direct labour hours are greater than budgeted there is a gain on capacity, which is favourable. The efficiency variance calculates the efficiency of the labour. If more hours are worked but less output is achieved, this is adverse.

Task 1.2

a)

	May 2006	*June 2006*	*July 2006*	*Aug 2006*
	£	£	£	£
Cost per 1,000 kgs	1,000	900	700	800
Seasonal variation	200	100	(100)	0
Trend	800	800	800	800

Tutorial note. The underlying cost is the Trend.

b) $$\left(\frac{(850-800)}{800}\right) \times 100 = 6.25\%$$

Tutorial note. The above calculation is the most normal way of calculating a change from one period to the next as a percentage of the original figure.

c)

	May 2007	*June 2007*	*July 2007*	*Aug 2007*
	£	£	£	£
Trend	850	850	850	850
Seasonal variation	200	100	(100)	0
Cost per 1,000 kgs	1,050	950	750	850

SECTION 2

Task 2.1

a) **Tutorial note.** The workings are shown for scenario 1 – the workings for scenario 2 are similar.

	Scenario 1	*Scenario 2*
Gross profit margin £ $\left(\frac{420,000}{1,200,000}\right) \times 100$	35.00%	10.00%
Operating profit margin £ $\left(\frac{246,000}{1,200,000}\right) \times 100$	20.50%	–2.33% or 0
Direct materials as a percentage of turnover		
£ $\left(\frac{300,000}{1,200,000}\right) \times 100$	25.00%	50.00%
Direct materials cost per unit £ $\left(\frac{300,000}{120,000}\right)$	£2.50	£2.50
Return on net assets $\left(\frac{246,000}{971,000}\right) \times 100$	25.33%	–6.15% or 0
Stock turnover in days (based on raw materials)		
$\left(\frac{50,000}{300,000}\right) \times 365$ or	60.83 days	20.28 days
Stock turnover in days (based on total cost of sales)		
$\left(\frac{50,000}{780,000}\right) \times 365$	23.40 days	11.27 days
Debtors' payment period in days		
$\left(\frac{150,000}{1,200,000}\right) \times 365$	45.63 days	30.42 days
Gearing (debt/(debt + equity)		
$\left(\frac{754,000}{(754,000+971,000)}\right) \times 100$	43.71%	60.41%
Gearing (debt/equity) $\left(\frac{754,000}{971,000}\right) \times 100$	77.65% or 0.78:1	152.56% or 1.53:1

b) **To:** Finance Director
Subject: Differences in key performance indicators
From: Accounting Technician
Date: 18 June 2007

i) The gross profit margin for scenario 1 is 35% but falls to 10% for scenario 2. There are two causes for this difference. The selling price has been reduced by 50% (from £10 to £5) which will have reduced the margin. The reduction in the selling price has however increased the volume produced and sold which has reduced the fixed overhead per unit which will have increased the margin. However, the effect of the increased selling price in reducing the margin has outweighed the beneficial effect of the fixed overheads.

ii) The operating profit margin for scenario 1 is 20.5%, this falls to a loss under scenario 2. The reduction in gross profit margin has fed down to the operating profit margin and the selling and distribution costs have increased due to the higher sales volume

iii) The direct materials cost as a percentage of turnover has increased from 25% under scenario 1 to 50% under scenario 2. This fall is caused by the 50% reduction in the selling price. Every unit that is sold under the two scenarios has the same direct material cost (£2.50) but the selling price in scenario 2 is only £5 giving a percentage material cost of 50%, whereas the selling price in scenario 1 is £10 giving a percentage material cost of 25%.

c)

Gross profit	£
Scenario 2 gross profit	180,000
Add back raw materials costs at £2.5 per unit (£2.5 x 360,000)	900,000
Less raw materials costs at £1.5 per unit for 360,000 units	(540,000)
Recalculated gross profit	540,000

Operating profit	
Recalculated gross profit	540,000
Less selling and distribution and administration costs £(122,000 + 100,000)	(222,000)
Recalculated operating profit	318,000

Net assets	
Share capital	725,000
Recalculated operating profit	318,000
Revised net assets	1,043,000

or

	£
Net assets under Scenario 2	683,000
Increase in stock of raw materials £(90,000 – 50,000)	40,000
Increase in trade debtors £(225,000 – 150,000)	75,000
Increase in short-term borrowing £(0 – 145,000)	(145,000)
Decrease in long-term borrowing £(1,042,000 – 682,000)	360,000
Decrease in creditors £(75,000 – 45,000)	30,000
	1,043,000

d)

	%
Gross profit margin £$\left(\frac{540,000}{1,800,000}\right) \times 100$	30.00
Operating profit margin £$\left(\frac{318,000}{1,800,000}\right) \times 100$	17.67
Return on net assets £$\left(\frac{318,000}{1,043,000}\right) \times 100$	30.49

e) **To:** Financial Director
Subject: Differences in key performance indicators
From: Accounting Technician
Date: 18 June 2007

i) The revised gross profit has increased to 30%. The increase in the gross profit is caused by the reduction in the cost of raw materials per unit.

However, although the reduction in cost per unit increases the gross profit of scenario 2, it is still below the gross profit of scenario 1 because the effect of scenario 2's lower selling price outweighs the advantages of its lower raw materials and fixed cost absorption rate.

ii) The revised operating profit for scenario 2 has increased to £318,000 from a loss. The operating profit margin is now improved to 18% which is fed through from the gross margin but this is still less than the 20.5% for scenario 1. Based upon the gross profit margin and the operating profit margin, the decision appears to be to adopt scenario 1.

iii) The revised return on net assets for scenario 2 is 30.5% compared to 25% for scenario 1.

Based purely on the above three indicators, the decision should be to set the price at £5 as per scenario 2 because the higher return on net assets indicates that the return on investment is (pound for pound) better in scenario 2 and therefore will increase shareholder value. The fact that scenario 1 still has better gross and operating margins is not decisive. These margins do indicate that there are better operating efficiencies in scenario 1 compared to scenario 2. However, the fact that the revised figures for scenario 2 show that it has a significantly larger operating profit than scenario 1 with net assets for the two scenarios being almost the same causes the return on investment in scenario 2 to be better.

Task 2.2

a) Lifecycle costing is a technique used to calculate the cost of an activity, project or piece of machinery over the whole of its economic life. The cost of acquisition is only one part of the lifecycle cost. Other costs include operating, maintenance, and decommissioning costs less any residual value.

Target costing is used where a company has to accept a price for its products, typically caused by competition in the market. Its target price may then be set either at the market price or a little below the market price if it is to gain a price advantage. The company will then decide on the profit margin it requires from the product and will calculate its target cost as target price less profit margin. The challenge is then to produce the product at the target cost or lower.

b) Target costing would be the most appropriate technique for the new cooler bottle as the selling price will be set by the market. Lifecycle costing would be most appropriate for the new production process because there will be design, set up, training, ongoing and decommissioning costs less possibly a residual value.

UNIT 8

PRACTICE EXAM 5

BETHERE AIRLINES

ANSWERS

ANSWERS

SECTION 1

Task 1.1

a) i) Standard price of materials per kg $= \dfrac{\text{Budgeted total materials cost}}{\text{Budgeted total materials usage in kg}}$

$$= \frac{£224,000}{56,000}$$

$$= £4 \text{ per kg}$$

ii) Standard usage of materials per meal $= \dfrac{\text{Budgeted total materials usage in kg}}{\text{Production (meals)}}$

$$= \frac{56,000}{112,000}$$

$$= 0.5 \text{ kg}$$

Tutorial note: The exam ner commented that a number of candidates flipped over some of the calculations in Task 1.1, so that , for example, the standard usage of materials per meal would have been 2kg rather than 0.5kg. Make sure you get them the correct way up and look at your answers to see if they are reasonable. A meal of 2kg is probably more than you could eat!

iii) Standard labour rate per hour $= \dfrac{\text{Budgeted total labour cost}}{\text{Budgeted total labour hours}}$

$$= \frac{£252,000}{28,000}$$

$$= £9 \text{ per hour}$$

iv) Standard labour hours per meal $= \dfrac{\text{Budgeted total labour hours}}{\text{Production (meals)}}$

$$= \frac{28,000}{112,000}$$

$$= 0.25 \text{ hours (or 15 minutes)}$$

v) Budgeted overhead abso-ption rate per hour $= \dfrac{\text{Budgeted total overhead cost}}{\text{Budgeted total labour hours}}$

$$= \frac{£84,000}{28,000}$$

$$= £3 \text{ per hour}$$

vi) Overheads absorbed into actual production = 27,930 hours x £3
= £83,790

Tutorial note: The examiner commented that many candidates calculated the overheads absorbed into production as

117,600 × 0.75 = £88,200

He further commented that the mistake could have been avoided by checking how the overheads are absorbed into production: in the question, it is stated that overheads are fixed and absorbed using direct labour costs. However it can be argued that since a standard cost system is in operation, the standard cost should be used, rather than actual labour hours.

vii) Total standard cost of actual production = $£560,000 \times \dfrac{117,600}{112,000}$

= £588,000

Alternatively:

	Standard cost per meal
	£
Direct material (0.5 kg × £4)	2.00
Direct labour (0.25 hours × £9	2.25
Fixed overheads (0.25 hours × £3)	0.75
	5.00

Total standard cost of actual production = 117,600 meals × £5 per meal
= £588,000

b) **Variance calculations**

Tutorial note: The examiner makes the point that you need to know these calculations inside out as in future exams you may need to work backwards from the variance to find another piece of information. Take care with the fixed overhead variances as these often cause problems.

		£	£
i)	**Direct material price variance**		
	Actual materials at actual cost	185,220	
	Actual materials at standard cost (61,740kg × £4)	246,960	
			61,740 (F)
ii)	**Direct material usage variance**		
	Actual materials at standard cost (61,740kg × £4)	246,960	
	Standard materials for actual production at standard cost (117,600 × 0.5kg × £4)	235,200	
			11,760 (A)
iii)	**Direct labour rate variance**		
	Actual hours at actual rate	279,300	
	Actual hours at standard rate (27,930 × £9)	251,370	
			27,930 (A)
iv)	**Direct labour efficiency variance**		
	Actual hours at standard rate (27,930 × £9)	251,370	
	Standard hours for actual production at standard rate (117,600 × 0.25 hours × £9)	264,600	
			13,230 (F)
v)	**Fixed overhead expenditure variance**		
	Actual cost	82,000	
	Budgeted cost	84,000	
			2,000 (F)
vi)	**Fixed overhead volume variance**		
	Actual production volume at standard rate (117,600 × 0.25 × £3)	88,200	
	Budgeted production volume at standard rate (112,000 × 0.25 × £3)	84,000	4,200 (F)

Tutorial note: This is a favourable variance because a greater production volume has been achieved than was budgeted-for. The two variances below are a further analysis of the volume variance and the sum of the two will therefore equal the volume variance. The capacity variance looks at how the actual production hours differs from the originally budgeted hours. The efficiency variance compares actual with the flexed budget, and is the same type of calculation as the labour efficiency variance.

		£	£
vii)	**Fixed overhead capacity variance**		
	Budgeted hours at standard rate (28,000 × £3)	84,000	
	Actual hours at standard rate (27,930 × £3)	83,790	
			210 (A)
viii)	**Fixed overhead efficiency variance**		
	Actual hours at standard rate (27,930 × £3)	83,790	
	Standard hours for actual production at standard rate (117,600 × 0.25 × £3)	88,200	
			4,410 (F)

c)

MEMO

To: Managing Director
From: Accounting Technician
Subject: Reasons for the variances
Date: 14 December 2006

Having investigated the materials and labour variances calculated for November 2006, I can suggest the following possible causes.

i) Direct materials price variance £61,740 (F)

This variance resulted from the purchase of materials at £3 per kg rather than the standard cost of £4 per kg. This material was cheaper and possibly of a lower quality.

ii) Direct material usage variance £11,760 (A)

The actual usage was worse than expected, and this could have been a consequence of buying inferior material.

iii) Direct labour rate variance £27,930 (A)

Direct workers were actually paid at £10 per hour , whilst we had only budgeted for a rate of £9 per hour. It is possible that the workers used were more skilled than we planned for.

iv) Direct labour efficiency variance £13,230 (F)

Actual production required fewer hours than were expected which is consistent with using more highly-skilled staff.

Tutorial note: There is more than one possible reason for each of the above variances, and marks would have been awarded for any reasonable suggestions.

Task 1.2

a) The expected price of fuel in:

December 2006 = $0.998 + 0.002 \times 12$ = £1.022 per litre
January 2007 = $0.998 + 0.002 \times 13$ = £1.024 per litre
February 2007 = $0.998 + 0.002 \times 14$ = £1.026 per litre

b) Standards are set in advance of the budget period and are based on historical information and our forecast of how these values will change over the next period. Variance analysis based on these standards is useful if prices are reasonably stable, but if prices are rising significantly, it will be difficult to set a standard cost which is relevant over the whole period, and variances will be inevitable.

c) An ideal standard assumes perfect conditions, with no wastage of labour or material. This would require the best quality materials and workers operating at maximum efficiency all the time. This is virtually impossible to achieve in practice as even the best workers cannot work to such high standards at all times, and the best quality materials and labour may not always be available.

It is not a good idea to set an ideal standard as this might demotivate the workforce. Faced with such high standards, they may well give up in the expectation of getting a negative variance no matter how hard they try. An attainable standard should be set to get the best out of the workforce.

SECTION 2

Task 2.1

a) **Performance indicators**

	September	*October*	*November*
Profit margin			
	$\frac{£148,687}{£690,000} \times 100$	$\frac{£154,125}{£697,200} \times 100$	$\frac{£125,480}{£672,000} \times 100$
	= 21.55%	= 22.11%	= 18.67%
Direct material cost as a percentage of turnover			
	$\frac{£185,000}{£690,000} \times 100$	$\frac{£185,100}{£697,200} \times 100$	$\frac{£185,220}{£672,000} \times 100$
	= 26.81%	= 26.55%	= 27.56%
Direct material cost as a percentage of turnover			
	$\frac{£274,313}{£690,000} \times 100$	$\frac{£275,975}{£697,200} \times 100$	$\frac{£279,300}{£672,000} \times 100$
	= 39.76%	= 39.58%	= 41.56%
Return on capital employed (ROCE)			
	$\frac{£148,687}{£1,211,000} \times 100$	$\frac{£154,125}{£1,218,700} \times 100$	$\frac{£125,480}{£1,204,700} \times 100$
	= 12.28%	= 12.65%	= 10.42%
Alternatively:			
	$\frac{£148,687}{£2,011,000} \times 100$	$\frac{£154,125}{£2,018,700} \times 100$	$\frac{£125,480}{£2,004,700} \times 100$
	= 7.39%	= 7.63%	= 6.26%
Meals produced as a percentage of orders			
	$\frac{115,500}{115,000}$	$\frac{116,200}{117,000}$	$\frac{117,600}{112,000}$
	= 100.43%	= 99.32%	= 105.00%
Meals produced as a percentage of capacity			
	$\frac{115,500}{125,000}$	$\frac{116,200}{125,000}$	$\frac{117,600}{125,000}$
	= 92.40%	= 92.96%	= 94.08%

b) **REPORT**

To: Managing Director
From: Accounting Technician
Subject: Performance of the Catering Division
Date: 7 December 2006

This report examines key areas of the performance of the catering division in November 2006.

1 Overall, the division performed significantly worse in November compared with the previous two months. Profit margin fell by 13% from 21.55% in October to 18.67%, and ROCE fell by 15% from 12.28% to 10.42% in the same period.

2 The problem in the division arises from the difference between meals ordered and meals produced in November. 117,600 meals were produced, which was 5% greater than the number ordered of 112,000. As the meals are perishable, excess production one day cannot be used the next day, and so leads to wastage.

3 The excess production in November meant that materials and labour costs were increased without the costs being recovered in increased sales.

4 The division worked at 94.08% of capacity in the month. We would not expect full capacity at all times as work should only be done to fulfil orders placed.

Task 2.2

a)

	Renting	*Purchasing*
	£	£
Turnover (120,000 × £6)	720,000	720,000
Cost of sales		
Materials (120,000 × £2)	240,000	240,000
Labour (120,000 × £1.50)	180,000	180,000
Fixed overheads	82,000	82,000
Rent	50,000	
Depreciation (£3m – £900,000)/(12 × 10 months)		17,500
Total cost of sales	552,000	519,500
Profit	168,000	200,500
Net assets		
(£1,204,700 + £168,000)	1,372,700	
(£1,204,700 + £1m + £200,500)		2,405,200

b)

	Renting	Purchasing
Profit margin =	$\frac{£168,000}{£720,000} \times 100$	$\frac{£200,500}{£720,000} \times 100$
	= 23.33%	= 27.85%
ROCE =	$\frac{£168,000}{£1,372,700} \times 100$	$\frac{£200,500}{£2,405,200} \times 100$
	= 12.24%	= 8.34%

c) Renting the machine gives a higher ROCE than buying the machine because the higher profit earned with a bought machine is outweighed by the large increase in net assets. Therefore the machine should be rented rather than bought. However, the ROCE is not necessarily improved when compared with the figures for October to November 2006, and further consideration should be given to whether the machine is obtained at all.

Task 2.3

a) Lifecycle costing considers costs over the whole lifecycle of a product rather than just looking at costs for short periods at some point in its lifecycle. It will include costs such as research and development at the start of the life of the product, production, selling, distribution and other costs to maintain the product, and the costs incurred in decommissioning production at the end of its life.

b) **Lifecycle costs of renting the machine:**

	£
Rental (£50,000 × 12months × 10 years)	6,000,000
Maintenance (£50,000 × 10 years)	500,000
Decommissioning	100,000
Total	6,600,000

Lifecycle costs of buying the machine:

	£
Purchase	3,000,000
Maintenance (£50,000 × 10 years)	500,000
Decommissioning	100,000
Scrap value	(900,000)
Total	2,700,000

UNIT 9

PRACTICE EXAM 6

GEEZER SCIENTIFIC

ANSWERS

ANSWERS

SECTION 1

Task 1.1

Note: The question asks for answers to be rounded, where appropriate, to two decimal places

a) The average selling price = Turnover / Units sold = £4,393,000/382,000 = £11.50

b) The number of instruments produced

= Units sold + closing stock – opening stock

= 382,000+15,000-4,000 = 393.000

c) The average material cost of each Pipstrelle = Materials cost / Number of instruments produced

= 1,650,600 / 393,000 = £4.20

d) The average hourly pay rate for basic hours = Basic Labour cost / basic labour hours

= £987,840 / 117,600 = £8.40

e) The average hourly pay rate for overtime = Labour overtime cost / labour overtime hours

= £18,344 / 1,456 = £12.60

f) The variable overhead cost per hour = Variable overhead cost / Variable overhead hours

= £190,489 / 119,056 = £1.60

g) The gross profit margin percentage = Profit / turnover

= £907,446 / £4,393,000 = 20.66%

Task 1.2

Operating budget for Pipstrelle Division year to 30 November 2009

a) **Sales volume**

	Units
Sales in 2008	382,000
Sales in 2009 (25% higher) 382,000 x 1.25	477,500

b) **Production of saleable units**

Sales in 2009 (see above)	477,500
Add: closing stock	5,000
Less: opening stock	(15,000)
Production units	467,500

c) *Cost of materials*

	£
Current price per unit (see above)	4.20
Price increase per unit	0.10
Price (2009)	4.30

Total cost:
Production units x price 467,500 x £4.30 = £2,010,250

d) *Units assembled*

	Units
Production of saleable units (85%)	467,500
Reject rate (467,500 x 15/85))	82,500
Number of units to be assembled (100 %)	550,000

e)

	Assembly	*Testing*	*Dismantling*	*Total hours*
Number of units	550,000	550,000	82,500	
Time required				
(mins each)	12.0	3.00	3.00	
(hours each)	0.2	0.05	0.05	
Hours required				
(units x hours each)	110,000	27,500	4,125	141,625

) *Annual labour cost*

Total hours required	141,625
Less: Basic hours available (75 staff x 1,680 hours per year)	126,000
Overtime hours required	15,625

	Hours	*Rate per hour (W1)*	*Cost* £
Basic labour	126,000	8.82	1,111,320
Overtime labour	15,625	13.23	206,719
			1,318,039

Working

2009 hourly rate = 2008 hourly rates per hour x 1.05

Basic = £8.40 x 1.05 = £8.82

Overtime = £12.60 x 1.05 = £13.23

) *Overhead costs*

2008 variable rate (per hours)	£1.60
2009 (add 5%) (per hour)	£1.68

	£
Total variable overhead cost (variable rate x total hours)	237,930
Fixed costs per question	750,000
Total overhead cost	987,930

h) *Cost of production for the year:*

	£
Materials	2,010,250
Labour	1,318,039
Overheads	987,930
Total	4,316,219

Therefore cost per unit = Total cost / production units = £4,316,219 / 467,500 = £9.23

i) *Profit per instrument:*

	£
Sales price (given in question)	11.00
Cost per unit (see above)	9.23
Profit per unit	1.77

Profit margin = (Profit per unit / Sales price per unit) x 100 = (1.77 / 11.00) x 100 = 16.09%

Note: You were NOT required to draw up an operating statement (unlike previous papers).

Task 1.3

a) Number of tests to be subcontracted

Tests required	550,000
Capacity (given in question)	425,000
Balance to be subcontracted	125,000

Therefore 130,000 tests need to be subcontracted (rounded up to next 10,000).

b) Additional cost of subcontracting over overtime:

Overtime cost:

Labour time per test = 3 mins = 0.05 hours

	£
Cost of overtime labour per unit = Hourly rate x 0.05 = 13.23 x 0.05	0.6615
Cost of variable overhead per unit = Hourly rate x 0.05 = 1.68 x 0.05	0.0840
Cost per test	0.7455

	£
Total cost of overtime = £0.7455 x 130,000 =	96,915
Total cost of 130,000 subcontracted tests (130,000 x £1.40)	182,000
Additional cost of subcontracting	85,085

Alternative solution. This solution rounds the cost per unit to 2 decimal places (and was the solution given by the examiner) **Note**: There appears to be no guidance on this part of the question whether to round or not)

Overtime cost

Labour time per test = 3 mins = 0.05 hours

	£
Cost of overtime labour per unit = Hourly rate x 0.05 = 13.23 x 0.05 =	£0.66
Cost of variable overhead per unit = Hourly rate x 0.05 = 1.68 x 0.05 =	£0.08
Cost per test	£0.74

	£
Total cost of overtime = £0.74 x 130,000 =	96,200
Total cost of 130,000 subcontracted tests (130,000 x £1.40)	182,000
Additional cost of subcontracting	85,800

(c)

	£
Original cost	4,316,219
Additional cost of subcontracting	85,800
Revised cost	4,402,019

Revised cost per instrument = £4,402,019 / 467,500 = £9.42

Profit per instrument = Selling price – cost per instrument
= £11.00 - £9.42 = £1.58

Profit percentage = (Profit per instrument / selling price per instrument) x 100
= (£1.58 / £11.00) x 100 = 14.36%

Tip: Questions such as this one will almost always use all the 'further information' provided. It can be beneficial to tick off the information on the question paper as it is used.

Task 1.4

From: An Other Student
To: Myra Benjamin
Sent: 4 December 2008
Subject: Subcontracting and capacity

a) i) Geezer has budgeted to produce 467,500 instruments. A 15% rejection rate means that we need to assemble and test 550,000 instruments. The maximum capacity of the Quality Control Department is 425,000 instruments. Given that orders to the subcontractors must be placed in multiples of 10,000 we would need to subcontract 130,000 units.

If we subcontract the cost of a test is £1.40 whereas if we do the work in-house, using overtime, the cost is £0 74. This will save us £0.66 per test.

ii) The profit margin for all instruments falls if we subcontract from 16.1% to 14.4%. For the instruments that are subcontracted the cost per saleable instrument will rise by £0.78 (£0.66 per instrument tested but 15% are expected to be rejected). The margin declines from £1.77 to £0.99. Thus the subcontracted instruments are still profitable.

b) Alternatives to subcontracting:

(**BPP Note**: You are only required to give ONE strategy. More are given here for demonstration purposes.)

- Improved quality of materials to reduce reject rates should be encouraged. This might be through offering higher prices for good quality materials; introducing penalties for rejects, or working with suppliers on a TQM programme.
- Capacity might be increased by introducing shift work. It may be that additional pay for shift work is less than that for overtime which would save money even on the first budget.
- Capacity might be increased by looking for other subcontractors who may be cheaper.
- Testing of the components could be done before assembly. Perhaps the assembly staff could do this. If the rejects could be detected earlier in the process this would reduce the volume to be tested in your area and to be dismantled.
- Alternative suppliers with better quality standards might be used to reduce the rejection rate.

Tip: Please note that Labour was NOT the limiting factor here, it was the lack of testing machine capacity.

SECTION 2

Task 2.1

a) Turnover per chargeable hour = Turnover / Chargeable hours

= £4,000,000 / 200,000

= £20.00 per chargeable hour

b) Variable cost per chargeable hour:

i) Materials = Increase in material costs / Increase in chargeable hours

= £25,000 / 50,000 hours

= £0.50 per chargeable hour

ii) Energy = Increase in energy costs / Increase in chargeable hours

= £20,000 / 50,000 hours

= £0.40 per chargeable hour

iii) Equipment hire = Increase in equipment hire costs / Increase in chargeable hours

= £25,000 / 50,000 hours

= £0.50 per chargeable hour

iv) Administration = Increase in administration costs / Increase in chargeable hours

= £5,000 / 50,000 hours

= £0.10 per chargeable hour

v) Collection & delivery = Increase in Collection & delivery costs / Increase in chargeable hours

= £12,500 / 50,000 hours

= £0.25 per chargeable hour

) Overtime costs per chargeable hour = Increase in overtime costs / Increase in chargeable hours

= £630,000 / 50,000 hours

= £12.60 per chargeable hour

) Number of workshops for maximum level = 250,000

maximum hours per workshop = 70,000 hours

Therefore need (250,000 hours / 70,000 hours) = 3.57 workshops = 4 workshops

e)

	Energy	Equipment hire	Administration
	£	£	£
At Minimum sales level:			
Total Costs	195,000	250,000	380,000
Less: Variable costs	£0.40 x 200,000 = 80,000	£0.50 x 200,000 = 100,000	£0.10 x 200,000 = 20,000
	80,000	100,000	20,000
Fixed cost	115,000	150,000	360,000

Task 2.2

Operating statement for the year to 30 November 2008

	Actual	Flexed budget	Variance
	£	£	£
Turnover (W1)	4,560,000	4,800,000	240,000 (A)
Costs			
Materials (W2)	123,500	120,000	3,500 (A)
Labour (basic hours) (W3)	1,390,000	1,470,000	80,000 (F)
Labour overtime (W4)	955,000	819,000	136,000 (A)
Energy (W5)	208,000	211,000	3,000 (F)
Equipment hire (W6)	297,200	270,000	27,200 (A)
Rent and rates (W7)	281,700	300,000	18,300 (F)
Administration (W8)	389,900	384,000	5,900 (A)
Collection & delivery (W9)	71,400	60,000	11,400 (A)
Depreciation (W10)	398,800	410,000	11,200 (F)
Total	4,115,500	4,044,000	71,500 (A)
Profit	444,500	756,000	311,500 (A)
Profit % of turnover	9.7	15.8	

WORKINGS

1) The budget is flexed on a sales volume of 240,000 hours.

   Flexed budget hours x Turnover per chargeable hour = 240,000 x £20 = £4,800,000

2) Flexed budget hours x variable materials cost = 240,000 x £0.50 = £120,000

3) Labour (basic hours) are a fixed cost

4) (Flexed budget hours – basic hours) x Labour overtime costs per chargeable hour = (240,000 – 175,000) x £12.60 = £819,000

5)

	£
Cost at Minimum Sales level	195,000
Less: Variable cost at min sales level (£0.40 x 200,000)	80,000
Fixed Cost	115,000
Add: Flexed budget hours x variable energy cost = 240,000 x £0.40	96,000
Total Energy cost	211,000

6)

	£
Cost at Minimum Sales level	250,000
Less: Variable cost at min sales level (£0.50 x 200,000)	100,000
Fixed Cost	150,000
Add: Flexed budget hours x variable equipment cost = 240,000 x £0.50	120,000
Total equipment hire cost	270,000

7) 4 workshops will be required. Flexed budget = 4 x £75,000 = £300,000

8)

	£
Cost at Minimum Sales level	380,000
Less: Variable cost at min sales level (£0.10 x 200,000)	20,000
Fixed Cost	360,000
Add: Flexed budget hours x variable admin cost = 240,000 x £0.10	24,000
Total admin cost	384,000

9) Flexed budget hours x variable collection and delivery cost = 240,000 x £0.25 = £60,000

10) Depreciation is a fixed cost.

Task 2.3

REPORT

From: An Other Student
To: The Board of directors
Sent: 4 December 2008
Subject: Divisional Performance

a) The flexed budget for the division shows a profit of £756,000 (15.3 % of income) compared with the actual profit of £444,500 (9.7%). This fall in profitability may be explained by the following

- Turnover was £240,000 below the flexed budget. This was because the revenue per chargeable hour was £19.00, £1 per hour less than budget.
- Labour overtime costs (see below) were £136,000 above budget.
- Equipment hire was £27,200 above budget.
- Collection and delivery costs were £11,400 above budget.
- These adverse variances were, however, offset by some savings, including £80,000 on basic labour hours, £18,300 on rent and rates and £11,200 on depreciation.

b) Labour (basic hours) costs are £80,000 lower than the flexed budget. This may be the result of:

- Employing lower grade / less skilled workers. This might result in more overtime being needed as these workers may be less efficient. In addition they may use more materials.
- Covering vacancies with overtime. Again this will be more expensive. The overall effect may be to the detriment of the organisation.
- Inaccurate budgeting.

c) A statistical process that could be used is Time Series Analysis.

Time series analysis is generally used for forecasting sales. By examining past sales data predictions may be made for future sales. Time series analysis separates out a number of factors that combine to make total sales. These are:

- Trend
- Seasonal variations
- Random variations.

This may improve the accuracy of the budgetary process and facilitate improved planning and control.

Tip: If you found this paper tricky practise more papers. The broad format of this paper is established and unlikely to change radically but each scenario is different. However, ensure that you have brushed up on any gaps in your knowledge and understanding before attempting another paper.

UNIT 9

PRACTICE EXAM 7

KEEPKOOL LTD

ANSWERS

ANSWERS

SECTION 1

Task 1.1

a) **Forecast sales of air conditioning units**

			Units	
Quarter	*Q1*	*Q2*	*Q3*	*Q4 (not asked for here but needed below (W1))*
Sales 2007/2008	15,000	5,000	5,000	20,000
2% increase	300	100	100	400
Sales 2008/2009	15,300	5,100	5,100	20,400

b) **Production budget in units**

	Q1	Q2	Q3
Sales (see above)	15,300	5,100	5,100
Less opening stock	(306)	(102)	(102)
Add closing stock (W1)	102	102	408
Net production	15,096	5,100	5,406
Add Rejects (W2)	76	26	28
Gross production	15,172	5,126	5,434

Workings

W1

	Q1	Q2	Q3
Closing stock = 2% of forecast sales in next quarter	£5,100 x 2% = £102	£5,100 x 2% = £102	£20,400 x 2% = 408

W2

Rejects = Net production / 199

Q1	Q2	Q3
15,096/199 =76	5,100/199 =26	5,406/199 =28

Note: 1 in every 200 items is rejected. So in above calculation net production is divided by 199 not 200. Also note that rejects are rounded up to the nearest whole number as required by the question.

c) **Cost of materials budget**

		Quarters	
	Q1	*Q2*	*Q3*
Gross production (see above)	15,172	5,126	5,434
Cost per unit (W1)	£575	£575	£575
Cost of production (gross production x cost per unit)	£8,723,900	£2,947,450	£3,124,550

WORKING

		£
Unit cost of components:	A	180
	B	255
	C	140
		575

d) **Labour hours budget**

	Q1	*Q2*	*Q3*
Gross production	15,172	5,126	5,434
Labour hours required per unit	1.5	1.5	1.5
Total hours required (gross production x labour hours required per unit)	22,758	7,689	8,151
Keepkool production staff standard labour available (480 hours x 25 employees)	12,000	12,000	12,000
Agency staff standard labour available (480 hours x 15 employees)	7,200	0	0
Overtime hours needed (Total hours required – Keepkool and Agency standard labour hours available)	3,558	0	0
Idle time (hours)	0	4,311	3,849

e) **Cost of labour budget**

	Q1	*Q2*	*Q3*
	£	£	£
Keepkool standard hours (12,000 hours (see above) x £12 per hour)	144,000	144,000	144,000
Agency standard hours (7,200 hours (see above) x £20 per hour)	144,000	–	–
Overtime worked (3,558 hours (see above) x £18 per hour (overtime is paid at 150% of basic labour rate = £12 x 150%))	64,044		
Total cost of labour	352,044	144,000	144,000

f) **Total cost of production budget**

	Q1	*Q2*	*Q3*
	£	£	£
Cost of material (see above)	8,723,900	2,947,450	3,124,550
Cost of labour (see above)	352,044	144,000	144,000
Production overheads (W1)	293,790	240,000	240,000
	9,369,734	3,331,450	3,508,550

Working

W1

	Q1	*Q2*	*Q3*
Variable overheads (£5 x labour hours)	£5 x 22,758= £113,790	£5 x 12,000= £60,000	£5 x 12,000= £60,000
Fixed overhead cost	£180,000	£180,000	£180,000
	£293,790	£240,000	£240,000

Note: Variable overheads are charged over 12,000 hours in Q2 and Q3 as this labour has to be paid even when idle.

Task 1.2

a) **Calculation of maximum number of units that can be produced in each quarter without using agency staff**

	Hours
Keepkool production staff standard labour available (480 hours x 25 employees)	12,000
Keepkool production staff overtime labour available (120 hours x 25 employees)	3,000
Hours available	15,000
Each unit takes 1.5 hours, so maximum units (15,000 hours / 1.5)	10,000

b) **Revised production budget (in units)**

	Units			
	Q1	*Q2*	*Q3*	*Q4*
Maximum production (see above)	10,000	10,000	10,000	10,000
Rejected units ((1 in 200) or x 0.005)	50	50	50	50
Total available for sale (maximum production less rejected units)	9,950	9,950	9,950	9,950
Forecast sales demand 2008/2009 (see above)	15,300	5,100	5,100	20,400
Shortage / (Excess)	5,350	(4,850)	(4,850)	10,450
Carry forward excess	–	4,850	4,850	(9,700)
Shortage	5,350	–	–	750
Less Opening stock (per question) which can be sold	(306)			–
Net shortfall of units	5,044			750
Rejects = Net shortfall / 199 (Note)	26			4
Gross production shortage	5,070			754
Hours required (gross production shortage x 1.5 hours per unit)	7,605			1,131
Agency staff required to produce shortfall (divide by 480 hours)	16			3

Note: 1 in every 200 items is rejected. So in above calculation net shortfall is divided by 199 not 200. Also note that rejects are rounded up to the nearest whole number as required by the question.

There are numerous ways of laying out this calculation. Candidates should ensure that their workings are shown clearly and that there is a clear narrative.

c) **Revised labour budget**

	Q1	*Q2*	*Q3*	*Q4*
	Units	Units	Units	Units
Gross production (W1)	15,070	10,000	10,000	10,754
Labour hours required (W1)	22,605	15,000	15,000	16,131
Keepkool production staff standard labour available	12,000	12,000	12,000	12,000
Keepkool production staff maximum overtime	3,000	3,000	3,000	3,000
Excess hours required	7,605	0	0	1,131
Costs	£	£	£	£
Keepkool production staff standard labour (12,000 hours x £12 per hour)	144,000	144,000	144,000	144,000
Keepkool production staff overtime (3,000 hours x £18 per hour)	54,000	54,000	54,000	54,000
Agency staff (W2)	153,600	0	0	28,800
Total cost of labour	351,600	198,000	198,000	226,800

WORKINGS

1)

	Q1	*Q2*	*Q3*	*Q4*
	Units	Units	Units	Units
Maximum production from task 1.2 b above	10,000	10,000	10,000	10,000
add gross production shortage met by agency	5,070			754
Gross Production	15,070	10,000	10,000	10,754
Labour hours required = Gross Production x 1.5 hours	22,605	15,000	15,000	16,131

2)

	Q1	*Q4*
Agency staff required to produce shortfall (see above)	16	3
Cost = Staff number x 480 hours x £20 per hour	153,600	28,800

Task 1.3

REPORT

To:	The Board of Directors	**Subject:**	Agency staff
From:	Accounting Technician	**Date:**	19 June 2008

This report explains the extent to which agency staff can be restricted, the implications this has for staff costs and ways to overcome restrictions on production.

a) The demand for Keepkool's output varies from quarter to quarter. Because of this seasonal nature of our sales we have been using agency staff. Agency staff will have to be used in quarters 1 and 4.

Please find attached to this report a table that shows the maximum number of units that can be produced without using agency staff. This shows that if we do not use agency staff then our output will be limited to below the amount required to meet demand in quarters 1 and 4. This is because of the restriction on overtime as well as the limit on the number of permanent employees.

The implications for staff costs is that the overall costs will be lower as Keepkool production staff are paid at an overtime rate of £18 per hour whereas agency staff are paid at £20 per hour. However there is an increase in costs in the first three quarters when we will incur a cost of £747,600 compared to the original budget of £640,044. There will be a saving in the fourth quarter as only three agency staff are to be used instead of 15 in the original budget.

b) Restrictions on production may be overcome by: (Note only two required)

- Smoothing out the seasonal nature of demand. This may be through the use of discounts in periods of low demand and increasing prices in periods of high demand.
- Production could be outsourced.
- Increasing the number of permanent staff.
- Negotiating an increase in the number of hours worked per member of staff.
- Employing part-time staff to cover peak periods.

Note:
Credit would be given for any two reasonable suggestions.
There are some easy marks here for setting out the report in the correct format.

SECTION 2

Task 2.1

a) Calculation of budgeted prices and costs

i) Selling price per litre =
Turnover / Sales volume =
£10,000,000 / 2,000,000 = £5

ii) Cost of material per litre =
Materials / Sales volume =
£1,600,000/2,000,000 = £0.80

iii) Cost of labour per litre =
Labour / Sales volume =
£1,800,000/2,000,000 = £0.90

iv) Variable cost of storage
Storage is a semi variable cost

As volume increases from 3,000,000 to 2,000,000 = 1,000,000
Costs increase from £870,000 to £1,030,000 = £160,000
Therefore, storage variable cost per litre 160,000/1,000,000 = £0.16

v) Storage fixed cost per year
At a budgeted sales volume of 3,000,000

Total budgeted cost	=	£1,030,000
Variable costs 3,000,000 x £0.16	=	£480,000
Therefore, storage fixed cost per year in		£550,000

b) **Flexed budgeted and actual operating statement for Kleanpacks Ltd for the last 12 months**

	Flexed budget		*Actual*	*Variance*
Sales Volume (litres)		2,600,000	2,600,000	
		£'000	£'000	£'000
Turnover (2,600,000 x £5)		13,000	14,300	1,300 (F)
Costs:				
Material (2,600,000 x £0.80)	2,080		1,950	130 (F)
Labour (2,600,000 x £0.90)	2,340		2,392	52 (A)
Power (2,600,000 x £0.65)	1,690		1,768	78 (A)
Storage (W1)	966		992	26 (A)
Transport (W2)	1,430		1,410	20 (F)
Maintenance (W3)	770		790	20 (A)
Depreciation (W3)	970		960	10 (F)
Admin expenses (W3)	650		658	8 (A)
Total expenses		10,896	10,920	–
Operating profit		2,104	3,380	1,276 (F)

WORKINGS

1)

	£
Fixed costs	550,000
Variable costs (2,600,000 x £0.16)	416,000
	966,000

2) Transport is a stepped cost

2,600,000 / 250,000 = 10.4 , so Kleanpacks will need 11 units (perhaps tankers)

Therefore transport costs are 11 x £130,000 = £1,430,000

3) Maintenance, depreciation and administrative expenses are fixed costs and remain unchanged from the draft budget.

c) **Explanation of variances**

Note: only one possible variance was required. Credit would be given for any reasonable suggestions.

i) The favourable turnover variance is a result of an increase in the selling price. The selling price may have increased due to an increase in demand perhaps because of fewer substitutes or changes in consumer taste.

ii) The favourable material variance may be due to either a decrease in the price being paid for materials, a decrease in the quantity of materials used per unit of production or a combination of the two.

iii) The adverse labour variance may have arisen due to using more labour, paying more per hour of labour, or a combination of the two.

iv) The adverse power variance may be a result of an increase in the price of power per unit, more power being used, or a combination of the two.

v) The adverse storage variance may be the result of an increase in the fixed cost element, perhaps an increase in rent or rates, or an increase in the variable component.

vi) The favourable transport variance may have arisen due to a decrease in unit costs, for example a decrease in the price of petrol; or more efficient use of transport.

Task 2.2

From: Accounting Technician
To: Jan Barry
Date: 19 June 2008
Subject: Budgeting matters

Hi Jan

I am e-mailing you with an explanation of how to improve the company's budgeting procedures:

a) i) At the moment the budgeting process is carried out by the accounts department. There would be a number of advantages if departments themselves were involved in the budget setting process. This is a bottom up approach and may allow for more accurate information as well as increasing motivation within each department.

ii) Currently we use periodic budgeting where a budget is set for a period and is then reviewed after the period end. An alternative to this is rolling budgets, this is where budgets are updated on a regular basis (monthly or quarterly). This enables the company to be more flexible and to ensure adequate resources are available.

iii) The company may consider the use of computer generated models. These can speed up the overall budget process and provide flexibility to respond to changes in markets.

b) In order to motivate managers to be more involved in preparing budgets the following methods might be considered: (**Note**: only two methods are required)

- Departmental managers should be educated and trained so that they understand the importance of budgeting and how their departmental budget fits with the achievement of the overall objectives of Kleanpacks.
- There should be recognition of the achievements of departments in meeting their budgets. This may be either financial or non-financial.
- Similarly there should be an acknowledgement, that if targets are not met then, this too is noted by senior management.
- The accounts department should offer support to departments when preparing their budgets.

Note: Credit would be given for any two reasonable suggestions.

Tip: try to ensure that answers relate to the question set and are not merely a brain dump of everything you know about a subject!

UNIT 9

PRACTICE EXAM 8

KARTONS LTD

ANSWERS

ANSWERS

SECTION 1

Task 1.1

Budgets for the four weeks ending 25 January 2008

a) **Production budget in units**

	250 ml cartons units	*500 ml cartons* units
Sales	250,000	100,000
Less: opening stock	(62,500)	(25,000)
Add: closing stock (W)	65,000	26,000
Production in units	252,500	101,000

WORKING

Closing stock

Next period sales:

250 ml cartons = 250,000 × 1.04 = 260,000
500 ml cartons = 100,000 × 1.04 = 104,000

Closing stock is to be equal to 5 days forecast sales

250 ml cartons = 260,000 × 5/20 = 65,000
500 ml cartons = 104,000 × 5/20 = 26,000

b) **Material quantity**

	250 ml cartons units	*500 ml cartons* units
Production in units	252,500	101,000
	Sq m	Sq m
Usage $252,500 \times \frac{40}{10,000}$	1,010	
$101,000 \times \frac{50}{10,000}$		505
Waste (W)	21	11
Material quantity required	1,031	516

WORKING

The final product requires 40 or 50 square centimetres of material but before this there is wastage of 2%. Therefore wastage:

250 ml cartons = 1,010 × 2/98 = 21
500 ml cartons = 505 × 2/98 = 11

c) **Material purchases in sq m**

	Sq m
Materials required (1,031 + 516)	1,547
Less: opening stock	(132)
Add: closing stock	145
Total material purchases	1,560

d) **Cost of materials purchases**

Materials purchases 1,560 sq m × £55 = £85,800

e) **Labour hours required**

		250 ml cartons units	*500 ml cartons* units
Production in units		252,500	101,000
		Hours	Hours
Hours required	$\frac{252,500}{200}$	1,263	
	$\frac{101,000}{160}$		632

f) **Basic labour hours and overtime**

Total basic hours available = 10 employees × 35 hours × 4 weeks
= 1,400 hours

	Hours
Total hours required (1,263 + 632)	1,895
Basic hours	1,400
Overtime hours	495
Total hours	1,895

g) **Cost of direct labour**

	£
Basic hours 1,400 × £8	11,200
Overtime hours 495 × £8 × 150%	5,940
	17,140

h) **Cost of production**

	250 ml carton	500 ml carton
	£	£
Materials		
1,031 × £55	56,705	
516 × £55		28,380
Direct labour		
1,263 × £9.045 (W)	11,424	
632 × £9.045		5,716
Overheads		
1,263 × £15	18,945	
632 × £15		9,480
	87,074	43,576

WORKING

$$\text{Average hourly labour rate} = \frac{£17,140}{1,895} = £9.045$$

Task 1.2

a) **Production units of 250 ml cartons**

	250 ml cartons units
Sales (250,000 × 1.08)	270,000
Less: opening stock	(62,500)
Add: closing stock (270,000 × 1.04 × 5/20)	70,200
Production in units	277,700

b) **Material purchases in square metres**

	Sq m
250 ml cartons (277,700×40/10,000)	1,111
500 ml cartons (101,000 × 50/10,000)	505
	1,616
Faulty production (1,616 × 2/98)	33
Add: closing stock	145
Less: opening stock	(132)
	1,662

c) **Basic labour hours and overtime hours**

	Hours
250 ml (277,700/200)	1,389
500 ml (101,000/160)	632
	2,021

Hours available		
Basic (10 × 35 × 4)	1,400	
Overtime (10 × 50)	500	(1,900)
Shortfall		121

Task 1.3

MEMO

To: Board of Directors
From: Accounting Technician
Date: December 2007
Subject: Revised sales forecast and production plans for 250 ml cartons

The revised sales forecasts for 250 ml cartons for the four week period ending 25 January 2008 now indicate that production levels will require 1,662 square metres of material and 2,021 labour hours. The production director cannot acquire more than 1,500 square metres of material in time for January production therefore there will not be enough materials for all required production. The shortfall in production due to the materials is 40,500 cartons (162 × 10,000/40). The production director also does not wish the 10 employees to work more than 50 hours of overtime during the period which would be the case with the revised production budget as there is a shortage of 121 hours of overtime. This would result in a shortfall in production of 24,200 cartons (121 hours × 200).

The main restriction therefore is lack of materials. Methods of overcoming the restrictions:

1. Decrease the amount of closing stock of finished goods that is required at the end of the month. At the moment the amount of closing stock is equal to 5 days of the following month's sales. If this requirement were reduced then production levels could be lower and the overtime limit would no longer be a problem. However even if all the planned closing stock of material were available for full production this would still not be enough to meet demand. If closing stock were reduced in January this would mean that in order to return to the required levels of closing stock then production would be higher in February.

2. In order to deal with the shortage of labour an additional employee could be taken on. This would then provide 140 additional basic hours (35 × 4) which would cover the deficit in labour hours.

3. A new supplier could be sought for the materials in order to increase the amount that is available in each month. This would have little effect on future production unless the materials were of higher or lower quality than the currently used materials and may also cost more than we currently pay if there is such a great demand for the material.

4. The materials and labour problems could be dealt with by subcontracting the additional production if there is a company capable of producing the extra cartons for us. The problem will be maintaining the quality of the sub-contracted cartons and ensuring the necessary timescale for production.

5. We could also consider decreasing the production of 500ml cartons in order to free up materials and labour hours for additional 250 ml carton production. If the additional materials are taken from 500 ml carton materials then this would see a reduction in production of 32,400 500 ml cartons (162 × 10,000/50).

SECTION 2

Task 2.1

a) i) **Budgeted selling price per unit** $= \frac{£15,000,000}{50,000 \text{ units}} = £300.00$

ii) **Budgeted cost of material A per unit** $= \frac{£2,500,000}{50,000} = £50.00$

Budgeted cost of material B per unit $= \frac{£990,000}{50,000} = £19.80$

Budgeted cost of material C per unit $= \frac{£1,365,000}{50,000} = £27.30$

iii) **Budgeted labour cost per unit** $= \frac{£2,700,000}{50,000} = £54.00$

iv) **Budgeted energy fixed cost**

	£'000
Variable cost (50,000 × £18)	900
Total budgeted cost	1,340
Fixed cost	440

b) i) **Actual selling price per unit** $= \frac{£16,500,000}{60,000} = £275$

ii) **Actual cost of material A per unit** $= \frac{£3,132,000}{60,000} = £52.20$

Actual cost of material B per unit $= \frac{£1,557,000}{60,000} = £25.95$

Actual cost of material C per unit $= \frac{£1,764,000}{60,000} = £29.40$

iii) **Actual labour cost per unit** $= \frac{£2,980,000}{60,000} = £49.67$

c) **Operating statement**

	Flexed Budget 60,000 £'000	*Actual* 60,000 £'000	*Variance* £'000
Turnover (60,000 × £300)	18,000	16,500	1,500 (A)
Material A (60,000 × £50)	3,000	3,132	132 (A)
Material B (60,000 × £19.80)	1,188	1,557	369 (A)
Material C (60,000 × £27.30)	1,638	1,764	126 (A)
Labour (60,000 × £54.00)	3,240	2,980	260 (F)
Maintenance (6 × 149)	894	987	93 (A)
Energy (W)	1,080	1,110	30 (A)
Variable costs	11,040	11,530	
Contribution	6,960	4,970	1,990 (A)
Energy – fixed	440	440	–
Rent and rates	940	945	5 (A)
Administrative expenses	850	800	50 (F)
Operating profit	4,730	2,785	1,945 (A)

WORKING

Energy is a semi-variable cost and therefore the variable element must be taken into account when determining contribution.

Flexed budget = 60,000 × £18 = £1,080,000
Actual = £1,550,000 – 440,000 = £1,110,000

An alternative method would be to treat the entire energy cost as variable in which case the operating statement would be as follows:

	Flexed Budget 60,000 £'000	*Actual* 60,000 £'000	*Variance* £'000
Turnover (60,000 × £300)	18,000	16,500	1,500 (A)
Material A (60,000 × £50)	3,000	3,132	132 (A)
Material B (60,000 × £19.80)	1,188	1,557	369 (A)
Material C (60,000 × £27.30)	1,638	1,764	126 (A)
Labour (60,000 × £54.00)	3,240	2,980	260 (F)
Maintenance (6 × 149)	894	987	93 (A)
Energy (1,080/1,110 ÷ 440)	1,520	1,550	30 (A)
Variable costs	11,480	10,970	
Contribution	6,520	4,530	1,990 (A)
Rent and rates	940	945	5 (A)
Administrative expenses	850	800	50 (F)
Operating profit	4,730	2,785	1,945 (A)

Task 2.2

MEMO

To: Gill Johns
From: Accounting technician
Date: December 2007
Subject: Annual performance variances

Variances

As requested I have compared the flexed budget at 60,000 units of sales and production to the actual figures and identified any variances. For those variances over £50,000 I have determined what action is required in order to investigate the variances.

Turnover £50,000 Adverse variance

This was caused by reducing the selling price from £300 to £275. Although more units were sold this did not outweigh the drop in unit price. It must be discovered why the selling price was reduced and why even more units were not sold at this reduced price. This will be the area of the sales manager.

Material costs
Material A £132,000 Adverse variance
Material B £369,000 Adverse variance
Material C £126,000 Adverse variance

There are two areas which must be considered when investigating these material cost variances:

- the price paid for the materials from the purchasing manager
- the amount of material used in production from the production manager or stores manager.

These large adverse variances could be price variances due to more being paid per unit of material or usage variances in that more is being used in production or a mixture of the two.

Labour £260,000 Favourable variance

Even though this is a favourable variance it should still be investigated. The personnel manager should be approached for information about the wage rates and the production manager about the employees used in production. This variance itself may partly be the cause of other variances. For example if lower grade employees are being used then they may be more wasteful with materials causing adverse materials variances. Alternatively the relationship between the variances could be the other way around. For example if new, higher quality and more expensive materials are being used then the labour force may be able to work more quickly causing the favourable labour variance.

Maintenance £93,000 Adverse variance

These costs are a stepped cost with a budgeted amount of £149,000 for every 10,000 binoculars produced. The reasons for this variance must be taken up with the maintenance department. Did they work more hours or were costs higher or perhaps the budgeted figure is out of date?

Reduction of selling price

The selling price of the binoculars is £25 less per unit than the £300 each that was budgeted. It is true that at this lower price 10,000 more binoculars have been sold but this does not make up for the lowering unit price leading to an adverse variance of £1,500,000.

The reduction in revenue from sales in conjunction with adverse variances in almost all cost areas has led to a much lower profit figure than was budgeted at £2,785,000 compared to the budgeted figure of £4,730,000. Therefore clearly the policy of dropping the price has not worked. It is also arguable that with so many of the costs of Miramar being variable costs rather than fixed costs that a drop in selling price in order to increase quantity sold is not a policy that it should be pursuing.

UNIT 9

PRACTICE EXAM 9

BRIGHTER COVERS LTD

ANSWERS

ANSWERS

SECTION 1

Task 1.1

a) **Forecast Sales (units) for August 2007**

	Model	
	Standard	*Luxury*
Sales	68,850	33,150

WORKING

Standard covers 67,500 x 102% = 68,850
Luxury covers 32,500 x 102% = 33,150

b) **Production Budget (units)**

	Model	
	Standard	*Luxury*
Sales	68,850	33,150
Add closing finished stocks	5,508	2,652
Less opening finished stocks	(5,303)	(2,507)
Planned production	69,055	33,295

WORKING

Closing stocks: Standard $\frac{68,850}{25} \times 2 = 5,508$

Luxury $\frac{33,150}{25} \times 2 = 2,652$

c) **Material purchases budget (grams)**

	Model	
	Standard	*Luxury*
Production units (each unit uses 20 grams)	69,055	33,295
Production material used (units x 20)	1,381,100	665,900
Wastage (4/96) (W)	57,546	27,746
Gross production material purchased(g)	1,438,646	693,646

WORKING

Calculation of wastage fraction

4% of material purchased is wasted. For 100 grams purchased the following applies:

Purchased	100
Waste	4
Used	96

Therefore the waste amount is 4/96 of the used figure

d) **Cost of materials purchases budget**

	Model	
	Standard	*Luxury*
	£	£
Materials purchases in grams	1,438,646	693,646
Cost of material purchases	£71,932	£173,412

WORKING

Standard $\frac{1,438,646}{1,000} \times £50 = £71,932$

Luxury $\frac{693,646}{1,000} \times £250 = £173,412$

Tutorial note

The Chief Assessor noted that some students had difficulty converting grams to kilograms.

There are 1,000 grams to a kilogram

Thus, 1,438,646 grams $= \frac{1,438,646}{1,000}$ kilograms

e) **Direct labour hours budget**

	Model		
	Standard	*Luxury*	*Total*
	£	£	£
Gross production (units)	69,055	33,295	
Labour hours required (× 1/15)	4,604	2,220	6,824
Standard hours available (W)	4,200	2,100	6,300
Overtime hours required	404	120	524

WORKING

Standard hours: Standard model 35 hours × 5 weeks × 24 = 4,200
Luxury model 35 hours × 5 weeks × 12 = 2,100

f) **Cost of labour budget**

	Model		
	Standard	*Luxury*	*Total*
	£	£	£
Standard hours x £10 per hour	42,000	21,000	63,000
Overtime hours x £15 per hour	6,060	1,800	7,860
Total cost of labour	48,060	22,800	70,860

g) **Budgeted operating statement**

	Model		
	Standard	*Luxury*	*Total*
	£	£	£
Sales (WI)	206,550	331,500	538,050
Material	71,932	173,412	245,344
Labour	48,060	22,800	70,860
Production overheads (W2)	55,248	26,640	81,888
Cost of sales	175,240	222,852	398,092
Profit	31,310	108,648	139,958

WORKING

(1) Sales: Standard 68,850 × £3 = £206,550
Luxury 33,150 × £10 = £331,500

(2) Production overheads: Standard 4,604 × £12 = £55,248
Luxury 2,220 × £12 = £26,640

Task 1.2

a) **Revised materials purchases and production budgets for luxury model**

i) **Revised production budget**

	Luxury (revised)
	£
Sales (33,150 × 1.4)	46,410
Add closing finished stocks $\left(\frac{46,410}{25}\right) \times 2$	3,713
Less opening finished stocks	(2,507)
Planned production	47,616

ii) **Revised materials purchases budget**

	Luxury (revised)
	£
Production units	47,616
Production material (× 20)	952,320
Wastage (4/96)	39,680
Gross production material (grams)	992,000

iii) **Revised direct labour hours budget (with extra staff)**

	Luxury
	£
Gross production (units)	47,616
Labour hours required (× $^1/_{15}$)	3,175
Standard hours available (with extra staff) (W)	3,850

WORKING

Standard hours with extra staff for luxury model:

35 hours × 5 weeks × (12 + 10) = 3,850

iv) **Revised operating statement**

	Luxury
	£
Sales (46,410 × £10)	464,100
Material (W1)	248,000
Labour (W2)	38,500
Production overheads (W3)	38,100
Cost of sales	324,600
Profit	139,500

WORKINGS

1) *Material*

$$\text{Luxury } \frac{992{,}000}{1{,}000} \times £250 = £248{,}000$$

2) *Labour*

Standard hours (with extra staff) 3,850 × £10 = £38,500

3) *Production overheads*

3,175 × £12 = £38,100

b) Email

From: AccountingTechnician@BrighterCovers.co.uk
To: TomFarrier@BrighterCovers.co.uk
Sent: 21 June 2007
Subject: Revised production and extra staff

As requested, I have revised the planned production and materials purchases budgets in line with the forecast increase in demand for the luxury model. I also include calculations showing the effect of taking on the additional staff that you asked for.

1) **Materials**

We need to ensue that there is a reliable supply of the materials needed for the new level of activity of the Luxury model. We can either do this by holding stocks ourselves or by entering into a new supply agreement whereby the supplier will hold stocks on our behalf.

The higher volume of purchases should enable us to negotiate a quantity discount with our supplier.

2 Labour

The decision to take on extra staff does not appear worthwhile if the production of the Luxury model is viewed in isolation. A saving of £1,375 could be made by not hiring the staff and relying on overtime (see working (a) below).

However, if extra staff were hired and it was possible to reschedule work so that the extra staff hired could be deployed to work on the Standard model when they are not working on the Luxury model then current overtime of £2,020 on the Standard model would be eliminated resulting in an overall saving of £645 by hiring the extra staff (see workings (b) and (c) below).

Please let me know if you need any further explanations.

Accounting Technician

WORKINGS

The following workings are relevant to the above memo

a) Standard hours (with extra staff) 3,850 × £10 = £38,500

Standard hours plus overtime (no extra staff) (see box below for calculation of hours)

(2,100 × £10 = £21,000) + (1,075 × £15 = £16,125) = £37,125

Gross production (units)	47,616
Labour hours required (× 1/15)	3,175
Standard hours available (without extra staff)	2,100
Overtime hours required	1,075

Therefore, saving by not hiring extra staff but using overtime ignoring effect of using spare staff on standard model = £1,375

b) Saving by hiring and using spare extra staff on production of Standard model

Spare hours available = 675 hours (see box below)

Overtime hours on standard model (see 1.1 e) = 404

Saving on overtime premium = 404 × £5 = £2,020

	Luxury
	£
Gross production (units)	47,616
Labour hours required (× 1/15)	3,175
Standard hours available (with extra staff) (W1)	3,850
Extra hours available	675

c) Net saving by hiring extra staff £(2,020 – 1,375) = £645

SECTION 2

Task 2.1

a) **Calculation of budgeted data**

i) Selling price per unit $= \dfrac{£14{,}000{,}000}{400{,}000} = £35$

ii) Cost of purchases per unit $= \dfrac{£4{,}800{,}000}{400{,}000} = £12$

iii) Variable cost of wages per unit $\dfrac{£2{,}600{,}000}{400{,}000} = £6.50$

iv) Variable cost of warehousing

Total cost – fixed cost = £(720,000 – 40,000) = £680,000

Variable cost per unit $= \dfrac{£680{,}000}{400{,}000} = £1.70$

v) Distribution costs per 100,000 blenders = £60,000/(400,000/100,000) = £15,000

b) **Calculation of actual data**

i) Actual selling price per unit $\dfrac{£20{,}000{,}000}{500{,}000} = £40$

ii) Actual cost of purchases per unit $\dfrac{£6{,}500{,}000}{502{,}000} = £12.95$

iii) Actual variable cost of wages per unit $\dfrac{£3{,}350{,}000}{502{,}000} = £6.67$

iv) Actual variable cost of warehousing = Total cost – Fixed cost = £(800,000 – 50,000) = £750,000

Actual variable cost per unit $= \dfrac{£750{,}000}{502{,}000} = £1.49$

v) Actual distribution costs per 100,000 blenders = £90,000/(500,000/100,000) = £18,000

Tutorial note. Be careful when calculating the above figures whether you use the sales quantity or the production quantity.

c) **Flexed budgeted and actual operating statement for the company's last financial year**

		Flexed budget		*Actual*	*Variance*
Sales volume (units) (W1)		500,000		500,000	
Production volume (units)(W2)		500,000		500,000	
	£'000	£'000	£'000	£'000	£'000
Turnover: Budget (500,000 × £35)		17,500		20,000	2,500 (F)
Variable costs					
Purchases: Budget (500,000 × £12)					
Actual (500/502 × 6,500)	6,000		6,474		474 (A)
Wages: Budget (500,000 × £6.50)					
Actual (500/502× 3,350)	3,250		3,337		87 (A)
Warehousing: Budget (500,000 × £1.7)					
Actual (500,000 × 1.49)	850		745		105 (F)
Distribution costs £(60,000 + 15,000)	75		90		15 (A)
		10,175		10,646	471 (A)
Contribution		7,325		9,354	2,029 (F)
Fixed costs					
Warehousing	40		50		10 (A)
Insurance	12		10		2 (F)
Rent and rates	15		18		3 (A)
Other administration	28		33		5 (A)
Depreciation	50		50		
		145		161	16 (A)
Profit		7,180		9,193	2,013 (F)

WORKING

The budgeted sales volume is flexed to 500,000 in line with the actual sales

The budgeted production and the actual production and both flexed to the actual sales of 500,000, even though actual production was 502,000. This removes the need to enter a figure for closing stock.

Task 2.2

REPORT

To: Clare Sands
From: Accountant
Subject: Analysis of results for last financial year
Date: 21 June 2007

a) **Significance of each of the variances and how they arose**

The actual selling price was £5 more than budgeted. This resulted in the favourable price variance of £2,500,000. The extra price would be due to additional demand for the product that allowed a higher price to be charged.

There is an adverse variance on materials used of £474,000. This arises from an increase in actual unit costs of materials (£12.95) over the budgeted price of £12.00. The rise in price may have been caused by the increased demand for the raw materials pushing up their price or by better quality materials being purchased.

The adverse labour variance of £87,000 is caused by the rate per unit increase from £6.50 to £6.67. This may be due to shortages of labour needed to satisfy the extra production pushing up the wage rate, or overtime working or the hiring of better quality labour.

The favourable variable warehousing cost may be caused by better use of resources at the higher production level that enables unit variable warehousing costs to be lower eg better scheduling of throughput enables less time to be spent packaging each item.

The adverse variance on distribution costs suggests that the budget may simply have been wrong and that such things as postage or delivery vans may have cost more than budget.

The other fixed costs while small in absolute terms are significant in percentage terms and would need to be investigated.

b) **Two procedures to achieve a better sales budget forecast (two of the following)**

Market research would give a better indication of the demand for the blender and its sensitivity to changes in price. A number of pricing options could be produced that would enable a better budget to be agreed.

Flexible budgets and expected out-turns could be produced on a more regular basis to enable the budget to be changed during the year if it appears to be significantly wrong compared to actual.

Time series analysis might reveal a trend that would assist in preparing a budget.

c) **Three steps to motivate managers to achieve budgets**

Maintaining motivated managers is an important aspect of setting and achieving budgets. Four ways of doing this could be (only three are required):

i) Involve managers in the budgeting process so that they will assume some ownership of the budget.

ii) Set budgets that are challenging but achievable – if a budget is too difficult managers will feel defeated before they begin – if too easy managers will not have to try to achieve the budget.

iii) Set performance targets inked to bonuses to motivate the managers.

iv) Ensure that managers are only appraised on the parts of the budgets that they control.

UNIT 9

PRACTICE EXAM 10

KANDO LTD

ANSWERS

ANSWERS

SECTION 1

Task 1.1

a) **Sales forecast**

	Period 1	2	3	4	5
Sales (units)	50,000	54,000	56,700	59,535	62,512

b) **Production budget**

	Period 1	2	3	4
Sales	50,000	54,000	56,700	59,535
Add: closing stock	18,000	18,900	19,845	20,838
Less: opening stock	0	(18,000)	(18,900)	(19,845)
Good production	68,000	54,900	57,645	60,528
Add: wastage – faulty items (production x 3/97)	2,104	1,698	1,783	1,872
Gross production in units	70,104	56,598	59,428	62,400

Tutorial note: Only good items can be taken into stock or sold, so the figure for good production represents 97% of what actually has to be produced. Wastage is 3% and gross production (what actually has to be produced) is 100%. This can be shown as a table:

Good production		97
Wastage	add	3
Gross production	=	100

So, given the figure for good production, we take 3/97 of this to find gross production. It is important that you understand this mini table above as it will help you later on in Task 1.2. This concept will is certain to appear in your exam.

c) **Materials purchases budget**

	Period 1	2	3	4
Gross production in units	70,104	56,598	59,428	62,400
Materials purchases (kg)	140,208	113,196	118,856	124,800

d) **Cost of materials purchases budget**

	Period 1	2	3	4
Material required (kg)	140,208	113,196	118,856	124,800
Cost of materials purchases (at £4 per kg)	£560,832	£452,784	£475,424	£499,200

e) **Direct labour hours budget**

	Period 1	2	3	4	Total
Gross production in units	70,104	56,598	59,428	62,400	
Direct labour hours required (at 3 hours per unit)	210,312	169,794	178,284	187,200	745,590
Standard hours available (400 employees x 35 hours x 12 weeks x 4 periods)					672,000
Overtime hours required					73,590

f) **Cost of direct labour budget**

	£
Basic hours (672,000 x £10)	6,720,000
Overtime hours (73,590 x £15)	1,103,850
Total direct labour cost	7,823,850

Tutorial note: Always read the question carefully to determine whether the overtime premium is to be charged to direct labour or overheads. In this exam is was part of the direct labour cost, but this is not always the case.

Task 1.2

a) **Revised materials purchases and production budgets**

	Period 1	2	3	4	
Materials required (kg)	140,208	113,196	118,856	124,800	
Materials available (kg)	120,000	120,000	120,000	120,000	
Excess/(shortfall) of materials	(20,208)	6,804	1,144	(4,800)	
Overall shortfall					
–materials (kg)					(17,060)
–finished goods (units)					(8,530)

b) **The effect of the restrictions on stock and production**

With raw material availability restricted to 120,000 kg per period, production is limited to 60,000 units per period. Looking back to the sales forecasts in Task 1.1 part a), this is sufficient to satisfy sales, but the stock levels originally budgeted-for can not be produced. The revised stock levels are restricted as shown in the table below.

Revised production budget in units

	Period 1	2	3	4
Sales	50,000	54,000	56,700	59,535
Add: closing stock (bal fig)	3,200	12,400	13,900	12,565
Less: opening stock	0	(8,200)	(12,400)	(13,900)
Good production	53,200	58,200	58,200	58,200
Wastage – faulty items (60,000 x 3%)	1,800	1,800	1,800	1,800
Gross production in units	60,000	60,000	60,000	60,000

Tutorial note: The first time the production budget was produced you had to work downwards from the Sales figures with the information about the stock levels that were given. This time you know the sales and the gross production figures, but you have to work back from the gross production figures to find the stock. This makes the calculation of the wastage slightly different as it is 3/100 x gross production. In other words, 1,800 (3%) of the 60,000 items produced will be rejected on inspection to leave 58,200 good items suitable for sale.

c) **MEMO**

To: Board of Directors
From: Management Accountant
Subject: Revised Production Budget
Date: 1 December 2006

Restrictions in the supply of raw materials have necessitated the revision of our production budget. This memo explains how the budget has been affected and how we can improve our forecasting in future.

i) The shortage of raw materials means that over the four periods to 30 November 2007 we would experience a shortfall in gross production of 8,350 units if we maintain stock levels at the originally planned level of 4 week's sales.

Our maximum production levels are limited to 60,000 per period, so if we reduce production from 248,350 units to 240,000 units in the four periods covered by the budget this will satisfy sales demand at present. However, it will not keep our stock at the required level and this could cause problems if our sales continue to grow in line with current predictions: we would eventually deplete our stocks and our budgeted sales levels would be subsequently be affected.

ii) In future we could make use of a number of techniques to improve our forecasting.

Strategic considerations: Market research and market analysis prior to the launch of a new product can be used to identify demand, competitors in the market and the availability and reliability of raw material supplies.

External Analysis: PEST analysis looks at political, economic, social and technological factors that affect the product. This could identify factors which would affect future availability and price of our raw materials and how long the current restrictions are likely to last. It might indicate whether it would be cost effective to start holding raw material stocks to cover any further foreseeable shortages.

Internal analysis: SWOT analysis identifies strengths, weaknesses, opportunities and threats. The threat of supply shortages might prompt an internal investigation into the stockholding policy for the new product and the effect of stock levels on working capital and cash flow.

(**Note**. Only two techniques were required.)

iii) Two factors that should be taken into account when considering the life cycle of the new product are outlined below.

Global competition: as major producing countries such as China and India emerge there is an ever increasing competition for raw materials. This could well shorten the product's life cycle.

Technological advances: competitors may well bring out more advanced products which will make ours obsolete and cut its life cycle short unless we research customers' requirements and invest in development to upgrade the products accordingly.

SECTION 2

Task 2.1

a) i) **Budgeted selling price per unit** $= \dfrac{6,000,000}{80,000} = £75$

or $= \dfrac{7,500,000}{100,000} = £75$

ii) **Budgeted material cost per unit** $= \dfrac{1,200,000}{80,000} = £15$

or $= \dfrac{1,500,000}{100,000} = £15$

iii) **Budgeted variable cost of labour per unit**

Increase in cost (2,700,000 -2,300,000)	£400,000
Increase in volume (100,000 – 80,000)	20,000
Labour variable cost per unit (400,000/20,000)	£20

iv) **Budgeted total labour fixed cost**

	£
Total labour cost for 100,000 units	2,700,000
Less: variable cost of 100,000 units (£20 x 100,000)	(2,000,000)
Total labour fixed cost	700,000

Alternatively:

	£
Total labour cost for 80,000 units	2,300,000
Less: variable cost of 80,000 units (£20 x 80,000)	(1,600,000)
Total labour fixed cost	700,000

v) **Budgeted variable cost of light, heat and power per unit**

Increase in cost (1,340,000 -1,080,000)	£260,000
Increase in volume (100,000 – 80,000)	20,000
Labour variable cost per unit (400,000/20,000)	£13

vi) **Budgeted total light, heat and power fixed cost**

	£
Total LH&P cost for 100,000 units	1,340,000
Less: variable cost of 100,000 units (£13 x 100,000)	(1,300,000)
Total labour fixed cost	40,000

(Again you could have based your calculations on a production volume of 80,000 units.)

vii) Budgeted variable cost of insurance, rent and rates per unit

Increase in cost (840,000 -760,000)	£80,000
Increase in volume (100,000 – 80,000)	20,000
Labour variable cost per unit (400,000/20,000)	£4

viii) Total insurance, rent and rates fixed cost

	£
Total IR&R cost for 100,000 units	840,000
Less: variable cost of 100,000 units (£4 x 100,000)	(400,000)
Total labour fixed cost	440,000

b) **Operating statement for the year ended 30 November 2006**

	Flexed budget		*Actual*		*Variance*
Sales and production volume	60,000 units		60,000 units		
	£'000	£'000	£'000	£'000	£'000
Turnover (60,000 x £75)		4,500		4,320	180 (A)
Less: expenses					
Material (60 x £15)	900		1,000		100 (A)
Labour (60 x £20) + £700	1,900		1,680		220 (F)
Light, heat & power					
(60 x £13) + £40	820		800		20 (F)
Insurance, rent & rates					
(60 x £4)+£440	680		650		30 (F)
Depreciation	500		500		0
		(4,800)		(4,630)	
		(300)		(310)	10 (A)

Tutorial note: The examiner noted that many people failed to include the fixed element of the semi-variable costs in the operating statement; look out for this in future. Also, you must show your workings.

Task 2.2

a) i) Actual selling price per unit $= \dfrac{4,320,000}{60,000} = £72$

ii) Actual material cost per unit $= \dfrac{1,000,000}{60,000} = £16.67$

iii) Actual variable cost of labour per unit $= \dfrac{\text{Total cost} - \text{Fixed cost}}{\text{Volume}}$

$$= \frac{£1,680,000 - £70,000}{60,000}$$

$$= £16.33$$

iv) Actual variable cost of light, heat and power per unit $= \dfrac{\text{Total cost} - \text{Fixed cost}}{\text{Volume}}$

$$= \frac{£800{,}000 - £40{,}000}{60{,}000}$$

$$= £12.67$$

v) Actual variable cost of insurance, rent and rates per unit $= \dfrac{\text{Total cost} - \text{Fixed cost}}{\text{Volume}}$

$$= \frac{£650{,}000 - £440{,}000}{60{,}000}$$

$$= £3.50$$

b)

MEMO

To: Victoria Andrews
From: Management Accountant
Subject: Analysis of actual results in the year ended 30 November 2006
Date: 1 December 2006

i) **Reasons for the loss**

The three main reasons for the loss for the year of £310,000 are

- The actual selling price achieved of £72 was £3 less than the budgeted price of £75.
- The sales volume actually achieved of 60,000 was 25% less than our lowest budgeted sales volume of 80,000 units units.
- An increase of £1.67 in the cost of raw material from the budgeted unit cost of £15 to the actual cost of £16.67.

The first two of these reasons have led to a £180,000 adverse sales variance. The current uncertain economic situation obviously means that customers are not prepared to pay as much for our product as we had thought, and some may not be spending on this type of product at all.

The materials cost increase has led to a £100,000 adverse materials variance. This could be due to unforeseen inflation specific to this material or we may not have qualified for bulk discounts if we bought less material as a consequence of lower sales and production.

In addition to the above adverse variances, there was a significant favourable variance of £220,000 on labour, the labour rate falling from £20 to £16.33 per unit. This could have resulted from fewer overtime hours being needed for reduced production, or from the use of less skilled workers. It could also be related to the materials adverse variance: if more expensive, but better quality material is used, this could enable the workforce to be more efficient, producing the same quantity in fewer hours.

There were also small favourable variances on light, heat and power costs and insurance, rent and rates costs. This could have been due to overestimates of cost rises over the budget period, no claims bonus build-up on insurances or a change of service provider.

ii) **General economic factors to consider in future**

Three important factors which we should consider to improve our budget forecasts in future are:

- The general economic environment. We need to look at the effects of inflation on our purchases and sales, competition from abroad where labour costs may be significantly lower and the impact of changes in technology in the sector in which we operate.
- Competition. We should look at competition both for purchases of raw materials and for the sales of our product. We should attempt to assess the strength of our brand and those of our competitors.
- The fiscal environment. Our budgets should take account of the effects of government policies and taxation, such as the availability of grants.

iii) **Control techniques**

To help prevent losses from occurring in future we should introduce the following control techniques.

- Flexible budgeting. On a regular basis, such as weekly or monthly, the actual results are compared to a flexed budget and variances are investigated to find the cause. Any corrective action can then be taken at an early stage
- Responsibility accounting. Managers are held responsible for the performance of their responsibility centre which may be a cost centre, a revenue centre, a profit centre or an investment centre. They will have to take action when there are adverse variances on costs over which they have control.
- Total Quality Management. The principle here is one of continuous improvement and reducing mistakes which carry a cost, such as wastage and idle time.

